T0330444

INNOVATION FOR
ENTREPRENEURS

To Max, Rosa, Miriam, and Kauen
Our most wonderful children

INNOVATION FOR ENTREPRENEURS

MARC H. MEYER

Robert Shillman Professor of Entrepreneurship and Matthews Distinguished University Professor, Northeastern University, USA

CHAEWON LEE

Professor of Business and Administration and Provost for International Affairs, Seoul National University of Science and Technology, South Korea

Cheltenham, UK • Northampton, MA, USA

Published by
Edward Elgar Publishing Limited
The Lypiatts
15 Lansdown Road
Cheltenham
Glos GL50 2JA
UK

Edward Elgar Publishing, Inc.
William Pratt House
9 Dewey Court
Northampton
Massachusetts 01060
USA

A catalogue record for this book
is available from the British Library

Library of Congress Control Number:
2022931709

ISBN 978 1 80037 509 3 (cased)
ISBN 978 1 80037 511 6 (paperback)
ISBN 978 1 80037 510 9 (eBook)

Printed and bound in Great Britain by
TJ Books Limited, Padstow, Cornwall

CONTENTS

ACKNOWLEDGMENTS

We thank the entrepreneurs profiled in this book for the care and attention to helping us with the preparation of their respective chapters. These include in order of appearance: Kevin Mureithi, Kate Weiler, Karthik Mahadevan, Brian Whittemore and Trevor Nelson, Josh Belinsky and Manny Lubin, Rob Van Sickle, and Deborah Gregg Suchman. A special thanks also goes to Neil Willcocks for his help editing the My M&M's case. He also contributed the chocolate chip cookie example in Chapter 9: Defining the Prototyping, as did Steve Golden who contributed the solar flashlight example, and Greg Collier the mobile app example. All are not only outstanding innovators but passionate in their desire to help the next generation of entrepreneurs.

INTRODUCTION TO *INNOVATION FOR ENTREPRENEURS*: MINDFUL, MEANINGFUL INNOVATION

This book teaches how to innovate to solve problems in the world around us. For those of you thinking about starting a new company, the best ventures are grounded in clever innovations that solve significant problems. Creating societal impact with these innovations can also go hand-in-hand with money-making and the more practical matters of conceiving, designing, and bringing new products and services to life and into the hands of users.

This book provides a set of methods to (a) think about problems experienced by people of far-ranging and different types, (b) find classmates who have shared interests in a particular set of problems, (c) deeply understand the users' needs and frustrations as the basis for innovation, and then (d) design clever, robust solutions for these people that solve their problems. This is a hands-on textbook designed for highly experiential learning. It is methods based and intended to both inspire and help students to achieve real impact with their innovations. And for us, innovating is a lot of fun. *We hope it is for you!*

Innovation is the application of science and technology to make life and work better across a wide range of fields, by industry and profession. The technology is not just software, or electronics, or biochemistry. There are also remarkable innovations occurring in food and nutrition, health and wellness, construction and buildings, and new materials with great functionality. And all the machines we see and use at home, at work, in the hospital, or during transportation are becoming smart and connected – the Internet of Things. Innovation impacts how we live, how we work, where we live and where we work, and how we commute or not. Innovation is genuinely everywhere if one cares to look. In other words, innovation impacts everything in the world around us – and if it doesn't yet, then in a particularly old-fashioned, problem-ridden area of existence, it will.

Due to this wide-ranging impact, innovation is a core skill to be learned and applied. Given the world's needs, this is a wonderful time for aspiring, young professionals to learn innovation methods, and then after, the technical and business skills needed to operationalize innovative ideas. The purpose of this book is to teach you how to become a powerful, effective innovator.

Over the years, our students have inspired us with their innovations. So much so that rather than teach methods like a traditional textbook, we want to show these methods through the innovation stories of these students. We think you will be inspired, too. If you do not say to yourself throughout this book, "that's cool," then we have missed the mark. A number of these stories will be of first-time innovators/entrepreneurs who set out to solve a broader societally focused problem and then landed on a specific product or service idea. We will also share some of our personal stories. Innovation has been our life-long passion and pursuit. We see it as a way to inspire young people to use their energy to help society and themselves by engaging in *mindful, meaningful innovation.*

The structure of the book is simple. Chapter by chapter, we present a set of methods that form a logical step-by-step process for innovating. Each successive chapter presents the next method or two, with each method is illustrated with an example of one of our students or using our own experiences. Then, towards the end of each chapter, we provide a small set of exercises to apply that chapter's methods to your innovation project with your teammates. For the final project presentation – which your teacher will expect you to deliver in a fine manner – you should be able to assemble the templates from various chapters into a first draft, then polish and personalize with your own style and character. If you commit yourself to the work from the very start and stick with it through each chapter, pulling everything together should be straightforward and provide a genuine sense of accomplishment. If you wait until mid-semester to kick things into high gear, perhaps not so good. You are in the type of course where it may be difficult, if not too late, to catch up.

Additional materials will be made available on the companion website: https://www.e-elgar.com/textbooks/meyer.

Nearly all innovation ideas transform through a learning process where teams ask a series of questions as hypotheses to prospective users. Answers are provided, insights gleaned, and the innovation idea takes further shape. Along the way, you will invariably *pivot* and sharpen your ideas. Every effective, impactful innovator does this, and so will you.

Fortunately, talking to users, understanding their problems, and designing exciting solutions to solve these problems are fun to do and enrich beyond just the wallet. If you do well, we promise that you will feel it in the heart as well as the mind. Using this book should allow you to make some of this quiet, personal discovery, to discover your passion and pathway to contribute to and help the world around you. Most university students take a decade or more to know if they want to be an innovator, how to do it, and where to do it with a specific industry or professional focus. Let's see if we can begin to answer these questions right now, in this very semester. If successful, you will have created the foundation for a productive, meaningful life and with it, the joy of making a contribution to society.

Please have a great journey and let us know where you land!

Marc H. Meyer and Chaewon Lee
Cambridge, MA and Pangyo, South Korea

1
Types of innovation

INTRODUCTION

There are many different types of innovation – and since this a course in innovating, perhaps it is best that we start by understanding these different types of innovation. And then, as an assignment, we will ask you have to look at companies, products, and services for an example of each type. These examples will then help you determine the type of innovation you may wish to undertake this semester.

LEARNING OBJECTIVES

After reading this chapter, you will:

1. Understand the different types of innovation.
2. Find strong examples of each primary type of innovation.
3. Begin to think through what types of innovation feel most comfortable to you, based on your experience, passion, an area of study at school, or simple fascination with one of the examples you have uncovered for your exercises in this chapter.

THE DIFFERENCE BETWEEN INNOVATION AND INVENTION

It is important to understand the difference between *innovation* and *invention*. Both are needed to advance society forward, but they *are different*. *Invention* is the discovery of new technologies, chemistries, materials, and the like. *Innovation* is the integration and application of both new and existing technologies to solve specific problems. For example, a new electric vehicle (EV) is an integration of complex chemistry (new technology in batteries), software and communications technologies (new technology for driverless controls), and electric motors (existing technology but continuously improving) to make EVs exciting to drive as well as sustainable.

To solve the pressing problems facing our world – such as climate change, the aging of the population in need of services, public health crises, the threats of crime and terrorism, the replacement of an aging infrastructure with smart, sustainable infrastructure, and to improve learning and income disparity around the world – we need *both* inventors *and* innovators.

The innovator cannot design brilliant new solutions without breakthrough technologies, usually invented by someone else, and the inventor needs the innovator to make his or her technological discoveries valuable and applicable.

WHAT ARE THE MAJOR TYPES OF INNOVATION?

Innovation has become a significant focus for most organizations, be they startups or large, multi-national corporations. In this book, we are primarily focused on startups, even though the methods you learn can just as easily be applied to jobs in product management or development in a big company. In other words, trying to differentiate innovation in terms of a big company versus small company innovation is a false separation – good innovation is good innovation no matter where its source. It is not even a matter of degree or the money needed for R&D.

We have seen some of the very best innovations occur in startups. Incredibly creative and disruptive innovations can emerge from just one or two individuals working in a startup – and that is in comparison to R&D groups in some of the largest corporations in the world. At the heart of every exciting startup is typically an exciting product or service innovation, branded and marketed in an equally compelling way.

However, different types of innovation involve different types of work. Let us take a quick tour through them with a few examples.

Product innovation

From the customers' perspective, people buy products on overall perceived benefit rather than just a specific feature or two. Products are purchased because of perceived *value*. One kind of value is purely economic: a new product or system saves users money. For example, connected cars or machines save their owners money by giving alarms about imminent failure points and initiating preventative service. Alternatively, a new product might allow users to generate more sales or revenue rather than save money. The eCommerce and social networking software innovations such as Shopify and Squarespace are good examples of revenue-enabling product innovations. Third, the value created by a new product might be experiential – in other words, providing the user with a fundamentally better, more enjoyable experience that does not necessarily equate to any type of cost savings or making more money on the part of the user. Disney has been a remarkable experience innovator over the decades with its films, theme parks, and web content. Similarly, that is why one of the authors, has over the years, owned a bunch of Mazda Miatas, the most fun one can have driving a small, economical sports car. In sum, a great product can have benefits that are economical, experience-based, or both.

Product benefits and value to the user are essential when considering a new "product innovation." A new product might look great, but you must ask yourself what it does and its benefits for customers. Many new products fail because they do not deliver distinctive value or significant "points of difference" from current competitive products.

Product innovation can come in different forms. We classify product innovation in two levels of change over current competitive products or product approaches.

- *Incremental product innovation* occurs in a product category that already exists and where the customer is not required to learn new behaviors to use the product. For example, toothpaste manufacturers have introduced toothpaste that, in addition to cleaning the teeth, "whitens" the teeth, or impedes gum disease. Major brands try to outdo one another with new benefits stacked on top of current benefits. The bulk of product innovation in today's marketplace tends to be incremental innovation. This is sometimes referred to as a product line extension. While incremental innovation is important in industry, focusing on it only leaves a company prone to more dramatic, dynamic innovations. One only needs to look at the havoc caused by Tesla over traditional car manufacturers.

- *Disruptive innovations* disrupt and obsolete all the current products in a given industry and/or market. No doubt, Tesla has been a disruptive innovator in passenger cars. At the time of writing this chapter, Ford disrupted the truck industry by introducing a powerful new EV truck. In fact, Ford is disrupting its own market leadership position, which was over $40 billion of its F-Series sales each year. Rather than let Tesla or upstart Rivian steal its sales, Ford decided to take matters into its own hands and disrupt its traditional designs. Amazon has disrupted both the distribution and Cloud services industries. Alternatively, mRNA-based COVID-19 vaccines are as disruptive and category-changing as any other product example.

Generally, disruptive innovations require changes in behavior on the part of the user. For example, driverless cars change driving behaviors. Furthermore, the time between introducing a disruptive product and its widespread adoption in the target market can be greater than five or more years. Consider solar panels on residential rooftops, which started in about 2010. In 2020, solar rooftop energy had risen to just 6% of all households in the United States, even though far more homeowners have given serious consideration to it, and no doubt that penetration will double over the next five or so years. Sometimes, however, a disruptive product innovation is cleverly designed not to require significant behavior or other usage changes by the user. One might say this about the mRNA vaccines – jabbed into the arm with a standard syringe. Similarly, most Cloud and cybersecurity software work behind the scenes. These are relatively seamless technology usages or integrations.

The authors have personal experience developing incremental and disruptive innovations in both large companies and startups. A great example of successful incremental innovation is a fun cupcake kit. Not that many years ago, we worked with a team to develop a new type of cupcake kit for moms and their children. The focus of the design was to improve the experience of learning to bake and having fun doing it with young children, featuring tunable frosting (butter content primarily for moistness), extra moist cake, and the ability to make crazy designs. Soon, children were making "alien" cupcakes and all sorts of fun stuff for Halloween and birthday parties. Designs were submitted onto a website to allow people to share their creations and even get free trips to bake their special cupcakes on TV. This cupcake kit was an incremental innovation because cupcake mix and frosting had existed for decades. However, this new design was just much better. The product line generated over $100 million a year in new revenue for the parent company (Dunkin Hines).[1]

The authors have also worked on disruptive product innovations. A more recent example is connected light-emitting diode (LED) lighting. LED lights have replaced incandescent and fluorescent lighting worldwide as LEDs use a tenth of electricity to produce the same amount of light. The LED is a truly disruptive innovation – obsoleting its predecessors. LEDs are tiny electronic diodes of different sizes, intensities, and colors that emit light when electrified – *connected LED lighting* is simply giving each LED light an I.P. address so that other programs can uniquely identify it on a network. Different types of sensors can be integrated into the printed circuit boards next to the LEDs. With these sensors, the LED light fixture can become a motion or occupancy sensor on the ceiling in an office space or conference room, or a pollution and traffic monitoring system in a street lamppost, or a security device in a spotlight in a retail store. With 50 million-plus LED lights now used worldwide, connected LEDs mean that the world will increasingly become sensored for public and private applications. This disrupts both contemporary lighting and other existing ways of monitoring the environment and people.

There are also times when you think that a new product is disruptive, but it is not. For example, as a young twenty-ish-year-old, one of your authors left MIT for five years to help build a software company that provided the first real-time Unix-based operating software for process control in factories, some of which were the most prominent beer-brewing production lines in the world. While we were indeed unique by having real-time open-systems software, the fact was that there were existing real-time proprietary operating systems from several other, much larger companies. We were faster and better but not genuinely disruptive. But it was so much fun! We helped some the biggest brewers in the world brew beer better and along the way, received a few kegs of beer it as a thank you back from our customers.

Services innovation

Like products, services innovation must also have clear functional benefits and value for the user. Services innovation is an increasingly important component of our economy because in Western economies, such innovation comprises the majority of gross domestic product (GDP) and employment, and therefore, is important for entrepreneurs to consider. In 2020, only 2% of the workforce in the U.S. was employed in agriculture, compared with about 20% in product-making and manufacturing, and about 78% involved in software and services. In fact, a product can be sold instead as a service. Consider the example of image analysis software that can help physicians in community or rural hospitals detect bone fractures. The entrepreneur could license this software as a software product to these emergency departments, or instead charge on the basis of each image scanned through the Cloud.

Incremental service innovations are the most common type of new-service innovation. This involves modest changes in the performance of the current service, like serving customers quicker with an improved help desk or customer call center. However, disruptive service innovations are becoming increasingly common through enabling Internet of Things (IoT) and Cloud-based communications. In South Korea, where your authors live half the year, there are stunning service innovators. These include Coupang, which many would argue is every bit as good as Amazon in that part of the world and, in fact, better when it comes to the supply of fresh fish, meats, and vegetables directly from the growers to your door. Another example is Kakao – the leading messaging or chat service. Kakao also provides direct wireless calling, a taxi finder service, a bike-sharing service, and even a drive-you-home-in-your-own-car service for those persons who drink a bit too much over dinner![2]

An example is another startup in which we participated in the healthcare space. This service innovation utilized a set of vibration and motion sensors for home health monitoring. By placing various sensors on mattresses, sitting chairs, and even toilet seats, we could learn all sorts of things about the residents' conditions: how long they slept, if they were not able to sleep, if they went to the bathroom too many times during the night, or worse case, if they never actually got out of bed in the morning. This software-as-a-service gave visibility into the health and well-being of the seniors, with a degree of granularity that had not existed before. In that sense, it was disruptive as a health monitoring service. The need for the elderly to age in their homes is only going to grow over time – home health monitoring will become an essential service innovation.[3]

Internal process innovation

Internal process innovation is like services innovation but performed inside a company. Process innovation is when a company improves the processes and procedures to create and deliver value to customers. It tends to be internally facing unless it is a call center automation for customer help centers. Modifying a manufacturing process is an example of process innovation.

Discarding large computers for Cloud services is another. Alternatively, process innovation can include a company's logistics for delivering products and services to customers. Many students in this course are likely to be studying engineering. Some of you are industrial engineers and process innovators, working to improve machines and other types of production processes. This work involves developing new ways to do things better, faster, cheaper, or more conveniently, using automation and intelligent machines. And just because the innovation is process-related does not mean that it is boring or less important than an externally facing product or service innovation – it is just different.

Externally facing process innovation can be equally important. Take healthcare. The methods for delivering healthcare services changed a lot during the pandemic, largely process-driven. For many months, patients could not quickly enter a hospital for care. Telemedicine progressed from rarely used before the pandemic to a more mainstream mode of care delivery for a broad range of outpatient services.

Process innovation occurs all the time in industries other than healthcare, of course. One of the most memorable instances for us was to see one of our students use the Microsoft HoloLens to automatically bring up all the electrical harness wiring diagrams for electricians wiring large airplanes in the company where he was working. Then, using another button on the smart glasses, he allowed an inspector at an entirely different location to do inspections of the completed wiring installations. His innovation saved his company as much as 50% of the time and cost for wiring a typically large cargo plane. This type of service innovation was disruptive in the technologies used and its impact on existing, traditional workflows. When we consider this student, Brian, his passion was to apply new technology to automate production and quality control. Internal process innovation is the area in which he truly excels. That might be you, too, in the future.

*** *** ***

While product, service, and process are the three primary types of innovation in industry and society, additional types of innovation are complementary to these three primary types. These major forms of complementary innovation are *platform innovation, business model innovation,* and *channel innovation.* That makes things easy to remember: three primary types of innovation and three complementary forms that help make the first three successful. Figure 1.1 shows a simple framework for connecting these types of innovation.

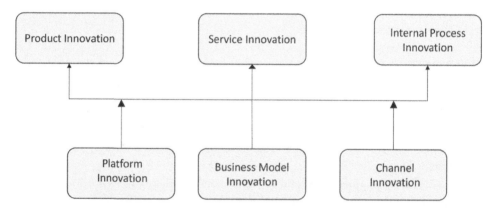

Figure 1.1   The types of innovation

Platform innovation

As noted, platform innovation is a complementary form of innovation for product, service, and process innovators – and it is mainly for engineers. Platforming is the "under the hood" strategy for getting specific products and services developed and manufactured fast and with high levels of profitability. A platform is a subsystem, module, or process used in more than one product, system, or service. For example, a product platform might be an engine design used across many car models. In software, it might be a library of graphic interface objects shared across a word processor, a spreadsheet, a database, or charting program. A platform might also be a common process, such as an underwriting process used across multiple properties and casualty insurance lines.

It takes innovative thinking to create platforms that can readily scale across different products, systems, or services. The payoff can be substantial. Most automotive manufacturers now design their engines to be shared across cars and sport utility vehicles (SUVs); Honda pioneered the effort to take it one step further, to share engines across passenger cars, SUVs, and small trucks. In the software industry, Microsoft has common GUI and Cloud services across most of its applications, such as Microsoft 365. Alternatively, in services, Uber has a single app covering various ride and food delivery services.

Platforming also allows companies to try new product and service applications relatively quickly and at marginal cost. Using a collection of standard building blocks, a company can innovate for a new application or type of customer without having to recreate the new product or service from scratch. Creating new products quickly, powered by underlying platforms to generate new revenue streams, is just what most companies want. Furthermore, it is a fun and challenging set of work for creative engineers and product planners.

New *core technologies* often become enabling platforms for products, systems, or services. There are many powerful examples in today's society. 5G is not a product or a service in itself. Instead, it is a communication protocol and international standard that enables more powerful cell communications by cellphones and other 5G devices.

Blockchain is yet another example of a new core technology that provides secure, encrypted tracking of transactions between two parties or many more parties. A product, component, or service transaction passes from person to person or company to company. Cloud-based registration adds each new step to a shared transaction log with a date-stamp, and information about what is being transferred and the monetary amounts of the transfer. Again, blockchain itself is neither a product nor a service; it is a method that allows new types of tracking and authentication.

For example, major companies are developing food blockchains to track the origin and date of the specific ingredients combined and processed in a box of cereal. When a government encounters a food safety issue, if a blockchain is in place for that food, the investigators can find the source. All the intermediary processors, shippers, packagers, and retailers for that single box of cereal manufactured in a particular "lot" or shift are available. Complex, yes, but increasingly necessary and a real Problem Space for many new process innovators.

The authors have had the opportunity to work on substantial platform innovations across multiple industries. These have been in hardware (such as a typical motor for various power tools, common engines, or seating for passenger vehicles) or software, including common databases for various financial or risk management services, or software libraries containing algorithms for specific situations. For example, there was another software venture that created "single sign-on" for hospital information systems. The system provided a standard database definition for doctors, nurses and patients that identified each person trying to use a clinical information system, and tracked everyone's utilization of that clinical software. Many healthcare software applications in the U.S. found themselves having to license and integrate this venture's software libraries into their own systems, in order to plug and play within the hospital environment. It was used in nearly 1000 hospitals to provide user and data security. When platforms work, be it in hardware or software, they can be very cool and very powerful.

Business model innovation

A business model is not a company's new products or services, per se, but how it makes money from its products or services. In that sense, business model innovation is a complementary or additional type of innovation for product or service innovation.

A business model generally includes: (a) the revenue model, and (b) an operational model. A revenue model includes how a company charges customers and the price it charges relative to competitors. The operational model defines the approaches and resources a company uses to produce that revenue, such as R&D manufacturing, selling, or customer service.

Uber and Airbnb are outstanding business model innovators in the ride-sharing and temporary lodging industries, creating their specialized marketplaces. Even though each has a specific set of service offerings, their common business model is as important as the service they actually deliver. The way Uber or Airbnb provides and charges for their respective services is a core element of the service. The salient feature of this business model is that each created a method to minimize their capital investments into the assets needed to produce the revenue. When you use Uber, you are driven in someone else's car, not Uber's. This creates a win–win between Uber or Airbnb, its suppliers and its customers. These marketplace companies make money by taking a percentage of the fees charged to users for the service.

Companies such as Uber and Airbnb are also called peer-to-peer or multi-sided marketplaces. There are other notable examples of these special marketplaces. These include peer-to-peer payment services. Friends can split the cost of dinner, for instance, with a single, easy-to-use app. This is quite disruptive in its relation to how payments worked in the past. Formerly, they would all have to be physically present with a credit card or cash, and the product or service provider would have to calculate the splitting of the bill. Venmo and PayPal are but two examples of the newer, innovative approach. As parents of children in college, we used specialized services like these to allow a half dozen roommates to split the monthly rental fee with electronic payments, made by the parents through electronic funds transfers. The same peer-to-peer rental payments provider also handled the rental leases for the landlord, saving that person all sorts of hassle chasing individual renters for signatures and money.

The same peer-to-peer model extends to many other marketplaces. Turo is a peer-to-peer marketplace for car owners to rent their vehicles to other individuals, allowing the consumer to bypass the standard procedures and car stock of the traditional rental companies. Crowdfunding platforms are another striking example. We have seen many of our students raise tens of thousands of dollars through Kickstarter campaigns. One raised over $1 million for a laptop screen extender![4]

In hindsight, there is no doubt that these peer-to-peer marketplace business models have had as disruptive an impact on our daily lives, as any given product or service. Just like technology platforms, these business platforms can be powerful. Note that behind all of these peer-to-peer business models is sophisticated back-end software to register and secure subscribers, a well-designed app, and a financial institution to handle any required financial transaction's regulatory and risk aspects in an exchange. Moreover, getting consumers to become members of these marketplaces is not easy – typically demanding large sums of invested capital for web and traditional media marketing and business partnerships. Building new marketplaces is tough!

Channel innovation

Channel innovation is also complementary to product and service innovation. It, too, can come in different forms. A big-box retailer that over time generates a significant percentage of its sales through eCommerce has innovated with its go-to-market channel, following in the footsteps of the true innovator in this field, Amazon. The other aspect of channel innovation is that most companies do not give up their older, traditional channels. A retailer such as Walmart maintains its stores but also invests heavily in eCommerce.

Managing two very different channels for the same consumers is called multi-channel and/ or omnichannel integration. One of the very best in omnichannel management, Staples, seeks to eliminate traditional in-store and online shopping and delivery barriers. If you order an item online or in a store, either way, you can either pick it up at the same or a different store, or have it delivered to your home or office. Companies such as Staples or Amazon invest heavily in database and analytics software to understand individual consumer behavior and preferences, allowing them to make recommendations for new purchases whenever the consumer visits the website. This approach helps maximize revenue from the same shopper.

In a later chapter, you will read about how we had as much fun as one can have at work creating a direct-to-consumer product for the Mars family, based on custom-printed M&M candies with text and photographs submitted by customers. This effort was a significant channel innovation for Mars because traditionally, nearly all of its products had been, and continue to be, sold through retailers at check-out counters or on shelves. Going to direct-to-consumer was a new and different way for Mars to interact with its consumers. Furthermore, with the customized M&M's, the concept took off like a race car, at a price point ten times the traditional, standard M&M candy price. *It was the epitome of channel innovation.*

*** *** ***

One last subtle point. We have shown that platform, business model, and channel innovation complement three major types of primary innovation – product, service, and process innovation. If we dig into matters a bit more, it is also true that both platform innovation and channel innovation can profoundly affect a company's business model. Platform innovation reduces materials and production costs – often called the cost of goods sold. A common engine across cars reduces the per unit production costs. The engine platform improves the operating expense side of the business model.

On the other hand, channel innovation primarily helps a company generate more revenue – the other side of the business model. If you think that some channel innovations can also significantly reduce the costs of selling – eCommerce versus bricks and mortar – well, you are correct. However, most entrepreneurs and corporate executives think about channel innovation as a way to reach more customers and drive revenue. With this in mind, we have got to correct our Figure 1.1 a bit (see Figure 1.2), so that platform and channel can impact business model innovation as an intermediary effect and still drive the product, service, and internal business process innovations above.

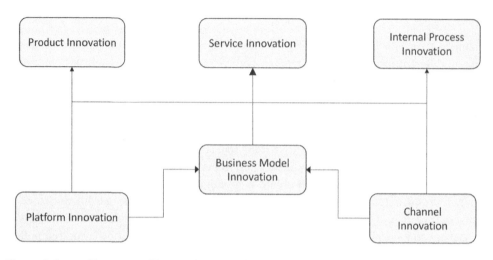

Figure 1.2   The types of innovation, modified a touch!

Reader exercises: it is your turn to find some inspirational examples

Your work for this chapter is simple, and hopefully, exciting and motivational. We ask you to find examples out in the real world of innovations representing each of the six types of innovation. Then tell a short story about the innovation that you think is the most powerful and most inspirational for you as a student of innovation and on the verge of becoming an innovator yourself.

There is one condition: the examples you select cannot be mentioned in this first chapter. This means not Tesla, not Uber, and not Airbnb. Nor Signify LED Lighting. Nor Staples or Amazon. Or Mars. Sorry – you must find your own examples. And then, identify the one that inspires you the most. Social innovations are just a way of describing a specific product or service innovation with a business model that typically sacrifices price and profit to allow greater accessibility by those persons or organizations in need of the product or service. Then, do some additional research to learn the story about the innovators themselves, how the innovation was conceived and executed, as well as its commercial or societal impact. Use Figure 1.3 as your guide.

Type of Innovation	Example - Company	Your reasoning
Product		
Service		
Internal Process		
Business Model		
Channel		
Platform		

Tell the story for your favorite innovation	
The innovator(s)	
The history or start of the idea	
How it took shape as a product or service	
Its impact	

Figure 1.3   Find examples of the six different types of innovation. Tell the story about your favorite example

NOTES

1. If you would like to read more about the cupcake kit: Meyer, M.H., Crane, F.G., and Lee, C. (2016). "Connecting Ethnography to the Business of Innovation." *Business Horizons*, 59(6), November, 699–711. It is a fun story.
2. South Korea is a country with widespread adoption of new 5G-enabled services. It was the top-ranked innovating country in the most recent Bloomberg Innovation Index; see http://www.koreaherald.com/view.php?ud=20210203000994. Published February 3 2021.
3. For those students interested in medical technology, we wrote a fun case on this that you might track down: Meyer, M.H., and Kursh, S. (2012). "Elder Alert." *International Review of Entrepreneurship*, 10(4).
4. Mobile Pixels, a plug-in dual monitor for laptops.

2
Finding the right problem to solve

PURPOSE

Innovation requires a purpose. What are the right innovation areas for us as individuals? Where can we excel? Where can we have clear impact?

This chapter provides a method for discovering your core values and understanding your natural skills. You will then learn how to match these core values and skills to contribute to society and the world. This approach will lead you to select a problem to solve through innovation that is not only "right" for your intended user *but suitable for you*. As said by Steve Jobs, people with passion can change the world. Find a problem for which you have a real passion and start learning and innovating to solve it – this is one of the keys to a successful, meaningful, and happy life.

LEARNING OBJECTIVES

In this chapter, we will learn a method to help you:

1. Understand your core values and why these are important for purposeful innovation leading to successful companies, NGOs, or government initiatives.
2. Understand your natural and learned skills.
3. Identify problems to solve that interest you. Then, make sure these are the *right problems* for you to solve based on your core values and personal skills.
4. Align core values, personal skills, and Problem Space is a great way to design innovations and start a meaningful, impactful venture.

INTRODUCTION

There are some opportunistic entrepreneurs who make money regardless of what their company does. They jump on any good opportunity that comes along and are masterful at making the most of that opportunity, turning it into a business of value, and flipping it typically by selling the venture to a larger company. This type of person is a sales-driven, opportunistic, "hit and run" entrepreneur who is driven by creating the next transaction, to sell the next product – whatever it is – and then sell the company. One could argue that historically, capitalism has been led by such opportunistic, serial entrepreneurs.

There is another type of entrepreneur. This type of entrepreneur is driven by the burning desire to solve a specific problem in society that requires deep thinking, innovation, and persistent teamwork to get something done and achieve impact. Not only is the problem "big" – which means many people or companies or governments are greatly burdened or suffer from that problem – but the problem has not been an easy one to tackle in the past or present. The problem is important and challenging. Taking it on is no trivial matter; solving it takes time, different skills and teamwork, and requires building more than just a good sales organization. And the desire to take on the challenge must be grounded in an inner, core value within the entrepreneur to help people by solving challenging problems they face at work or at home. This core value keeps the entrepreneur passionately thinking and working for years to achieve the desired impact, a process that could be a life-long journey.

We think of this type of entrepreneur as an innovator, a builder of both things and teams to solve big problems. Her or his interests are based on deeper personal care and empathy for people experiencing these problems. The journey is more than just making money. And we believe that this type of entrepreneur is the best hope for our challenged, struggling world. In the decades to come, we hope that people will talk about such entrepreneurs not just for how much money they have made but for the problems they have solved and the clever designs developed to solve these problems. The new generation of electric vehicle (EV) entrepreneurs are but one example, just as the scientists who developed COVID-19 vaccines at breakneck speed.

We hope you want to become this type of mindful entrepreneur. The world needs innovators who can understand problems and change the world for the better. And we hope that this book helps you in this journey. *Society needs innovative thinking.*

As an example of this type of entrepreneur, let's meet Kevin (Figure 2.1).

KEVIN REALIZES A PURPOSE FOR HIS LIFE'S WORK

Kevin Mureithi grew up in a rural village in Kenya. Through his work in school and his parents' determination, he made his way to a university in Kenya, Maseno University, where he decided to study environmental science. When he thought about working for an environment-related company in Kenya, such as a utility serving Nairobi, it did not truly excite him. It seemed

Source: Kevin Mureithi, Eco Blocks & Tiles. Used with permission.

Figure 2.1   Kevin Mureithi

a long way off from his core values and goals, helping people back in the villages that were part of his own upbringing.

What was Kevin going to do with his life? How would he help people and, more specifically, improve the environment in which they lived and worked? He was determined to figure it out.

UNDERSTANDING AND ACTING ON YOUR CORE VALUES

While in the small school serving his rural community, Kevin knew that he wanted to get educated to help himself, and his family and his community. And when he later entered university, this core value of helping people in rural communities was continuously on his mind when he chose his course of study. His journey was to discover a pragmatic way to make that core value a reality.

Kevin had a second core value: a deep inner drive to "prove things to himself," almost stubbornly, even as other people told him that it couldn't be done. Innovation and proving that his ideas could work became both a passion and a core value, as great as the desire to help rural communities throughout Africa.

Kevin was always coming up with new engineering ideas, even at a young age, and he was never shy about talking to people about them. It might be a new housing idea, a new power generation concept, or a water purification system designed for poor rural families and communities. But nearly all of these conversations ended up with someone telling him why these ideas could not be done, for one reason or another. So, when he started learning engineering as a college student, he realized he would have the skills to prove to himself that the naysayers were wrong. Kevin turned "helping people" into a more direct, mindful form of "impact" through clever engineering, and in the process, prove to himself that his ideas could be made into workable solutions.

If, at that very moment, you were to ask Kevin what type of life pursuit would make him most happy, it would be a fusion of these two core values – helping people and proving things to himself.

We are confident that some magic combinations will work just as well for you, so let's discover and make them visible now.

Please complete Figure 2.2 with up to five areas that you might consider your core values. Most people have two or three core values. This might feel a bit odd at first since you probably have never been asked to think about yourself in this way and in this structure – but heck, give it a try and see what comes out on the piece of paper! Think of this as personal discovery through entrepreneurship and innovation!

Now, let's prioritize. If you had to pick just one or two core values that are most important to you – nearest to your heart – core values that you know will motivate you and inspire others around you – what would these core values be?

We read that for Kevin, his two top core values were to help people and to prove things to himself, regardless of what other people said was possible or not. A more fine-grained spin on his core values might be helping rural communities through creative but pragmatic

Your Important Core Values

1.

2.

3.

4.

5.

If it is hard for you to list five core values, take a look at the list below to get some ideas.

Compassion for people, eating healthy, wellness and fitness, education and helping others learn, creating a clean environment, innovation and the design of new things, making things around you more efficient, curing or stopping diseases, traveling and exploring the world, finding new friends and building community, social justice and politics, taking responsibility for yourself and others, carrying on the family tradition, being independent, being a big success financially.

Figure 2.2   Your important core values

engineering innovation. He realized these core values as he started college. This realization has propelled him forward ever since.

Now, it's your turn. What are the one or two core values that you know will drive you over the coming decade? Look at the list you made in Figure 2.2 and try to summarize them into just one or two core values as the next Figure 2.3. There is no right or wrong core value. –What motivates you may not motivate anyone else sitting next to you, although we suspect there will be a kindred spirit or two. Some people care about making money more than contributing to society, and some care about social status and reputation. And yet others want to create a sustainable world, and others, to cure terrible diseases. Your authors teach and write books to help young people discover themselves and contribute to society – it is our own core value that keeps us passionate about our work even though we have been doing it for over thirty years! If your work is your passion, and your passion is based on a core humanistic value – that is what we wish for each and every one of you. All values are meaningful in different ways. So please don't be afraid of other people's judgment. We all are different from others and special in these differences.

Your Two Most Important Core Values

1.

2.

Why do these two core values rise to the top?

What real-life experiences support this conviction and compassion?

Figure 2.3   Choose your two most important core values

BUILDING UPON NATURAL SKILLS WITH LEARNING THROUGH CLASSES AND INTERNSHIPS

Upon entering university in 2004, it is no surprise that Kevin decided to focus on environmental science as the right path to help rural communities. He always loved the natural beauty of his home in Kenya, the fresh air, and the magic of the natural environment. And in the same thought, all the trash that villagers would throw away on the side of the road made him mad. It was an environmental injustice that people inflicted upon themselves.

Kevin worked his way through various courses. He began picking up the engineering skills he needed to "prove things for himself" and particularly liked mechanical engineering. He also took courses in chemical engineering – which would prove crucial later on. And his favorite projects had a community improvement focus. Already he was working to serve his two core values of helping people with innovation and to build things that other people did not think was possible.

As Kevin progressed through his classes, he was anxious to get more real work experience. Many call this "experiential education," which can occur in internships or by starting your own company inside a university-based incubator. This type of experiential learning can be as powerful as any classroom education. If you have a chance to grab an internship with a company or organization that seems to connect with your core values, by all means, do it!

In Kevin's case, he took an internship with a local Kenyan nongovernmental organization (NGO) working with local farmers on sustainable farming practices. Working with local farmers and the staff of this NGO, he fell in love with the word "impact." Helping farmers translated into impactful innovation and achieved by counseling farmers on new methods and new technologies.

Kevin also learned about the challenges most NGOs face, particularly in raising the money needed to do good and achieve the desired impact. The managers of the NGO saw Kevin's passion and ability to connect with people. They invited him to participate in the fund-raising process. He learned what later became an important skill: presenting to external audiences, donors, or investors. The internship initially intended to be just a couple of months turned into a full year.

A realization entered Kevin's mind: It would be great to create an impactful product or service housed in a company that could generate its own cash flow instead of always relying on donors' and governments' goodwill. Kevin realized that knowledge of financial matters was as important as engineering. To create a successful innovation for rural society, he would also need to create a sustainable business model that did not rely just on government or NGO handouts, e.g., he should try to create a commercial enterprise to achieve societal impact.

To summarize, the essential skills that Kevin realized he needed to achieve impact based on his core values were: (1) environmental science, (2) communications, primarily speaking well and effectively, and (3) the future goal of learning how to design and implement a cash-generating business, all still focused on helping the poor. His university provided the first skill set; his internship provided the second. By the time he graduated from college, he was reasonably proficient in #1 and #2. As for #3, Kevin knew he would still have to learn about money. That journey would come later, from yet another job experience.

Now, let's turn to you.

- When you ask a young person what their expertise is, most times s/he or will answer "I'm not an expert in anything." If that is true for you, it's okay! Let's try another way.

- When do you feel the most pleasure accomplishing something?

For example, did you feel great pleasure getting into college? Building a computer model? Did you ever feel good helping a poor person? Were you proud of yourself when you taught a child something new? Did you experience your most fun and "success" scoring goals in soccer with close teammates? (In fact, this was one of your author's story – leading to one of his skills as an entrepreneur building strong, diverse teams, just like in soccer.) Or, did you experience real achievement selling some products during a summer job in high school? Building something with your own hands? Raising a wonderful garden full of healthy things to eat? In other words, what have been the moments in your life when you stepped back a bit and said to yourself, "That's great, and I did it." You can also think about accomplishments such as getting an A in a class, or even getting a scholarship for college. Fill in the left column of the chart in Figure 2.4 as best you can.

Next, think more in-depth into what was behind those accomplishments – and not just your drive or core values, but rather, the specific types of skills or knowledge need to make that accomplishment. Fill out the right column of the chart. Teaching a child a new language, for example, takes both language proficiency and excellent communication skills. Or, building a new shed requires design and engineering skills. Or winning the state championship

Articulate Your Natural and Learned Skills

	My accomplishment	Abilities, skills, knowledge needed for that specific accomplishment
1		
2		
3		
4		
5		

Figure 2.4   Articulate your natural and learned skills

in soccer requires not only physical skills but teamwork, and more teamwork! If you won a prize at a computer programming competition or created a mobile app, the common skill is "computer-related knowledge." You might feel proud of having taken care of an elderly or physically impaired person – and the essential skills here attention to detail, patience, and some medical awareness.

Now, go through Figure 2.4 one more time. We want you to think about the two or three accomplishments that felt the very best. Look at the skills you exhibited that enabled these accomplishments; write them down on the list in Figure 2.5.

Next, are there any common skills that seem to be coming up in these top three accomplishments? There may be common threads. These are important to identify. For example, in Kevin's case, it was building things with his own hands.

How does this list look? Everyone on this Earth is good at *something*. Understanding your strength is important, for young people like yourselves to realize their natural skills, hone them, and join with people *with other complementary skills* to solve problems through innovation and entrepreneurship.

We think you will agree that it is a lot easier to find your strengths by reflecting on the skills emerging from your past accomplishments rather than simply agonizing over what you might do best in the future. A great baseball hitter has a natural swing coupled with training and practice; a game developer, a natural imagination coupled with studied programming skills, and again, practice; a musician has a natural ear for melody, training, and time on the keyboard. We believe that the most accomplished people build on natural skills that they sharpen through study and application.

Define Your Natural and Learned Skills

1.

2.

3.

Are these just functional or technical skills, e.g. programming or design?

Or do you have some natural people skills, e.g. building a team, negotiating, running a process, or selling?

Figure 2.5   Define your natural and learned skills

FINDING A PROBLEM TO SOLVE THAT ALIGNS WITH YOUR CORE VALUES AND PERSONAL SKILLS

It is far more preferable to pick a problem to solve in a world where you have deep motivation and some natural skills to solve that problem. In this way, the problem becomes more doable for you and the team you build around yourself.

For example, someone who does not like the sight of blood should probably not become a surgeon. Or, someone with no flair for music should not become a professional musician. And as you students can probably attest with one or two personal experiences as students, someone who does not have a passion for teaching and cannot communicate clearly should probably not become a teacher!

Finding the *right problem* takes time. The right problem means: (a) that a large number of people experience the problem and it is important to them, (b) that solving that problem fits with your core values, and (c) that the innovation and marketing of that solution builds on both your natural and learned skills. This is 1–2–3: an important problem; alignment with core values; and leveraging your abilities.

Kevin is a good example. He had his core values and the two skills of engineering and communicating well established by the time he finished college, with a degree in environmental

engineering. He had learned machine design and mechanical engineering. He also had significant knowledge about local and global environmental issues and regulations, and emerging
technologies for environmental remediation. But with all these skills, he still needed a specific
problem to solve, one to which he could apply his passion and skills. Where and how could he
help rural communities with impactful engineering innovation?

Kevin looked hard in Nairobi and the surrounding area for a good environmental engineering job. Such a position was tough to find, especially in the 2004–05 time frame. The
Kenyan government was not focused on environmentally friendly manufacturing processes
or remediation. And the few jobs he was able to track down in environmental science were in
areas such as water sanitization for the rapidly expanding capital city – Nairobi – and not for
the rural poor.

Kevin took a bold step. He teamed up with several similarly-minded friends from Maseno
University to create their own NGO. Their focus was to develop a trash collection service for
the villages and small towns back home. His first partner, Anthony, was quite different than
Kevin: Anthony had a natural skill for deal-making and negotiations. Kevin's second partner,
Hope, had studied accounting and finance. She was good at managing the money flowing in
and out of the NGO. Different but complementary skills are *a good thing* for any business or,
in this case, NGO. Their concept was simple. Collect trash, charge the local communities or
citizens for the trash removal, and bring the garbage to major transfer stations that sorted out
reusable waste and ship it off to China (which used to be the destination point for much of the
glass and plastic discarded in Africa). These transfer stations would pay Kevin's team some
money for the trash, and together with small user fees, the three friends would make enough
money to live and employ a few villagers. At least, that was their original idea.

Unfortunately, people didn't collect trash in these rural communities. Villagers would burn
paper and discard glass and plastic by the sides of the road. And there it would sit. There was
no history of these villages paying anything to deal with their trash. For these reasons, Kevin
and his partners realized that there wasn't sufficient money to sustain the NGO. After a year of
trying to create cash flow, reality set in, and Kevin had to temporarily put the venture on pause
and find a job that would pay a reasonable salary.

A well-paying position in the environmental science area was unlikely in his country, other
than a government job. Kevin also wanted to learn about managing money, which would
not happen as a government employee. Kevin convinced the manager of a commercial bank
back in Nairobi to hire him as a commercial loan officer. He received training in commercial
lending and finance, learned spreadsheets, and how to interact with banking clients. He
worked in commercial lending for four years, and did well. The bank manager had big plans
for Kevin's future.

Kevin's burning core values remained, however. To everyone's surprise, this fast-track loan
officer took his savings, warmly thanked his superiors and peers, and quit his job. When Kevin
shared that he would build a profit-making business to help clean up the trash of Kenya, his
friends thought he was crazy. (Now, they don't – Kevin still does his banking with the same
bank and sees his old colleagues regularly.)

During this transition period, opportunity knocked again. Mentors at his university told
him about a special Master's Degree in Environmental Science and Technology in one of the

FINDING THE RIGHT PROBLEM TO SOLVE

finest engineering schools in Europe – the Delft University of Technology, otherwise known as TU Delft. Even better, there were full scholarships available to support students from Africa with a passion for achieving social impact with technology.

Kevin was a natural for the program, so off he went – from the hot, sunny days of Kenya into the cold, windy rains of the Netherlands. He studied, made new friends, he got a world view on climate challenges and environmental science and technology. One of the signature aspects of TU Delft Master's programs is the Master's thesis project. These are not just research papers. At TU Delft, students typically have to design and build real things within their area of study. Kevin saw this as an opportunity to transition from a trash collection business into creating a new product that would use recycled trash. He was surrounded by accomplished engineering professors, excellent prototyping facilities, and bright, engaging students from around the world. It was time to innovate.

FROM THE PROBLEM TO SOLVE TO A PRODUCT IDEA, AND THEN TO A NEW BUSINESS

Kevin's problem to solve was environmental remediation. His old way of solving this problem was collecting trash and getting it to a transfer station that would ship recyclable material to other countries. Kevin wanted to develop a higher-order product with commercial value that used these materials to do something of value back in his home country. Also, at about this time, China stopped taking in the trash for recycling from Africa. Kenya needed another way to recycle: glass and plastic. Timing can often be everything for the entrepreneur; when opportunity knocks, you've got to recognize it and jump on it.

For his applied Master's thesis at Delft, Kevin began experimenting with equipment to mix crushed glass with melted plastic to extrude things such as roofing tiles or paving stones. Extrusion is the process of melting materials together and pushing them through molds while still hot – like Play-Doh – and then cooling it to form the desired shapes. He figured he could mix in sand for color and as a binder. A roof tile made this way would be a lot lighter than the current clay tiles used in Kenya. And, the new composite tile would also be a lot less fragile than a clay tile. These should be big wins for builders, who could pay standard prices for roofing tiles but get something better – a lighter and stronger tile (Figure 2.6).

Kevin also posited that builders with lighter tiles could use considerably less supporting timber underneath a new roof and build these supports in less time – increasing their house-building efficiency. The builders would not have to buy extra tiles to make up for inevitable breakage in transportation over rough roads or during installation. And for Kevin's societal concerns, the raw materials could be collected by villagers, who would earn money for cleaning up their villages. The concept was not just a new product with a compelling use case; it was a sustainable business model that would collect waste products from rural Kenya. And if Kevin was successful, eventually, he might hire hundreds of employees to pick up the glass and plastic, work the machines, and deliver finished products to building sites.

During his summer break from school at TU Delft, Kevin returned to Kenya. He made numerous prototypes by hand in very low volumes to validate the composite tiles with builders back in Kenya. Talking to people was one of Kevin's natural skills and he enjoyed the process. He found that, as expected, traditional clay tiles were heavy and fragile. His prototypes would be half as heavy and many times more robust. As standard practice, the builders were buying an extra 30% tiles to cover probable breakages. And the weight was just as important: to roof a typical four-bedroomed house in Africa required 2000 roof tiles. With clay, the calculations came out to about 10 tons of tile weight on the roof; with Kevin's composite tiles, just 4 tons. The savings in structure support beams was almost 50%.

Upon returning from Kenya to finish his Master's degree, Kevin took a "clean tech" entrepreneurship class at Delft, where he created a business model and financial projections for his venture and a proper pitch deck. (This is where your authors first had the pleasure of meeting him). Kevin knew he needed a high-volume extrusion machine which, when combined with a small manufacturing facility, would cost approximately $200,000 in Kenya. Without assets to use as collateral, his old bank in Nairobi was not an option.

Source: Kevin Mureithi, Eco Blocks & Tiles. Used with permission.

Figure 2.6   Roofs with Kevin's composite tiles

As fortune would have it, Kevin was introduced to a Dutch NGO located adjacent to TU Delft. Over a few months, he worked with the managers of this NGO, ValorWater, which supported environmental programs and related ventures in developing countries. Managers at ValorWater helped him improve his business plan, particularly the operations and financials in the plan. In the process, they saw Kevin as a bright, fully committed environmental entrepreneur. A few months after his graduation, ValorWater gave Kevin a grant to buy his first machine and build a facility. This grant was nonequity dilutive and served as seed financing. ValorWater shared Kevin's values and thought his mission worthy.

Yes, you readers might say that Maseno University, TU Delft, and ValorWater, and even China's cessation of recycling trash from Kenya, were all bits of good fortune for Kevin – but you must also agree that Kevin did a lot to make his own luck and take advantage of the opportunity in front of him. *Entrepreneurship is often making the most of some good luck.*

Upon graduation, Kevin returned home, re-engaged his old partners, and built his facility. He sent us a picture the very day he broke ground for the new factory (Figure 2.7).

While Kevin was having the factory built, he bought machines and a trash collection truck, all used equipment – and after two and a half years of planning, experimenting, and fundraising, Eco Blocks & Tiles was in business.

Kevin targeted his home village, Gilgil, as the first territory to pay villagers for gathering plastic and glass. And now, he has about a dozen employees working the crushing and melting machines and extruding composite tiles (Figure 2.8).

Source: Kevin Mureithi, Eco Blocks & Tiles. Used with permission.

Figure 2.7   Kevin purchases land for his production plant!

Source: Kevin Mureithi, Eco Blocks & Tiles. Used with permission.

Figure 2.8   Kevin and team at Eco Blocks & Tiles

NOW, IT IS YOUR TURN

Hopefully, you have taken inspiration from Kevin's journey and have started to think about what it means for you at the beginning of your journey. Like Kevin, such journeys are as much about your personal discovery about who you are, what fulfills you as a person, and how you might contribute to society as well as your livelihood.

We have three fundamental questions to guide this personal discovery of innovation:

1. What is the problem you want to solve?
2. How does that problem align with your core values?
3. Do your skills, either natural or learned, apply well to solving that problem?

Question 1: define your Problem Space

Take a look at the list of potential areas in which your instinct and experience tell you that you want to explore seriously and potentially work during your career. If we have not listed your area of problem–passion, please write it down in the blank space at the bottom of the template (Figure 2.9).

The big problem you want to solve

☐ I want to help people learn better   ☐ I want to improve transportation

☐ I want to improve nutrition/wellness   ☐ I want a food/nutrition/or wellness product innovator

☐ I want to improve agriculture   ☐ I want to create new computing and communications technology

☐ I want to be an energy/environmental innovator ☐ I want to create systems to help companies run more efficiently

☐ I want to help the disabled   ☐ I want to create new medical therapies to cure diseases

☐ I want to innovate in gaming & entertainment ☐ I want to improve personal and/or cyber safety

☐ I want to improve home/building construction ☐ I want to improve sports products or services

Or, I want to _____

Figure 2.9   The big problem you want to solve

If you have selected two or three areas in which you want to work, please narrow this down to a single area, not just for this course, but a problem area you wish to explore over the next four to five years while in school and perhaps doing internships. We will call this your Problem Space (see Figure 2.10). There are numerous specific problems within that space, each with its own "use cases" and potential innovations – one of which you will focus on with teammates in this course. And you do not have to use all the words we used above or even the same words.

Make this Problem Space your own.

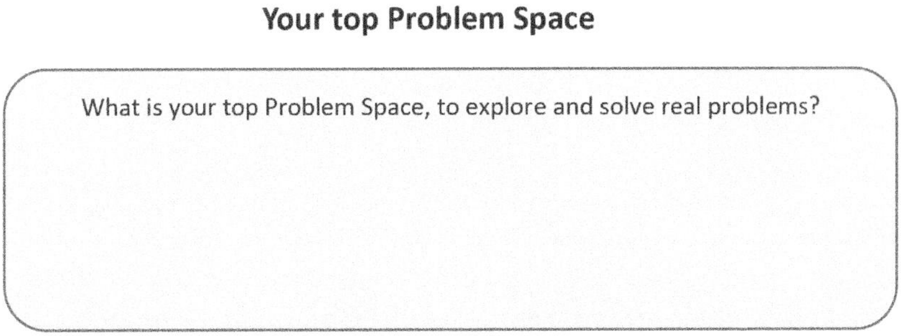

Your top Problem Space

What is your top Problem Space, to explore and solve real problems?

Figure 2.10   Your top Problem Space

Question 2: connecting your core values to a Problem Space

The next step: for the Problem Space you have selected, does it resonate strongly with your core values?

Let's say that you were home for dinner with your family or with your closest friends. Someone asks you about what area you are working in as a student that might lead to a sustained venture. As you respond, how excited and passionate are you? How much does that Problem Space resonate in your gut, with your core values? And if that uncle or friend says, "that sounds ridiculous!" or "I can think of more important problems to solve," how strongly would you argue back, "Not so!" In short, do you have passion and conviction that comes from selecting a Problem Space that directly touches your core values?

One way we can assess this is by filling out the template in Figure 2.11. Use a scale of 1 (no conviction) to 5 (a lot of passion and conviction) to fill in the middle box in the figure. For the idea you have in mind, does it really score a 5, or is it a really a 3? Can you then redefine the Problem Space to create a stronger fit with you core values, just as Kevin pivoted his business idea and engineering for the composite tile made from recycled glass and plastic.

Connecting Your Core Values to a Problem Space

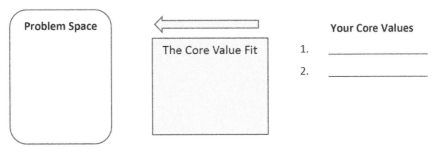

Figure 2.11   Connecting your core values to a Problem Space

If you don't feel conviction and passion for that Problem Space – well, perhaps you should think of another that resonates more deeply. You will be a lot happier and more effective. The passion and skills with which we do our work is the essence of a meaningful, happy life.

Question 3: your skills and the Problem Space

Do your natural and learned skills seem to lend themselves to innovate in the Problem Space you identified above, a Space that resonates with your core values? Regarding skills, do you feel that you can get a running start designing a new product or service for your chosen Problem Space? Are your natural and learned skills a good fit, perhaps even a strong fit?

Can you make a list of those skills that fit well, and other skills that you are clearly missing? Often, missing skills can be gathered by convincing certain other people to join your team. On the other hand, if you have no natural or learned skills that fit your Problem Space, you should think about another Space that takes better advantage of your skills (See Figure 2.12).

This is an iterative process. The driving question is, where might you be most effective as a problem-solver? Solving a problem, carefully chosen, becomes a great source of internal satisfaction – *for any one at any age.*

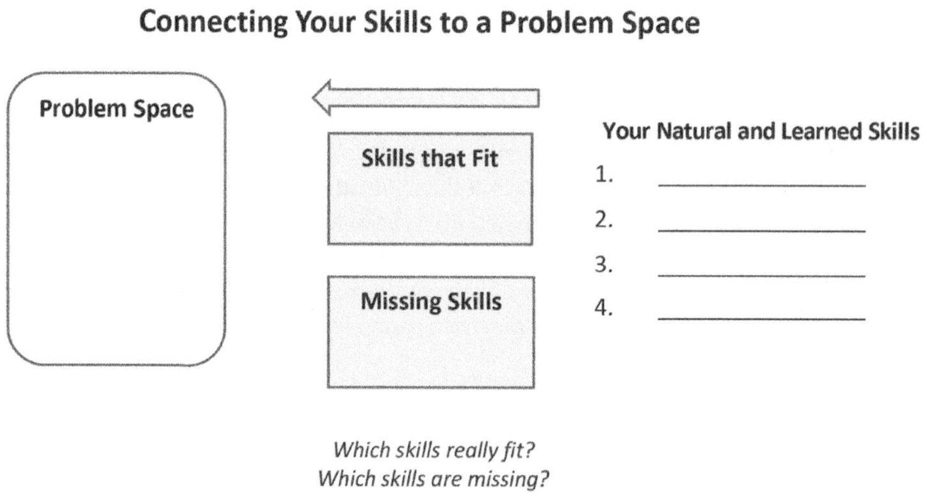

Connecting Your Skills to a Problem Space

Which skills really fit?
Which skills are missing?

Figure 2.12   Connecting your core values to a Problem Space

DEFINING PURPOSE, FULFILLMENT, AND HAPPINESS

Now, try to find a fusion of problems to solve, core values, and natural or learned skills. Use the template in Figure 2.13 to define the synergies between core values, skills, and problems to solve. Keep working on all three dimensions until you arrive at a sweet spot that not only makes sense but makes you feel good.

Connecting a Problem Space with Personal Values and Skills

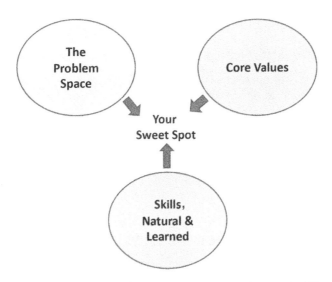

Figure 2.13 Connecting a Problem Space with personal values and skills

Take some time to think about this chart and what it means for you. The answer will lead to the right problem to solve, not just for your innovation's intended users but also *for you*. It is the essence of mindful innovation, which in turn often leads to both happiness at work and success. People who can make such a connection have a certain energy and glow that lasts throughout their lives. Let's reflect on the case study used in this chapter. Kevin is living his dream – helping the rural poor by bringing to market superior building materials made from recycled trash, employing villagers as well as staff in the plant, and driving the collection trucks. Just look at his smile at the beginning of this chapter as well as the other pictures of him on his new land, and then with his team. Anyone who knows Kevin knows that he is not just posing for the camera. It is the type of smile that can only be achieved by realizing one's core values through work, enhancing one's natural skills through classes and experiential learning, and creating an innovation that solves an important societal problem.

We want to see these smiles on your faces. Let this course be a start.

STEP 1: SHOW HOW KEVIN CONNECTED PROBLEM SPACE, CORE VALUES, AND SKILLS

Go back and draw Figure 2.13 for Kevin, with just a few bullet points next to each circle.

STEP 2: SHOW ANOTHER EXAMPLE

Do you have another example of an individual who has created a wonderful marriage of an important problem to be solved, core values, and personal skills for their own life's work? Is there someone you admire for this?

- Spend an hour talking on the phone or Zoom to them about their journey and its meaning to them personally and professionally – and then write down a one-page reflection for yourself and to share with others.
- What critical events in that person's life help create the realization and fusion of core values, skills, and a significant problem to solve?
- Where does this person's journey go next?

STEP 3: APPLY THE TEMPLATES TO YOUR OWN PROJECT

- First, identify the Problem Space where you think you would like to apply yourself over the coming ten years, if not more. Complete Figures 2.9 and 2.10 for yourself.
- Next, focus on your personal core values. Complete Figure 2.11 for yourself. A way of thinking about this is that if you create an impactful innovation for the Problem Space, will your personal guiding principles be emphasized?
- And last, take an inventory of your natural and learned skills that might apply to your chosen Problem Space. Complete Figure 2.12 for yourself. What skills do you have that lend themselves to problem-solving and innovation in your chosen Problem Space? And just as important, what are the implications for other people you want to include as team members for your venture?

Finally, after applying these templates to your thinking, please take a final step of integration to construct the synergy of Problem Space, Core Values, and Skills as shown in Figure 2.13.

The result should feel good in three ways: first, in your core or belly; second, in your heart; and third, in your head. In the Asian/Eastern tradition, the core in our bellies contains our internal energy and power. Our heart contains compassion. And our head – our thinking and spirit on how to achievemeaning and purpose that connects with the world around us for a greater good. *Find all three and nothing can stop you!*

While these templates might look simple, they require some careful thought in a quiet place. Most people do not think enough about these matters as they plan their careers and lives. Kevin did, and he is living a meaningful life as an entrepreneur and a social innovator. This thinking goes well beyond entrepreneurship. A doctor who brings compassion, conviction, and learned skills to her/his patients is no less mindful, no less a contributor to society, even though the doctor is unlikely to be an entrepreneur. Each type of career is its own form of creating a purposeful, fulfilling life.

Prepare a few PowerPoint slides to share your ideas and self-assessment with your classmates.

From here, we will next form innovation teams who share a common Problem Space, similar core values, and yet, have complementary skills needed to build a strong team.

3
Forming a team

INTRODUCTION

While there are many great solo inventors, *innovation* – the application of science, technology, and good old-fashioned common sense to solve real-world problems – invariably *takes a team*. In this course, you will be far more effective innovating for a real-world problem if you form a team where people (a) have a common interest for innovation in a given Problem Space, (b) share core values, and (c) have complementary (but not necessarily identical) skills. The purpose of this chapter is to help you form these teams and get you to work, stretching your innovative minds on a practice problem and then starting to get down to business for your team's Problem Space.

LEARNING OBJECTIVES

In this chapter, we will learn:

1. Shared Problem Spaces as the foundation for effective teams.
2. The principles of good team design in terms of shared core values and complementary skills.
3. Building a team with your classmates with compatible core values, complementary skills, and a strong interest in a specific Problem Space for innovation and venture development.

BUILDING AN INNOVATION TEAM

Now it's time to create innovation teams for this class. It is far more productive and fun to work in teams for innovation, as long as those teams share a common purpose, passion, and a commitment to share the work fairly. You've already done a lot of this thinking and self-realization in the previous chapter. Now, we want you to share this work with your classmates and, through this, to create teams with shared interests in Problem Spaces, compatible if not mutually reinforcing core values, and some different skill sets that can lead to a winning team – just like any team sport. An excellent basketball team has centers, forwards, and guards – each specialized in specific areas; a soccer team has its forwards, wings, midfielders, fullbacks, and a goaltender. Most teams need a good team to succeed. So do most ventures.

Your teacher will help facilitate discussion around your problem interests, core values, and skills. The best way is to organize by Problem Space first and proceed from there.

Also – and so very important – we ask you for a moment to set aside former friendships that you might have with classmates before this course. Start with a fresh page. This might be the time to meet new people and perhaps long-term teammates with whom you will innovate and venture.

The approach we want you to take is:

- First, find other people who have the same interest, and hopefully genuine passion, for a common Problem Space. For example, if you want to innovate in healthcare, it is preferable to find other team members who have a substantial interest in exploring healthcare innovation. If it's environmental remediation and climate management – the same thing, as it would be for next-generation gaming or entertainment, agricultural innovation, or water resources management on this planet. If it is new social services for helping the poor, that's great too. It doesn't have to be all about making money. The bottom line is that you want to build a team of aspiring *changemakers* for a given Problem Space.

- Second, once you have a group of people with a keen interest in a given Problem Space, we want you to understand and then find harmony amongst the core values of these potential teammates. If there is one person who cares first and foremost about making money for him or herself, that's fine, but this might not be a match for a team focused on health services for the disadvantaged. Or, if the Problem Space is health and wellness through better food and drink, if a potential member has no genuine interest or demonstrable activity of eating healthily – well, the passion for the project is unlikely to be there. Brewing a new type of craft beer might be a better alternative for that person! There are plenty of other Problem Spaces where a better match can be made. Matches for building teams need to be based on core values-based behavior by team members. This type of alignment keeps the team going through thick and thin.

- Third, and the critical icing on the cake, try to build a team that has a balance of skills. Many years ago, actual research into successful venture companies showed that a balance of skills was one of the essential factors in a team.[1] The most common way to think about this is to balance technical, customer-facing, and business/financial skills in a venture team. For a project such as the one in this class, where we focus on *innovation projects* that may or may not lead to an actual venture, we can have a somewhat looser definition. You should have someone who loves technology and might be studying the science or engineering used in your Problem Space. Then, perhaps, other team members whose skills are finding and talking to potential users of your innovation. And you might have others who enjoy thinking about the design of the business side of innovation – how one charges for a new product or service, how it is manufactured or supplied, and the costs of doing so, e.g. defining the business model. Since you are admittedly just starting your careers, no one will be an expert in any of these things – but already, you have some evidence and early experience in your natural skills, plus the courses you have enjoyed taking already. As we learned in the prior chapter, young people should try to understand and build upon their natural strengths. Try to build a team with people who are naturally good at different things, rather than just at the same thing.

CREATING DISCUSSION GROUPS BY PROBLEM SPACES

In Chapter 2, we asked you to select one or two favorite Problem Spaces. For convenience, that template is shown again here (Figure 3.1):

The big problem you want to solve

☐ I want to help people learn better ☐ I want to improve transportation

☐ I want to improve nutrition/wellness ☐ I want a food/nutrition/or wellness product innovator

☐ I want to improve agriculture ☐ I want to create new computing and communications technology

☐ I want to be an energy/environmental innovator ☐ I want to create systems to help companies run more efficiently

☐ I want to help the disabled ☐ I want to create new medical therapies to cure diseases

☐ I want to innovate in gaming & entertainment ☐ I want to improve personal and/or cyber safety

☐ I want to improve home/building construction ☐ I want to improve sports products or services

Or, I want to _____

Figure 3.1   Finding your Problem Space

This list is by no means exhaustive. Add others that most interest you. For example, you might be interested in helping to improve the way building, or homes are constructed. Or innovate in the field of sports, with equipment, athlete recruitment, and so forth.

Note that saying that you want to build a web app is not a sufficient answer. A web app is just a means to an end. State the end goal of the app first! What larger problem area will the app address? And while tempting, designing a new service to help students cook or deliver food to other students – well, that idea has been tried a thousand times and never really worked. Same with finding an apartment or roommates. There is too much competition, fragmented as it is, to make a significant impact. Try to focus on areas that will substantially impact society and are not just a student-to-student venture.

Your teacher will probably organize the teams into these interest areas. If your class is virtual, you should work on the Problem Space template and then gather in virtual groups to discuss:

- How do group members define the different dimensions of that Problem Space? In other words, what are the major problems that might be potential projects within the Problem Space?

- Which of these specific problems already have emerging solutions? What are these emerging solutions? What are people doing today to try to contend with or solve the problem? Which ones don't seem to have any real answers? (These might be high potential projects for your team.)

- Are there two or three specific problems that seem most interesting to at least three people in the discussion group? Is this the makings of a team?

The groups can then share their conversations with the rest of the class, report possible teams for specific problem areas, and see if other people might wish to join their team. The teams should not be set in stone yet, especially until we look at the following two steps.

FINDING SHARED, COMPATIBLE CORE VALUES, AND PASSIONS

In the last chapter, you were also asked to consider your core values deeply. Another way to think about core values is as your passion for improving something in society or succeeding in a particular industry, for example, to be the next Steve Jobs to make computing so much easier for the rest of us.

Core team members need to have compatible if not identical core values. If you want to create a societally focused venture, founders and employees genuinely need to buy into that social mission because it will directly affect what you create and how much money you are comfortable making. Suppose you want to start a company designing the world's most innovative, efficient buildings. Everyone on the team needs to cherish the environment as well as attractive building design. Otherwise, people will be working at cross purposes and clients will be poorly served. In one of the author's first companies, our clear shared core value and passion was (a) entrepreneurship, and (b) innovation in the open systems software environment (Unix/Linux), and the problem to solve was to create great software tools for building real time process control applications for things such as medical equipment or brewing beer! Also, we shared a common university – in this case, MIT – and felt a companionship of problem-solving "nerds" who wanted to tackle hard problems with software.

Discovering common share values does not happen through a simple questionnaire. It takes thought, iteration, and openness. Fortunately, you have already worked through that process in the previous chapter. You have come to understand your core values – the attitudes and behaviors you cherish above others. This type of awareness is a huge accomplishment for someone just starting their career. Now, you just need to share this with your classmates.

Another important aspect of core values is the type of business that might be created from an innovation. Imagine a spectrum that ranges from a purely mercantile to a purely nonprofit enterprise. And in the middle is a hybrid organization that wants to generate profit but also wants to contribute some of its profits back to societal causes. If you look at Figure 3.2, one might consider an old company such as Monsanto as being on one extreme, well known for purely commercial interests with little demonstrated care for small farmers or the environment (Monsanto was sued extensively for its behavior). The Red Cross or Doctors without Borders are on the other extreme. And in the middle of the spectrum, there is a company such as Patagonia, with founders and executives committed to sustainable, environmentally-friend practices.

Patagonia manufactures outdoor and sports active apparel that is premium-priced but produced with a green global supply chain (Figure 3.2). Plus, Patagonia contributes a percentage of operating profit to environmental causes (Figure 3.3).

When talking about Problem Spaces and personal motivations for pursuing a career in a particular Problem Space, you should also see if there are shared values amongst your class-

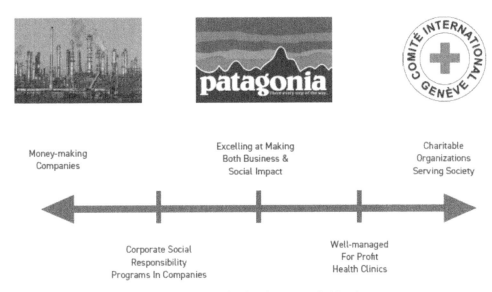

Money-making
Companies

Excelling at Making
Both Business &
Social Impact

Charitable
Organizations
Serving Society

Corporate Social
Responsibility
Programs In Companies

Well-managed
For Profit
Health Clinics

Figure 3.2   The spectrum of an organization/company's identity

Patagonia: Called the World's Most Responsible Company

There are those rare companies that excel both in making money and helping the larger society. In fact, helping society becomes part of their core mission and the branding for their products and services. And making money helps provide the extra cash to allow these companies to help society more. Rather than be in conflict, the founders figure out the magic recipe for making these two goals synergistic. Such companies "create value" in more than one way, good for their shareholders, good for their customers, and good for society.

The first picture on this page is Yvon Chouinard, the founder of Patagonia. His company is a stunning example of success in both areas, now approaching $1 billion in annual revenue and over 1000 employees. Also shown is Rose Marcario, the long-time CEO until 2020. She is a Buddhist, environmentally and socially concerned, and also a tremendous manager.

Patagonia strives to achieve sustainability through careful, detailed practices in its global supply chain, ranging from the recycled materials it uses, to the labor practices of its suppliers, to the carbon footprint of its manufacturing and distribution process. Patagonia has contributed nearly $100M to environmental causes and continues to allocate 1% of its sales to such causes.

Patagonia has a synergistic mission, to provide the best quality apparel for outdoor enthusiasts, and in turn, help protect those very outdoor environments in which its clothes are used – be it on the mountain or on the bicycle ride to work. It has created a compelling brand that attracts actual or aspiring outdoor enthusiasts – as well as employees who seek to actively contribute to this mission.

Figure 3.3   Patagonia, the world's most responsible company

mates for specific points on the spectrum shown in Figure 3.2. Even the most mercantile of companies must now embrace environmental and societal awareness in the design and management of their operations because this is a primary concern of their consumers and business partners. Learn about how your potential team members feel about this balance.

In a meeting with prospective team members, already aligned by Problem Space, take the step of sharing your core values. Is there compatibility? Is there authenticity in the form of direct personal experiences that are the grounding for that core value? Often that comes from family history or an earlier educational or internship experience.

Listen carefully. Are there any apparent incompatibilities? For example, a potential team member who cares about personal reputation and financial success will not be compatible with team members driven largely by social mission. Or, a climate-focused Problem Space needs team members who are passionate about climate change and sustainability. Otherwise, there will likely be frustrations down the road in doing the work for this course, and beyond in an actual venture. This is important because many ventures start precisely in early-stage courses such as this course. You just never know what might emerge from bright minds and good hearts!

Keep listening. Does one team member seem to have an excellent way of expressing her/his core value that is authentic, inspirational, yet grounded in the real world? That approach might help imbue a new venture with rich core values and also, design practical product or service that will have a real impact – much like Patagonia or eyeglass manufacturer, Warby Parker, Tesla, or Apple.

Listening with care is a crucial skill. Ask "why is that important to you?" when someone shares a deeply held idea. Find the underlying motivations and the grounding experiences of your potential team members. This is an important step in self and group awareness. You will be spending a lot of time working together – so choose wisely and thoughtfully. Core values may sound "soft" to some readers, but we assure you that ventures are expressions of the character, skills, and human quality of the people who start and build them.

BUILDING THE TEAM: MEL'S PRINCIPLE

We've considered shared Problem Space and core values. Now, the last all-important step in team building is to strive for a diversity of skills.

Early on in one of your author's first ventures, we formed a Board of Directors to bring some outside perspective to help our business. This included several non-founder outsiders. One of these was Mel Litvin, known as "the Captain" around Boston. Your author had met him near MIT through friends. Mel was tough and direct, having flown fighter planes off the decks of aircraft carriers. At that time, he was in his mid-50s, running a computer printer manufacturer near Boston. From the $300,000 high-speed printers made by that company to the $3 silk flowers he imported from China in his next company, Mel was incredibly versatile as a business person. Above all else, he cherished cash in a company, whether it was high-tech or low-tech. He was old-school, tough as nails, and just what we needed.

From Day 1, the Captain proceeded to teach us "smart kids" about the real world of business with expressions such as "You guys think you are so smart, but really, you ain't all that smart." Such talk, with action demanded, formed how we charged customers and collected our money, how to create a selective approach to selling and qualifying resellers, and how to build out our product line with value-added services. The most important thing he taught us, however, was how to round out our team. Let's apply this thinking to your innovation teams.

Mel walked into one of your authors' offices one day and had him write down all the things he was genuinely good at doing on the left side of a blank piece of paper as a set of bullet points. At that time, your author was only 24 years old.

Then, he had your author write down all the things that he was not so good at doing on the right side of a piece of paper, also as a set of bullet points. And of course, Mel proceeded to add more "not so good" bullet points that he knew would be important for the growth of the company. *We were young and did not fully know what we needed to know.*

Figure 3.4 provides a simple template for you to make your own list of personal skills. Take a moment to take a first pass now.

Then, Mel did something rather shocking. He took the author's completed template and ripped that piece of paper in half, right down the middle, splitting the list of things the author thought he was good at doing with those in which he lacked skills and experience. Even more shocking, Mel then crumbled up the half with the strengths listed into a little ball, and with obvious delight, threw your author and his skills into the trash can in the corner of the office! The good things didn't matter? What a shock! Of course, that was not the point. Mel then said, "I'm getting sick of coming in here and watching you guys interview programmer after

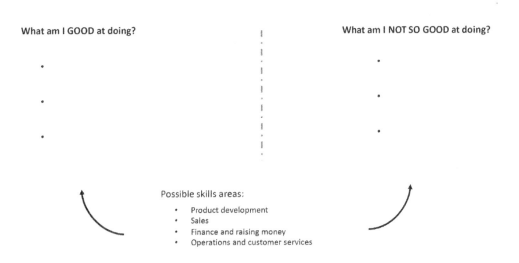

What am I GOOD at doing?　　　　　　　　　　　　　　What am I NOT SO GOOD at doing?

Possible skills areas:
- Product development
- Sales
- Finance and raising money
- Operations and customer services

1. Candidly list the your strengths on the left side

2. Just as candidly, list your weaknesses on the right side

3. Now focus on the right side. Who should you be trying to speak with as you form your team?

Figure 3.4　　　Personal skills assessment

programmer. You need to start hiring people who are not like you, with very different skills and experiences. If this company is ever going to grow into a real business, it needs to be more than an R&D shop. That's right, some folks who can wear a suit to go sell a big company, who have a nice pair of shoes, and have a good haircut!"

To make his point clear, he then took the remaining, uncrumpled piece of paper and taped it on the side of your author's computer screen and made a pretty big deal of the same with the other partners in the venture. He told us to look at it every time we picked up the phone to talk to someone who was not a customer. Of course we were going to continue to hire great programmers. At the same time, however, we needed to start addressing our weaknesses with experienced people who were good in areas where we were lacking, and every bit as good in those areas as we excelled at programming. This meant sales as well as working with spreadsheets, managing cash flow and budgets.

Focus on creating a team with a diverse set of skills. Mel's voice rings to this day: "You guys want to talk to people just like yourselves, a bunch of nerds. That's fine, but nerds most often don't know how to sell, belly to belly. With all the people you plan to hire, you had better find a few that can hit the streets and produce revenue, real revenue, and double it year after year."

Mel's template also showed that we had to hire dedicated customer support personnel and other technical staff to work with big customers to integrate our software with their software and machines. It made no sense for the programmers to fly to a different city or country to do complex systems integration – which would make our development schedules for products instantly irrelevant. Or to have our fastest, most creative programmer spending hours each day handling trivial support calls just because he loved to talk with people and cared so much about the software they were using.

In hindsight, such moves were pivotal to our company's growth. The Captain made decisions brutally clear – and insisted on action – or otherwise, with his heavy Boston accent, "I'm out the door." And the thing was that he meant it.

Mel's intervention with his simple framework was the most important advice he gave us in those early years. If it worked for us, it will also surely work for you.

NOW, RECRUIT TEAM MEMBERS ONTO YOUR TEAM

Who is going to be "your" team? You want a team with diverse skills and an *esprit de corps* that comes from shared goals, values, and passions.

We also want you to organize yourselves in a way that takes the best advantage of every team member's skills. This means collectively deciding which individuals are best at doing some things, and other individuals, other things – the work products of which are then brought together for mutual understanding and integration. Not everyone needs to do the same set of work, but everyone needs to do their agreed set of work. In this way, every team member contributes where they have capabilities and genuine interest. And any free-rider needs to be given a warning or two and then asked to find someplace else to work. Set the ground rules for your innovation project work up front and live by them.

Being part of a dysfunctional team is an awful experience; being part of a high-performance team is one of the best experiences in the world. It takes some careful thought, listening, and maturity to build a high-performance team. Use this course to enhance your skills in team building and team self-management.

Reader exercises

STEP 1

Hold conversations both within and outside of class to find individuals who also have a primary focus on your Problem Space. Ideal team sizes are between three and five individuals. If you have more people than that number in your class who have the same problem interest, work further to divide that Problem Space into subspaces. Every single area listed in our template (shown in Figure 3.1 above) can be subdivided.

For example, Education as a Problem Space can involve subsets that include online services, new types of dynamic courseware, and even age segmentation, for example, high school, college, the elderly, the learning disabled, etc. Smart buildings and infrastructure can include commercial versus residential structures, IoT systems, security systems, and so forth. And nutrition and wellness – that Problem Space segments into a half-dozen different areas.

STEP 2

As you gather in these teams to share ideas, spend time talking about your respective core values. What are people's personal experiences in that Problem Space, and their visceral, compelling passion for solving problems in it? And perhaps as important as anything else, are there different perspectives on the type of venture that might be created through innovation?

STEP 3

Do a skills assessment of potential team members. S*trive for a diversity of natural and learned skills.* And don't forget to go beyond classes or jobs. Find out what people "love to do" and are also "good at doing," whether by studying it, having some type of current or prior job using that skill, or is just a "natural" by virtue of genetic or some other type or predisposition. Construct the three- to five-person innovation teams. Your professor will help guide this team formation and will invariably have his or her preferred team sizes.

NOTE

1. Roberts, E.B. (1991). *Entrepreneurs in High Technology.* Oxford: Oxford University Press.

4

Ideation – for and with the user

THE PURPOSE OF THE CHAPTER

The purpose of this chapter is to have your team develop its first innovation concept for its Problem Space. This innovative concept will improve throughout this book, refined through market, competitive, and in-depth user research. However, we must have a starting point that serves as the hypothesis to guide further work. This starting point will be either a new product or service concept that purposefully and pleasingly solves a specific target user's problem(s). Hopefully, after they start using your innovation, these early users will want to share their discovery with other potential users, creating a certain buzz around your innovation that is a prelude to a larger marketing and communication effort. This starting point is called the Customer Value Proposition. It is literally the refinement and narrowing of your original Problem Space into a more specific problem focus for which you then create a new product or service. On one simple page, the Customer Value Proposition helps you define the "who, what, where, and benefits" of your new product or service.

LEARNING OBJECTIVES

After reading this chapter, you should be able to:

1. Develop a Customer Experience Map for a specific use case in your larger Problem Space.
2. Develop a Mind Map of different innovation pathways to solve the user's problems.
3. Develop a Customer Value Proposition for a specific innovation concept – a new product or service – that solves user problems based on one of the innovation pathways in your Mind Map.

LET'S GET STARTED: MEET KATE

Kate was 27 years old and the year was 2009. She had worked as a technical sales representative for three years in a large company, with over $20 billion-plus annual revenue in the enterprise storage space. She was young, intelligent, good at her job, with a promising career path in technical sales.

However, the job was not satisfying her inner values and dreams of creating and running something herself. She knew it deep in her heart. Selling complex technology to store terabytes of data was not fulfilling her deeper core values. She cared most about two things: (1) health and wellness, and (2) having a job that she felt passionate about and which would make a positive impact in the world. She thought of herself as a "doer," which later became a way that she also thought about her target users. Kate was afraid of waking up at the age of 35, stuck in the same job. She began to think about alternatives. However, she also knew that she had learned the valuable skill of "selling" products to other businesses. That skill would come in handy later.

Kate lived her passion for health and wellness, perhaps to the extreme. She was a dedicated triathlete (combining long swims, bike rides, and runs). Figure 4.1 shows Kate running with her triathlete partner and, later, her business partner, Jeff. She prided herself on competing in "Ironman" triathlons 2.4-mile swims, 112-mile bike rides, and 26-mile runs! However, as she competed in long-distance training and actual competitions, she experienced several frustrations as a consumer, one of which was energy recovery snacks and drinks. The energy bars were full of mysterious chemicals and carbs, beverages were not much better, with bucket loads of sugar in each bottle. When she looked carefully at the ingredient decks of the major brands, she was hard-pressed to call them "healthy." Moreover, they were complicated, just like the storage systems she was tired of explaining to people in business sales.

Figure 4.1　　Kate and Jeff, triathletes first, entrepreneurs next

Kate started reading books on health and wellness in her spare time, lots of them. One that touched her inner core was Mike Pollan's *Food Rules*, with the basic idea that foods and drinks were far too complicated, filled with unhealthy chemicals, sugars, and fats. He encouraged readers to avoid all foods that have more than five ingredients. This minimalist approach to food became part of Kate's thinking.[1]

She made the fateful and bold decision to leave her tech sales job to pursue her passion for health and wellness. "Heck," she thought to herself, "I am young, and if not now, when? Besides, I can always go back to selling tech." She enrolled in the Master's of Science in Applied Nutrition at Northeastern University, quit her storage sales job, and worked part time at Lululemon Athletica as she was going to school. In her mind's eye, she saw herself as a health and wellness entrepreneur and somehow involved in nutrition – she just did not know the specifics yet.

In sum, Kate went back to learn what she thought she needed to pursue her core values and passions in the Problem Space of new products for health and wellness. Now, she just had to figure out the new product or service. It was her time to innovate.

DESIGN THINKING AND RAPID PROTOTYPING – TO IMPROVE THE EXPERIENCE OF THE TARGET USER

Innovation is a special word for your authors. It is more than scientific or other technology invention and discovery. Instead, it is the application of science and technology to improve the human condition, be it at work, or play, or simply living. Moreover, when we use the word innovate, we think about engineering not just to make things a little better but *a lot better* for the intended user.

The popular expression for the major method for this type of impactful innovation is *design thinking*. The innovator develops a strong empathy with target users to deeply understand their needs and problems and then designs impactful solutions – be these new products, services, or new processes within a company. One can also think of design thinking as use-inspired innovation or experience design.

That context for design thinking involves a specific type of situation or activity for a target user. This is called a use case. Going to class is a use case in education, with innovations such as hybrid or online learning. Reading materials or watching videos is another specific use case. Students working on group projects versus individual assignments are two very different use cases. Assessing work – for example, tests or presentations – is yet another specific use case. Sometimes, people refer to use cases as the jobs-to-be-done. People also sometimes refer to the user's problems as their "pains" and the improvements delivered to users as "gains." Use the language that works best for you. Make sure your teammates are on the same page!

The target user is also an important term. There is no universal target user for an innovation. Instead, through careful thought, different types of users can be segmented into distinct groups, whether by age, or gender, or position in a company, or even psychographic behaviors – such as an older person who is "young at heart." It is best to identify these different target user groups and select one group for your initial innovation project. The more specific you are, the clearer and more purposeful your innovation will be. Should you launch a company, you can then broaden your initial innovation into a product line or a suite of services that can address different user groups with slight variations that suit them better than your first user group.

Since this is user-centered design, as innovators, you now need to get out of your seat, spend some time with your target users, and observe and talk to them about their experiences in their use case. The use case might be as simple as going shopping to see the frustrations incurred getting to a store, finding certain products, perhaps adjusting them (such as clothes), and getting them home. The central idea is that through direct contact with target users, you as the innovator develop empathy with them and a deep understanding of their problems and frustrations. Only then can you make a difference in their lives with passionate and compassionate innovation. No one, even the most accomplished professor, is so smart that he or she can know the answer for a new target user and use case. Only by listening, observing, and conversing can you hope to develop the insights needed to create breakthrough, impactful solutions. This general approach is shown in Figure 4.2.

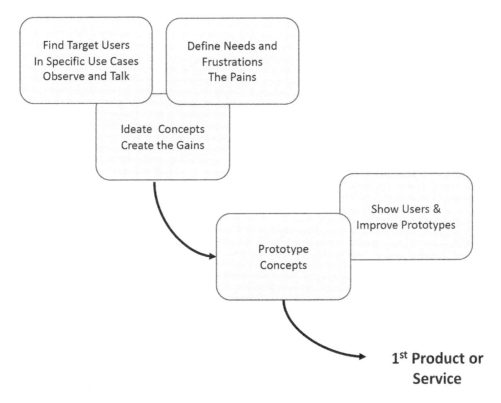

Figure 4.2   The process flow of design thinking

The other essential ingredient of design thinking is iterative, rapid prototyping of a new idea. Prototyping means not trying to make the final version of something right away. You get an idea – inspired by a target user – and you try to build it. Then you show it to that user, and hopefully several or more similar users, and then make the product or service features even better. This is different than traditional engineering or software development where developers try to learn everything needed in a product, write a formal specification with features, functions, and price, and then build the product or service to that precise specification, followed by a separate cycle of thorough testing and bug fixing. This traditional approach has come to be known as a waterfall approach to development.

Over the past several decades, people have started approaching new product and service development in a more modular, incremental approach. Developers work closely with target users to identify specific "use cases," find the problems encountered in those use cases and then innovate specific features to solve those problems. And rather than try to make everything perfect right from the start, designers and developers try to create "quick and dirty" prototypes, show these to target users, learn more, and work their way towards an excellent product or service. In many, if not most, categories of products or services, this is a more effective way to learn user problems. Product and service development becomes much like discovering a new recipe for traditional food. The chef tries a little bit of this or that, be it a unique combination of spices or other ingredients – tastes it him/herself, has others taste different varieties, and then, after repeated trial and error, sticks the new recipe on the menu![2]

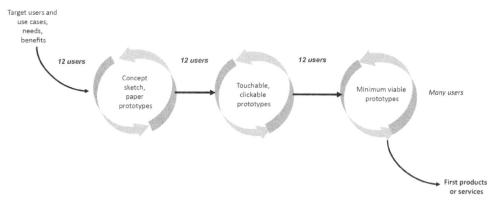

Figure 4.3   From concept sketches to initial prototypes to functional prototypes

Fortunately, there are many tools for prototyping in different fields of endeavor. There is no reason not to build a quick and dirty prototype for a new product or service in this day and age. And making a first prototype might take a week or two, not the months or years of some ten or twenty years ago. These tools include wireframe builders for mobile apps or websites, 3D printers for physical products, and food prototyping kitchens now found in many major cities with machines for creating foods, testing them for basic safety, and to design packaging. Recursive design and testing are essential. This is known as lean or agile design.

Immersion with target users – also known as the customer discovery process – takes real work, but it is also fun. We will want you to talk initially with just several target users in your Problem Space to help identify your project's fundamental solution pathway. Once you have done this, we will teach you the customer interviewing process that includes the types of questions you should ask to guide initially your new product or service design. We will then ask you to talk to a dozen more target users to learn more deeply what they think and feel, creating design drivers for your innovations. We will then design your new product or service on a piece of paper (or digitally). Ideally, we would like you to show your paper or electronic drafts to a dozen more target users and get their feedback. We will then want you to prototype your design – whether it is for a new product, a new web app, or a service. Last, we want you to walk another dozen users through that first stage prototype to gain even more feedback. In summary, this is three rounds of target user interviewing to get to an improved initial proto-type of about a dozen persons each round.

The goal is to create an MVP. Most people refer to this as the minimal viable product. We think that for new concepts, this is a bit of a misnomer. The correct way of thinking about an MVP is as a minimal viable prototype. In no way is this MVP ready for prime-time commer-cialization. Instead, it is a working, functional prototype that can be used for rigorous trial and testing with end-users. It is excellent for gathering specific user feedback. It is also ideal for understanding the final packaging types for food or consumer packaged goods or any potential systems and data integration for software and services. Therefore, in this course, our goal is to design MVPs – and we want them to be excellent prototypes. In fact, let us call the MVP the MVLP: a minimal viable, lovable prototype.

Getting to an MVLP is not exactly a walk in the park (unless you are designing new dog snacks, in which case the user research environment might well be a dog park!). It will take several months of this course, and probably another two to six months following it, to build the prototypes for more extensive user testing (depending on the product's technical complexity or service). At some point along the way, you will sit back with your team, and with all the supporting user feedback needed, you will say, "Heck, this prototype is good enough, more exciting in fact than anything else on the market. Let us now productize the prototype, button everything down, and get this into the market." That race should result in your first dollar/euro/renminbi/peso/won of revenue!

Thus, it is a journey, and it will take some work. At the same time, this is a fun type of work. Ideating, talking to real users, creating a new product or service from scratch, showing it to people, and hopefully seeing a smile on their face – taken all together, it is a most enjoyable activity and it can go well beyond just a class project. At least, that has been our own experience and we hope you find the same. We will have you engage in these user immersions, step by step, applying specific methods in this book's chapters. And don't worry; you will be working in teams. However, if someone is not pulling their weight, you should let them know! And if nothing changes, perhaps let your teacher know it.

To get user insights, we want you to think about going deep. One of our teaching colleagues over the years is a highly experienced designer, Craig McCarthy. Craig led practices in two highly successful design firms (Continuum and Altitude, both in Boston). He then took a job as an innovation leader at Fidelity Investments. Craig has excellent experience and wisdom about initial ideation and follow-on innovation. He picks the initial target users carefully – they must be truly representative of the user and use case in the Problem Space – and then go deep, very deep to learn from them. Do this with a genuine, passionate interest so that you can say to yourself, "I have fallen in love with my customer's problems." Only then can you become an effective, systematic innovator to solve these problems. Real-user insight is an essential but rare commodity. Become a master of uncovering it and communicating it. And throughout the process, show respect and empathy for your target user, even if they are very different than you.

LET'S START TO IDEATE, WITH METHODS

Our mindset is to innovate for the user, as opposed to just ourselves. Many smart people think they know better than anyone else and believe they can innovate without really talking to the target users for whom a new product or service is intended. Perhaps this why so many new products or services fail (by some estimates, upwards of 85%!). As noted above, we will instruct you to spend time with users in iterative, recursive rounds of interviewing to learn about the issues and problems in specific use cases from *their eyes* and with *their voices*. As the late and forever great Steve Jobs (Apple and Pixar) said, always start with the customer experience first, then apply the technology to improve that experience.

This leads to the four steps in this chapter. First, we will create an initial project hypothesis for our chose Problem Space. Second, we will then learn how to create a Customer Experience Map by actually having you do your best to spend a couple of hours with your target users in a *specific use case* within your Problem Space, and from this, improve your initial project idea. For example, planning a vacation is one use case, taking that vacation is another use case, and creating a visual memory of that vacation is another use case. Your solution might be a web app that helps plan, experience, and create real-time and lasting videos and chats around your holidays. We want you to consider all the various use cases to start. Then, learn about it directly from the target users. We want you to see problems through the eyes and ears of these users rather than just your own thinking.

Third, rather than fixate on a single innovation too early, we will learn how to explore different possibilities for innovation in that Problem Space using a technique called *Mind Mapping*. Your team will sit down in some quiet meeting space or Zoom room to create a Mind Map of your collective thinking on different innovation pathways to solve the user's problems and improve their experience. One path might be creating a new product or a new type of material. Another path might be a new service, or even a new social innovation. Or your team might come up with an entirely different, disruptive business model, such as Airbnb or Uber, e.g. a sharing-economy type of innovation. It's all up to your team, based on your understanding of the target users and the team's passion for pursuing a particular type of innovation.

The fourth method in this chapter is to select just one of these innovation pathways to begin more focused, detailed design. We will express this as the Customer Value Proposition, an important design template. We will use this Customer Value Proposition as the anchor point for the rest of the work you will do in this book. In fact, chapter by chapter, you will continue to refine your Customer Value Proposition.

As teams begin to innovate, some may decide to discard their original idea to pursue another idea that they think is better. That's okay and even expected. Continue to follow the prescribed process: talk to additional target users, understand their use cases and their pains, create a Mind Map of alternative approaches to solving their problems, and *only then*, write a new Customer Value Proposition and give it to your teacher to review and provide additional feedback. (Figure 4.4). This process of pivoting on innovation ideas happens all the time. It shows authentic learning and often leads to a better result. This is the nature of customer discovery.

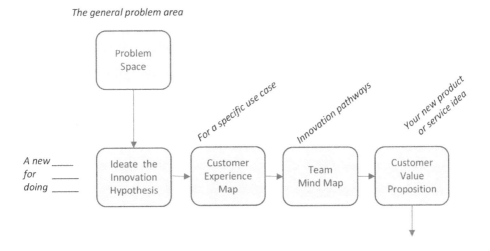

Figure 4.4   Ideation methods

IDEATING: COME UP WITH THE INITIAL INNOVATION HYPOTHESIS

Kate had decided on her Problem Space: healthy foods with minimal ingredients. You also have your Problem Space from the previous chapters and a team of innovation soulmates this journey. Now, let's work on creating your team's initial innovation idea.

First, identify the target end-user in your Problem Space. This is not always as easy as it sounds. For example, in the Problem Space of healthcare, some of the end-users might be the elderly, other middle-aged people, others your age, and yet others children. These differences become important if you think about the Problem Space of telehealth, where the elderly might need different solutions than everyone else. Or a new Internet of Things (IoT) medical monitoring device that will require a different form factor suitable for different populations by age and activity level. The same with food innovations: nutrition, flavors, and even packaging can vary widely by the general population's demographic segments.

Next, you need to think about the specific *use case*. A use case is the particular activity undertaken by your target user within your Problem Space. There are typically multiple, if not a dozen, of different use cases within any Problem Space. For example, in food, there are breakfast, lunch, dinner, and snack occasions at different times of the day. There is also sit-down versus on-the-go modes for each eating occasion. These differences can lead to very different food or drink solutions.

The same general idea applies to healthcare: use cases exist by type of disease, diagnosis versus treatment versus ongoing preventative care, and in-the-home versus in-the-hospital modalities. Each combination suggests a different specific use case, such as a new type of home diagnostic blood laboratory kits, or a portable dialysis machine that patients with chronic liver disease can finally can take on vacation. The more specific you are about the use case, the more effective you will be innovating to improve that use case. For example, you can't make a single product, really, for breakfast, lunch, and dinner all together (please don't say McDonald's French fries). However, we can create interesting new food concepts for breakfast, others for lunch, and yet others for dinner, and others for snack or party occasions.

With target user and use case in hand, the next step is to have in mind a hypothetical solution. Think about a general solution approach. Is it a new product, a new web app, or software, or is it a new service? In other words, what is the general direction in terms of the actual innovation where you want your team to head?

Then ask yourself and your team three basic questions:

● What are the most significant problems our target users face in the use case upon which we have decided to focus? There is bound to be more than one problem. Make a list and then prioritize the top one or two problems and the use cases they represent.

● How do current products, systems, or services match up against these problems? Are any doing a reasonably good job? What are the implications of this for your own innovation project? What are the most significant gaps?

● Then, what could you create that would make the user say "WOW?" What would put a smile on that person's face, to be so good that they tell their friends or workmates about it?

By considering these questions, you can then start focusing on the general direction of "the solution" that you think would please your target users. The way we think about this is as:

"Wouldn't it be cool if we were to create _____ (a new product, app, or service)
that did _____ (major features or functions)
to help _____ (the target users)
do _____. (the use case)"

Take a look at Figure 4.5, a simple template to help you focus your initial innovation hypothesis. Try to express your initial idea in this format.

Problem Space: _____

Target User: _____

Use Case: _____

Innovation Focus:
____ a new product,
____ a new system/app,
____ a new service,
____ a combination of the above

The innovation:

Wouldn't it be cool if we created a _____

that did _____

for this type of person (or company) _____

Figure 4.5   The initial innovation hypothesis

Create this "wouldn't it be cool if we could …" statement for your class project. Representative statements might be:

- I want to create a story-based animation app to learn languages. That app is a learning-style adaptive and social. It helps young students learn how to speak a new language in a more expressive, natural manner. It also adapts to their learning style and allows them to practice with friends in a social network around the app. (Target user: young people. Use case: learning to speak a new language – and the solution is a next-gen web, adaptive language app with a Zoom-like chatroom.)

- I want to create a new set of intelligent, Cloud-connected glasses that blind people can wear to tell them the type and price of the food they are looking at in a grocery store.

- I want to create a vision AI system in a microscope that can look at water samples and detect the growth of harmful algae and bacteria in water wells from which people drink or the ponds in which they swim.

Use Figure 4.5 to create this type of initial hypothesis for the target user, the use case, and the innovation pathway. It might be a good idea to do this quietly on your own and then gather with your team over coffee or tea to listen to each other's ideas. As you review one another's initial project hypotheses, which seem most impactful? Give everyone on the team a reasonable amount of time to share their ideas and to provide feedback. All must participate; each person must contribute.

This should result in an initial project pathway for your team. With it, we turn to the next step: Customer Experience Mapping with actual target users.

CUSTOMER EXPERIENCE MAPPING

It was August 2013, and Kate and her training partner, Jeff, were preparing themselves for an Ironman competition in Quebec, Canada. Hydration was an important part of this. Kate and Jeff stopped into a convenience store and looked at the racks of chilled drinks. They saw all the brands arrayed before them, just like in any other convenience store: Powerade, Gatorade, Monster, Red Bull, and so on; with Coconut Water displayed as well. But by this time, Kate had been studying nutrition science and was aware of the importance of clean, simple ingredients. She would rather drink water.

Then she and Jeff *got lucky*. They walked across the street to a little country store. On display were bottles of maple water (the sap extracted from maple trees). They grabbed a few bottles and hydrated with them for the race. As fortune might have it, Kate ended up having her fastest race ever, and with it, qualified for the Ironman World Championships in Hawaii! After the race, they stopped by the convenience store to buy a few more bottles of maple water. "This is special," they thought. Really special. And their thinking turned to not just race recovery, but to any intensive workout recovery. From this, a venture was born. To hear the story in her own words, please visit https://youtu.be/Slql2z1ZGZg.

Kate and Jeff's story of participating in a race is an example of a specific use case, hydration for muscle recovery, being lived by target users – in this case, two high-performance athletes. The use case of thirst and muscle recovery before and after a race is part of a more extensive use case. First, there is the pre-race, such as getting hydrated and getting other fortification (often with snacks) while driving up to the race; then there is *during* the race itself, often also with hydration with water bottles; and then, post-race recovery. Innovation can happen at any of these steps within the extended use case of before the race, during the race, and after the race – e.g. before the race, during the race, and after the race.

New product or service designers have come to use a technique called Customer Experience Mapping. Sometimes this is also called Customer Journey Mapping – but do not confuse them. Journey Mapping is for sales and marketing; Customer Experience Mapping is for initial design. A Customer Experience Map captures the total user experience as input into the design process. Then, *when you innovate*, your goal is to improve that experience in precise ways.

The process is quite simple. You array all the significant steps in the users' process of experiencing your target product or service category, tag along with a few of these target users, and then observe when and what makes them happy or sad, or even incredibly happy or angry! Then, you note the ups and downs of the user experience along the way and make some notes about why the users were happy or sad, and add this insight to your Customer Experience Map. This framework is simple – but it can show exactly where you, as an innovator, need to focus on impacting to improve things for your target users.

A colleague, Philippe Sommer, shared a Customer Experience Map he likes to teach. It is for buying a cup of coffee. Take a look at Figure 4.6. Note how Philippe stages the steps and provides additional detail on the figure. Then look at the boundary between Happy and Sad, and how Philippe scored each step based on his observations of target users while getting his own coffee one day. He identified actual "pain points," such as finding a place to park, waiting in line during rush hour, or waiting in the same line for really complicated drink formulations versus the simple black coffee he likes to drink.

From this simple mapping of a use case, you can begin to see areas that dissatisfy the user, here a consumer of coffee. In fact, we have had student projects for Dunkin', one of the world's largest coffee brands. Several of these projects have focused on improving the customer experience by building on experience maps such as the one shown above. One team developed a new mobile app, and another higher-capacity drive-throughs for the morning rush. A busy Dunkin' store might receive 75% of its total daily business before 9 am, and some studies have shown that 20% or more of people coming in to buy a cup of coffee or about to enter the drive-through lane turn around and leave without a purchase because the line is too long. Now, *that* is an opportunity to design new processes to improve the user's experience and make more money for the stores! Using Kate's story, let us develop a Customer Experience Map from the perspective of an active athlete. The major steps in the use case span include before, during, and after the race is completed. Various types of hydration/rehydration and refueling are done along the way, including on the drive home or to the hotel and during the week of recovery. Look at the details in Figure 4.7, using Kate's own words as a triathlete.

There are certain addressable need areas in Kate's pre- and post-race use case, *for healthy hydration*. This is a particular use case for X-thoners such as herself. The X-thoner was her initial, inspirational design focus, someone who competed in triathlons and other long duration competitions. This use case was highly focused, intense, and inspirational for start ing a company based on a new product or service. Later on, Kate broadened her strategy to more general, post-workout rehydration. However, if you focus on the general occasion first, you often miss the clear, inspirational need against which to design something rather special to improve the user's experience.To get this inspiration, the innovator needs to spend an hour or two with a few target users experiencing and perhaps suffering a bit in the use case to develop a powerful Customer Experience Map. You cannot just sit down and say, "I am that target user and I can draw my Customer Experience Map." That does not count because there is too much room for personal bias and risk. Even Kate set aside her personal time clock ambitions at a few races to talk to fellow racers about their hydration needs and preferences. Later on, she did the same at gyms.

For example, you might think that ready-to-serve, microwavable organic meals are terrible and frustrating, just because you have never actually eaten good products of this sort. Alternatively, you might want to create a new type of mobile app for finding an apartment because you have never found a good one yourself. Having these personal insights might be a way to get started to generate some initial innovation hypotheses. However, you have to validate your experience and be open to finding other, more significant problems to solve in a Problem Space. There are frozen vegan meal solutions, as there are apps for apartment and roommate finding. You must quickly broaden from your own experience to learn from that of other users.

Here is a simple challenge: you must spend an hour with at least two target users face-to-face on Zoom to talk about their problems in the specific use case. This holds true for each member of your team. Then, meet as a team to produce a consolidated, integrated Customer Experience Map, showing as many Happy and Sad moments as your user research has revealed.

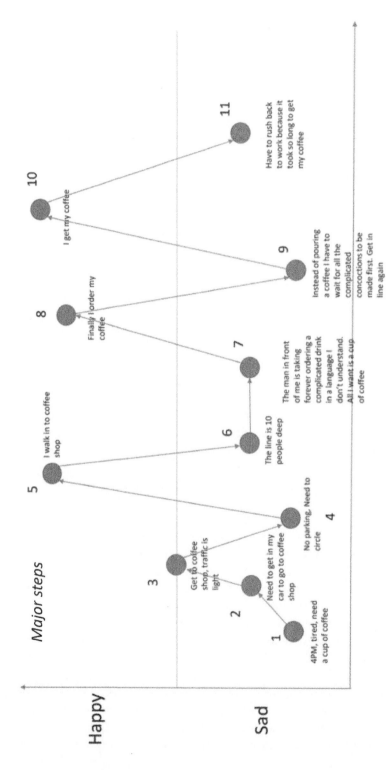

Customer Experience Map illustrated with getting a cup of coffee

Figure 4.6   Customer Experience Mapping

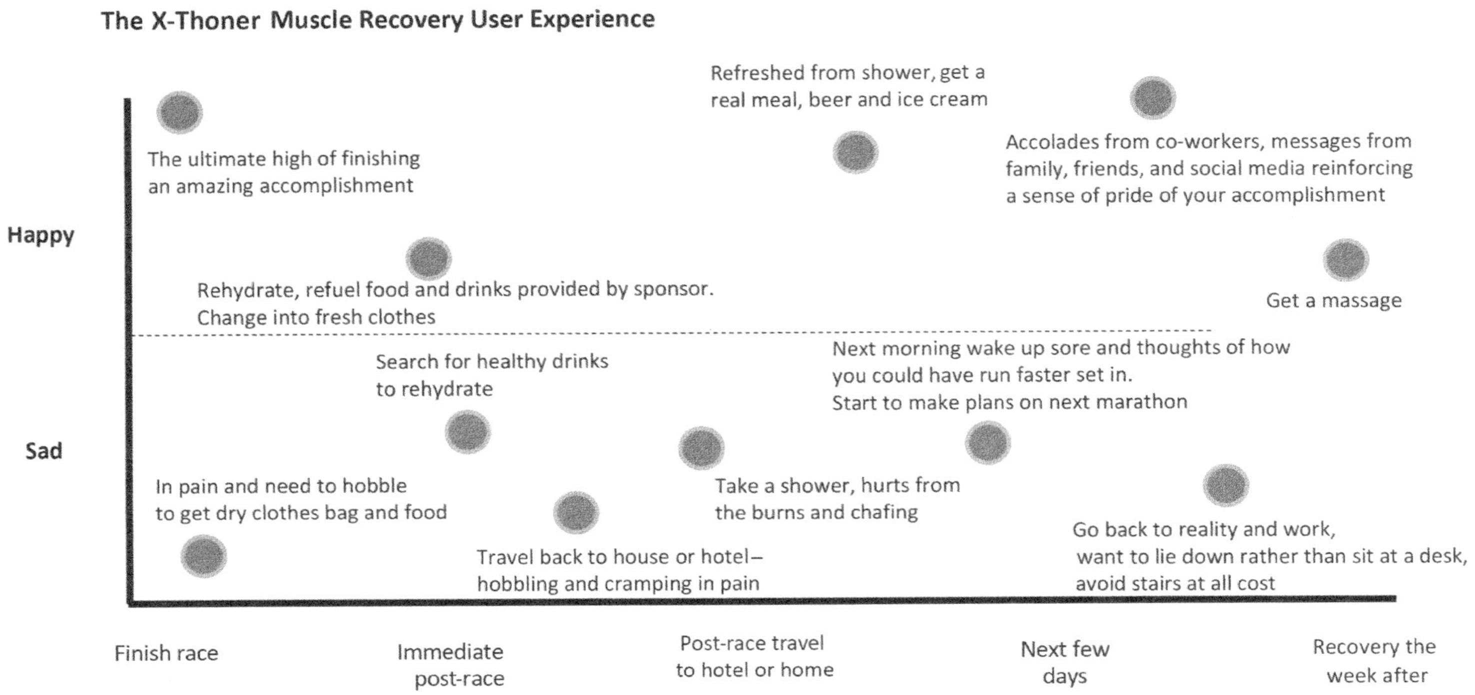

The X-Thoner Muscle Recovery User Experience

Happy

Sad

The ultimate high of finishing an amazing accomplishment

Rehydrate, refuel food and drinks provided by sponsor. Change into fresh clothes

Search for healthy drinks to rehydrate

In pain and need to hobble to get dry clothes bag and food

Travel back to house or hotel— hobbling and cramping in pain

Take a shower, hurts from the burns and chafing

Refreshed from shower, get a real meal, beer and ice cream

Accolades from co-workers, messages from family, friends, and social media reinforcing a sense of pride of your accomplishment

Get a massage

Next morning wake up sore and thoughts of how you could have run faster set in. Start to make plans on next marathon

Go back to reality and work, want to lie down rather than sit at a desk, avoid stairs at all cost

Finish race

Immediate post-race

Post-race travel to hotel or home

Next few days

Recovery the week after

Figure 4.7   User experience – the X-thoner muscle recovery

Start doing this over the next few days, or over the weekend. Don't delay. Bring paper and a pencil with you to take notes or an electronic tablet.

NEXT, MIND MAPPING FOR LOOKING AT DIFFERENT SOLUTION PATHWAYS

Mind Mapping is a relatively free-form technique for getting a range of possible solution pathways to address user needs in a use case that are revealed on a Customer Experience Map. A Mind Map is pretty simple – so please, do not make the ones you create overly complicated!

A Mind Map puts the Problem Space in the middle and then surrounds it with major potential solution pathways. For example, within the health and wellness food industry, the problem that Kate wanted to more specifically address was how to rehydrate and achieve muscle recovery for high performance athletes. As an another example,Kevin's Problem Space was sustainable building construction, and within this, his focus became how to create building materials from recycled glass and plastic. In these two examples, the Problem Space is refined and sharpened by targeted the user and use case.

Identifying different solution pathways is free form, broad thinking. Sometimes, it is easier to think about solution pathways as fundamentally different types of solutions for a given problem. For example, drinks relieve thirst, energy bars (as well as drinks) restore energy, and massages help muscles relax for faster recovery. And then, many athletes now turn to meditation to achieve similar effects!

Once you have defined different types of solution pathways, you can then ideate around potential product or service ideas. These become the potential solutions to address a Problem Space. Take a look at the Mind Map template in Figure 4.8.

You must let your creative juices flow. If you just put in just one solution pathway branching from the Problem Space at the center, and then only one product or service idea for that solution pathway – well, that is not putting sufficient creative effort into the process. There should be two or three different product or service ideas for each solution pathway, and there should more than just a single solution pathway for any given problem to be solved. You must force yourself to think broadly and outside the traditional box for problem-solving. Create solution pathways and new product or service ideas *that are interesting and different, please!*

How might we apply this method to Kate's use case of muscle recovery post-race? Let's say we become her design partners and help her create a new product or service for her Problem Space and the more specific target within it: healthy rehydration for athletes. To generate innovation ideas, we proceed to make a Mind Map showing different possible solutions – healthy drinks for muscle recovery (the use case), by high-performance athletes (the target user), within the health and wellness category (her general Problem Space).In the years leading up to Kate's startup, she had been running all sorts of X-thons and, at the same time, trying to think of different innovative ideas for athletes like herself. Creating a new healthy drink to accelerate hydration pre- and post-race was one of these ideas. She wanted an idea that could also be locally sourced, minimally processed, and include electrolytes and antioxidants known to help in muscle recovery.

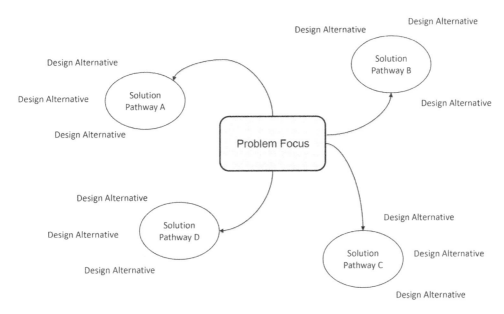

Figure 4.8   The Mind Mapping template

Kate came across a few options, but they did not meet all of her criteria. For example, Beachbody, the producer of several popular home exercise videos (P90X, Insanity, and so forth), had a very successful lineup of powders mixed with water and other ingredients, branded as Shakeology. Within the Shakeology lineup is a plant-based Chocolate Recovery Powder for post workouts and a *Recharge* product engineered to restore muscles at night during sleep. These products were scientifically engineered, with clinical studies supporting the claims in an extensive ingredients list. However, with its long ingredients list, its "powder" format, and the human-engineered science around it, Shakeology was not what Kate was looking for as part of her core values and mission.

Then, there was the old standby – easy to purchase from a Dunkin' coffee shop – a large iced coffee loaded with some extra sugar for a double hit of caffeine and sugar. Not very healthy – but actually, quite a bit healthier than popular energy drinks. These energy drinks claim to have two to three times the caffeine of a single cup of regular coffee plus loads of added sugar and artificial flavors. Freshly brewed coffee, at least, is natural! As Kate's partners in design, we write down these possible solution pathways. Please look at the Mind Map for muscle recovery shown in Figure 4.9, which focused on race recovery. Look at the bottom circles in the figure for thirst and muscle recovery.

As we work through her specific focus in her Problem Space – X-thon Muscle Preparation and Recovery – we must also think more broadly about other solutions. In addition to drinks, we consider energy bars. Kate had visited hundreds of energy snack bar aisles in grocery stores and eaten quite a few herself. Now, she went shopping with an entrepreneurial eye. She visited stores like Whole Foods Market to see the "healthier for you" types of snack bar options on the shelf. Perhaps with the right flavor, she thought, and a bottle of fresh mountain spring

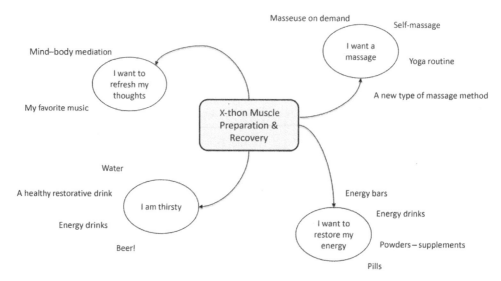

Masseuse on demand

Self-massage

I want a massage

Yoga routine

Mind–body mediation

I want to refresh my thoughts

A new type of massage method

My favorite music

X-thon Muscle Preparation & Recovery

Water

A healthy restorative drink

Energy bars

I am thirsty

Energy drinks

Energy drinks

I want to restore my energy

Powders – supplements

Beer!

Pills

Figure 4.9   A Mind Map for muscle recovery post workout

water, she would have her "clean" muscle recovery solution. Upon examination, however, all the snack products on the shelf did not meet her constraints: they were all heavily processed, had loads of sugar and fat, plus an extensive list of other chemicals such as food dyes and preservatives. Kate also tried the fruit leathers sold in these stores, but none tasted great due to the processing and lack of moisture. "Dry" was just the opposite of what an athlete wants, particularly after a race. Now, take a look at the muscle recovery Mind Map and locate "Energy bars".

Kate thought even more broadly *towards services*, and specifically, web-enabled services. From her Customer Experience Map, we can see that X-thoners regularly seek massage as part of the muscle recovery process. We begin to think, "Hmmm, maybe a massage, delivered at home or in the hotel, on-demand by masseurs who know something about body pain and exercise recovery." Kate had received numerous massages post-race and knew a helpful massage versus one that was not very effective. Accordingly, as her design partners for this example, we go to the Mind Map and write down "massage service" as a possible solution pathway. We might create a web-based intermediary as a booking portal to massage practitioners by geographical location, market the service through race managers, generate bookings on demand by athletes using the mobile app, and take a commission for placing a booking. Even back in 2013, there were already a few such attempted "multi-sided" ventures, but none had yet achieved scale. *Perhaps she could*. There are exciting startups in the area today.

Other recovery *services* were possible. There was mind–body meditation, with energy flow techniques such as Tai Chi or Gi-Gong. Could there be an app that provided such sessions, on-demand, for athletes that focused on meditation techniques for muscle recovery? If you check the web, you will see today that entrepreneurs are trying to do this, and some have achieved scale, such as Headspace and Peleton. With the web providing the distribution channel, innovating in this area meant coming up with a better muscle recovery mediation routine, getting well-known personalities to teach or use it, and targeted social marketing.

Possible, but very different than Kate's experience base. Nonetheless, playing the role of her design partners, we write it down on the Mind Map.

Mind Mapping is a recursive exercise. To do it well, you need a combination of user insight within the use case and creativity as a designer. The user insight comes after making an effort to spend time with several target users in their environment or context of use. For example, if you want to help children with their teeth brushing, spend time with some kids in the bathroom, observing their behaviors in the morning and night. Or, if you want to design for Kate and her fellow triathletes, get yourself to a race, not to run it, but to be with athletes to observe and talk in the hour after the race.

With a robust Mind Map in hand, you proceed to the next step – creating an initial Customer Value Proposition for a specific innovation idea that comes directly from one of the branches in your Mind Map.

PRIORITIZING SOLUTION PATHWAYS AND DESIGN ALTERNATIVES

When you meet with your team to share Mind Maps and select a specific solution path, your prioritization of possibilities needs to be grounded in some substance and not based on just whim.

To use Kate as an example, why did she land on a new type of drink; why didn't she get into supplements or pills; or a new type of yoga routine; or an on-demand massage service; or the energy bar business? There are usually several reasons why innovators head down a particular direction. Let us examine a few:

- **Applicable capabilities, such as learned knowledge and natural skills:** Kate had already begun studying nutrition and health as part of a graduate program at Northeastern University. Going from selling software for a tech company to enrolling in a graduate program in nutrition shows just how committed Kate was to her venture, what people refer to as having "skin in the game." In contrast, while she loved receiving a sports massage, she did not know much about giving massages, nor was she an expert in creating a web business, social marketing, and other skills needed to create a portal for on-demand massage "delivery." The same considerations came to play for the mind–body meditation pathway. From Chapter 3, it should be clear that you have accomplishments already, which suggest current and future capabilities, and that you are studying or planning to study specific areas of in-depth knowledge in college. In other words, you are already good at some types of thinking and work and will be getting better at them. And like Kate, some of you might already be knowledgeable about certain areas from your hobbies or passions (but please, don't use starting a bar for your innovation project!).

- **Competition that is too large and fierce:** If there is a large, dominant competitor precisely in a specific solution pathway with a wide range of product or service solutions already – well, you might want to try something else. Or otherwise, you have got to learn as much as you can about the failings of that competitor's products or services and figure out how to design something substantially better and more impactful on your target users' lives or work. Sadly, many entrepreneurs look at new consumer eCommerce opportunities and then see Amazon and Walmart rearing their enormous heads and even larger commercial appetites. This happened with Kate as well. Her insight as an athlete and from nutrition courses could have well-positioned her to create a new energy bar type. Possibly back in 2013/14, when she was starting her company, she might have had a chance to develop an energy bar as a muscle recovery solution. Even then, however, the competition was intense and concentrated. There were Powerbar, Luna, and private label brands such as those from Trader Joe's. And today – well, there is Kind Bar, a $1 billion-plus brand, which can spend considerable sums on R&D and has the Mars, Inc. global distribution channel to sell its products. Most successful serial entrepreneurs – the most competitive types of people you might ever encounter – will, in a quiet moment, admit that they do not like competitors with any scale for their next new venture. Entrepreneurs look for spaces without dominant, super successful competitors, affording plenty of running room to try new things, get traction, and then scale.

- **Government rules and programs:** The government can have a significant impact on innovation and entrepreneurial opportunities. Whether we like it or not, this impact will only grow over time if your Problem Space and your specific target within it has a clear societal impact. The government can cut both ways. Specific innovations can be fueled by the tailwinds of government rules, subsidies, and grants. This is often true for new energy technologies or conservation services and in some countries *more* than others. Conversely, there might be regulations that would create substantial headwinds for innovation. For example, around the world, there is a need to clean up hazardous and other waste created by society, manufacturers, and miners. The regulations for transporting this waste after a clean-up run a mile deep in North America and Europe. Similarly, fire codes mandate the use of certain materials in building materials and office furniture for those of you who might want to design better furniture for your dorm rooms than the terrible stuff you have now! This does not mean that you cannot be an innovator in these areas – but you will have to become experts in the rules and regulations governing your category of products and services.

- **A compelling crisis that demands your help:** Solution pathways and specific design ideas sometimes rise to the top by the sheer size and urgency of the market need. For example, the pandemic of 2020/21 is driving a tremendous amount of diagnostic and tracing innovation, literally around the world, with government and institutional money supporting R&D. Antibiotic resistance will also soon rear its ugly head, leading to new opportunities for bioscientists. Or climate change has made EVs a mainstream option. How else could a small, struggling startup called Tesla suddenly become more valuable on the stock market than traditional, more prominent automotive manufacturers? And with climate change, traditionally "boring" industries will transform into dynamic ones: the design and engineering of civic infrastructure, buildings, transportation systems, agriculture, and mariculture – all of these will be disruptive by demand-driven, user-inspired innovation. As the oceans rise and our lands dry, innovators must address water management. Current estimates are that between 20% and 50% of all water used in cities leaks underground from old pipes. These crises demand our attention and lead to inspired, impactful innovation. As an innovator, such circumstances can create powerful demand, government grants, and venture capital for innovative, scalable concepts.

Now, with your team's aggregated Mind Map, you must select a solution pathway and pick a design area – a new product or service – upon which to focus. This might take some quick research on the web regarding competitors, government plusses or minuses, or a compelling societal need – gathering some facts and not just based on your personal passions. You can get this information in 30 minutes or less, especially if you are working as a team. You can have one person look at each of these areas and reconvene to consolidate the information and make some decisions to rule some solution pathways out or push others to the head of the line. Please keep a record of your reasoning and the data supporting it. As the innovation project proceeds, you will learn more about all these areas and will want to update your team's collective understanding of them for your final presentation.

LET'S DEVELOP A CUSTOMER VALUE PROPOSITION

Sometimes, you simply have to have an open mind for innovation, to be on the hunt, learning from your users and their environment, and then *just get lucky*. Something or someone or some company inspires an idea in your head. If you are ready for it, magical things can happen. Let's get back to Kate's story.

The little country store in Mont Tremblant, Canada, that Kate and Jeff visited was the source of their inspiration. They walked and saw the different local, unique products that country stores tend to offer, not the big brands in most convenience stores. There, sitting on a shelf all by itself, were bottles of purified, filtered, pure maple tree water. The store owner told her the maple tree water was locally made and fresh. Buying several bottles before the race, Kate and Jeff consumed and found the taste delightful, with a bit of natural sweetening sugar but still very "clean." No heavy sugars and caffeine of existing energy drinks. They bought a few more bottles to take home, which they also soon consumed. The store owner told them to keep the bottles chilled because the shelf life was not that long before the taste soured.

Hmmm. Pure maple tree water, natural sugars (it turns out that the maple tree water has half the sugars of processed drinks). Upon further research on the web, maple tree water was loaded with natural electrolytes and other goodies to help muscle recovery. And it was locally sourced, straight from nature with minimal processing – just heating and filtration before bottling. Perhaps Kate and Jeff could also add flavoring from natural sources, unlike most current sports energy drinks. Holistic health, achieving life balance with a positive view for improving self and society through healthfulness, environmental closeness, and sustainability. And perhaps Jeff, who was so good with his hands and machines as a professional tradesperson, could figure out how to extend the shelf life to the six months or so needed for commercial distribution. This could be *it*!

When Kate got back home, she immediately wrote down these basic dimensions for the new drink concept that she would at first call *DrinkMaple*. The pure freshness of tree water, the sweetness of maple water, and its natural ingredients for muscle recovery. There was a lot of work to do indeed. But it appealed to her core values of minimalism in healthy foods and leveraged her acquired knowledge in nutrition science. The apparent marketing hurdle would be to create awareness and confidence that maple tree water was healthy; current maple-tree associated products had baggage. Aunt Jemima and Mrs. Butterworth's ("maple syrup") were anything but healthy, being mainly corn syrup with artificial flavoring.

Kate began breaking the concept down into its specific elements. She created what is called a Customer Value Proposition. This was her first Customer Value Proposition. Over the coming months, she would continue to refine it, just like Jeff began working to secure a maple tree water supply and improve its shelf life by tinkering around with the manufacturing process. And he would do the same with the packaging, seeking to step away from plastic to cardboard, a more readily recycled form of packaging.

The Customer Value Proposition is intended to be a simple, powerful way to express the target customer, the products or services to be provided to that customer, and the distinctive benefits from using your products or services. The clearer and more concise, the better. So please, make your team's Customer Value Proposition simple and straightforward!

Take a look at Figure 4.10, it shows the major elements:

- the name or brand of your products or services;

- the problem you wish to solve;

- the specific types of users and specific use cases you wish to serve;

- the needs you wish to solve and the benefits you wish to provide;

- how solving these needs and providing these benefits provide clear differentiation from current competitors;

- and finally, a summary statement of two or three sentences (at most) that integrates all of the information above into a concept statement that can be discussed with target users. It might also eventually be put into a customer survey to test the idea with a larger sample.

Kate began jotting down her phrases for these critical aspects of her new concept. When she saw it all on one page – simply and powerfully stated – she was excited. And so was Jeff. They then began to think about broadening their market, first from X-thoners to sports-active performance-seeking consumers. This could be anyone going to the gym, riding a bicycle, or going for a weekend hike who sought a healthier, tasty form of hydration without added sugar and other "junk."

As time has progressed, Kate and Jeff continue to broaden their consumer target to include any health-aspiring "thriver" – an active person who takes a holistic view on personal health and where rehydration plays an important part – even working at the office and not just the gym or outdoor exercise. The phrase "sports-active performance seekers" was replaced with "thrivers," with a Generation Z, Y, X focus. Kate and Jeff landed on the Customer Value Proposition as shown in Figure 4.11.

Refine the Customer Value Proposition

ABC *(give it a name)* is a family of (products/services/solutions)	
That *(solves what problem)*	
For *(which target users)*	
For *(which target buyers)*	
The needs we expect to solve *(name primary needs)* and benefits we wish to provide *(name major benefits)*.	
And is different than current *(competitors/products)* because of *(why target users will buy it)*	
Now, put it all together:	

Figure 4.10   The Customer Value Proposition template

With this "use-inspired" innovation concept, their entrepreneurial journey then took flight. As stated before, a Customer Value Proposition is intended to be refined and improved over time.

DRINK SIMPLE TAKES FLIGHT

While completing her nutrition studies, Kate entered her University's incubator with its concept design and business planning methods, as well as the mentorship provided by seasoned industry hands. She received a grant to develop a website, design the bottle label and another packaging, and get samples produced for a test market in the Boston area with Whole Foods and a few other retail partners. DrinkMaple launched officially in 2014. Soon, Katie and Jeff added additional flavors to the original version (Figure 4.12).

Consumers loved the concept – the most important thing for an entrepreneur. The pilot's success provided the data needed to convince the leading healthy foods distributor to take DrinkMaple across the country, reaching other Whole Foods stores and other premium outlets. Meanwhile, the website began to generate revenue as well. While Kate handled the marketing and financial side of the business, Jeff tacked the shelf-life challenge and aligned a secure supply from maple tree farmers. He began experimenting with more sustainable types of packaging. $1.4 million of angel money flowed in 2015, followed later by $4.6 million in 2017, led by a venture capital firm specializing in new food products and restaurant innovation. And with this money came experienced advice to broaden the brand. DrinkMaple became Drink Simple, where the maple tree water remained the underlying platform to which

ABC (give it a name) is our product/service:	• Maple Water
That is a solution for (what specific problem):	• Dehydration/lack of healthful hydration on the market
For (which target consumers/users):	• "Aspiring Thrivers" – people looking to thrive naturally
Sold to/through (which target buyers/resellers)	• Retailers such as Whole Foods, Walmart, Grocery channel, eCommerce, Amazon; sold through distributors.
The needs we expect to solve (name primary needs) and benefits we wish to provide (name major benefits).	• Functional–hydrating functionality, plant-based, antioxidants • No added sugar/low natural sugar • Tastes great
And is clearly different/better than competitors' products or services because: (This is your basic competitive positioning)	• Tapped from a tree with natural functionality and delicious taste. Not created in a chemistry lab.
Now, put it all together, in two concise sentences. Add a concept sketch on a second page if appropriate.	
In a world where so many products have additives and junk ingredients, we at Drink Simple are proud to tap refreshment directly from nature to help people thrive naturally.	

Figure 4.11   The Customer Value Proposition for Drink Simple

Source: www.drinksimple.com. Used with permission.

Figure 4.12 Drink Simple's products

Source: www.drinksimple.com. Used with permission.

Figure 4.13 Drink Simple's expanded product portfolio

different flavors and a carbonated line of drinks were added in 2019/20 (Figure 4.13). More products, more shelf space, more visibility led to more revenue. Kate began to think of her target consumers as "doers" rather than "thrivers," which broadened the use case beyond just sports. It could be anyone on the go, to the gym, on a hike, or to school or work, who wanted a clean, healthy, great-tasting drink.

Looking at the company business in mid-2020, Kate and Jeff knew that their next step was to break into major national distribution, working through one of the big beverage players that "own" the shelf space in hundreds of thousands of grocery and convenience stores in the United States alone. This is called "direct store distribution," or DSD. Achieving it is a big mountain to climb for entrepreneurs.

But then again, these two are X-thoners! So Kate's journey continues. Please check the company's website at www.drinksimple.com. And yes, even if you are not a triathlete, we think you will love the product.

Now, using the methods in this chapter, let us get to work building your own Customer Value Proposition, one that will improve as you advance through the semester. Be inspired by Kevin's and Kate's stories. And they would be the first ones to tell you that *if they did it, you can do it, too.* Do your own thing in your own Problem Space with your new team. Focus on your target user, their use case, and the problems they are experiencing in it. Develop your specific focus within that Problem Space, think about different solution pathways, and then create a design concept for one of the pathways that presents the best opportunity to innovate for your team. This will typically be a new product or service concept.

Reader exercises

Now, it is your turn. Your reader exercises will take a day or two of initial customer research and several or more hours of sense-making, integration, and PowerPoint-making with your team. Sense-making is a term used to refer to making sense of diverse information from different sources towards a specific set of conclusions and actions.

STEP 1: DEFINE YOUR INITIAL PROJECT HYPOTHESIS

Use the template in Figure 4.5 to shape and further focus your team's idea. This is best done in a team meeting. Be succinct, but more ideas are better than fewer at this point, specifically for the "wouldn't it be cool" section of the template.

STEP 2: CUSTOMER EXPERIENCE MAPPING

Use Figure 4.6 as a template. Each person on the team should identify at least two target users in your Problem Space and document their complete, end-to-end experience in the use case upon which you have chosen to focus. In Kate's case, this was post-sports rehydration, where race prep, during the race, and post-race is the complete view, and where muscle recovery is as essential as quenching thirst. Working in a team should have benefits: for example, you might have different team members focus on different types of target users (younger, older; female, male; poor, affluent; or for business-to-business (B2B), workers, managers); or, you might have team members focus on different use cases within your Problem Space, such as "renting a car" versus "buying a car." Build a Customer Experience Map based on your observations and conversations with target users.

STEP 3: BUILD A MIND MAP AND CREATE A FOCUS FOR YOUR INNOVATION

Next, as an entire team, and using your Customer Experience Maps, build a Mind Map. Refer to Figure 4.8. Within the general Problem Space, you want to create a more specific problem focus within it for a specific type of target user in a specific use case. Then, identify (a) major solution pathways, and (b) specific new product or service design ideas for those pathways. Again, look at Kate's example first, then use the template to build your team's Map.

Re-read the several pages in this chapter on decision criteria and dimensions for prioritizing solution pathways and product or service ideas within them. Of course, personal passions are most important for prioritization – *what you want to do the most carries a lot of weight. Be mindful of external competitive and market realities.* It makes no sense to invest your team's time in a new product or service area where there is excessive competition or regulatory barriers. Conversely, a really "hot" booming market for specific new product or service categories is more worthy of your time than low growth markets. Step 3 is to prioritize the different ideas on your team's Mind Map. You can use color codes or numbers to show that prioritization.

STEP 4: CREATE A CUSTOMER VALUE PROPOSITION

Last, create your Customer Value Proposition, using Figure 4.10 as a template. This is just your initial version – your working hypothesis. Chapter by chapter, we will improve it. Or, you might pivot the Customer Value Proposition more profoundly, such as changing your innovation to a service model as opposed to selling products. It's okay, just try as a team to create your first Customer Value Proposition as best you can. At this point, *the perfect gets in the way of the good.*

NOTES

1. Pollan, M. (2013). *Food Rules: An Eater's Manual.* New York: Penguin Group.
2. Having been a seafood chef while in college, one of your authors was having dinner with a Pakistani who introduced the pleasures of the spice cardamom. We had it that evening in a mild curry. Back at the restaurant, we mixed cardamom seeds with the butter, wine, and tomatoes for cod and flounder dishes, slow-cooked until the fish just began to flake. The result was and remains a little bit of heaven. This type of innovation was encouraged and occurred frequently amongst our kitchen staff.

5

Users, buyers, and use cases

THE PURPOSE OF THE CHAPTER

Segmenting potential users is one of the most potent thinking processes that an entrepreneur can do at the beginning of her or his journey. Add to that an understanding of different use cases – or *occasions of use* – and that makes an entrepreneur's focus even more powerful. Then, adding the actual buyers or a new product or service, who may or may not be the actual user, makes the "customer segmentation" for an innovation complete. When some people use the term "customer segmentation," you must ask yourself whether they mean users, buyers, or specific use cases – for each can be different and are too often mushed together without specific meaning.

This user/buyer/use case segmentation will fuel the rest of your innovation journey. It will also be helpful when it comes time for you to plan the marketing and sales processes needed for your innovations.

In the previous chapter, you spent time with one or several potential target users in your Problem Space to develop a more specific definition of it, a solution pathway, and an initial new product or service concept. We are now going to think about these first several target users as a larger user group. You also focused on learning a specific use case and the problems in it to generate an initial Customer Value Proposition. This chapter will take things to the next level, digging into segmenting your market by further users, buyers, and specific use cases. This upfront work will greatly increase your innovation effectiveness.

LEARNING OBJECTIVES

After reading this chapter, you should be able to:

1. Segment your customers in terms of different types of users for your idea.
2. Understand that the buyers for an innovation are not always the end-users. The motivations and concerns of these buyers are just as important as those of the end-users.
3. Further segment your users by specific use cases.

CUSTOMER SEGMENTATION: USERS, BUYERS, USE CASES

We design products and services to please users and to also satisfy the buyers if they are different from the end-users. We then work just as hard to figure out the best way to reach and sell to as many people as possible.

People use the word customers to refer to both users and buyers loosely. For your enrollment in this particular course, you are the user, and your parents are probably the buyer. If you are taking this as a graduate elective, however, then it is most likely that you are both the user and the buyer. And just as users and buyers can be different, there can be multiple types or users in any given product or service situation. Dog food innovators now target different breeds of pets. Or, there are multi-sided marketplaces. For example, if you create a mobile app for car sharing such as Turo, there are two types of users – the car owner and the car borrower, and your company is sitting in the middle collecting a percentage of rental fees.

The basic idea: not all potential customers for a company's products or services are the same in (a) who they are in terms of age, gender, income, or pervasive attitudes, (b) what they wish to buy, (c) how much they want to buy, (d) when they wish to buy, (e) where they wish to buy, including online, and (f) how much they wish to pay. *Who, what, how, when, where, and how much* – are essential dimensions for understanding the differences between users for the purposes of new product or service design.

For example, as a first-time entrepreneur, you might think that all college students are the same in finding an apartment, buying furniture, or getting a car. But that assumption is incorrect. Consider your friends. Are they all the same in their purchase preferences? Young men are often very different in their consumer tastes and preferences than young women; international students sometimes quite different than local ones. While this makes innovation challenging, it also makes it fun: users and/or buyers can be hugely different in their basic needs and preferences for a new product or service. They can also be miles apart in how they prefer to buy a product or service and what they are willing to spend. If you have a sibling of a different gender, think about how you differ in your preferences for beer or even coffee; and then, consider the differences between you and your siblings from your parents! You want to design specific products or services for particular types of users. And then beyond this, for particular types of occasions or use cases. For example, many consumers prefer a different strength and style of coffee in the morning versus later in the day or evening.

Customer segmentation is the process of understanding and organizing these differences for different user groups or *consumers*. Dividing a very broad group of potential users into more specific groups, each with its clear set of needs, attitudes, and preferences, keeps a new product or service focused on each segment's requirements. Sometimes those needs are the same, but more often than not, in certain aspects, they are different. The car you might prefer to buy after your first job is probably quite different than the vehicle chosen by your parents for their own needs and price tolerances. These differences then get expressed in interior and exterior styling, and for some driving enthusiasts, in the acceleration of the vehicle. When one of your authors thinks about his dream car, a small, quickly accelerating, stick-shift convertible comes to mind; his wife, a luxurious SUV; and when we ask our own Millennial children, two say an "EV" right away, and the other,

"Do we really even need to own a car when renting one for just a morning is so easy to do?" Here, the difference in underlying attitude is as important as the demographic category. In other words, people even in the same demographic category can be completely different as users and buyers based on a pervasive attitude they possess, such as "outdoor active" versus sedentary, or technology adept versus technology resistant.

THE FUNDAMENTAL IMPORTANCE OF UNDERSTANDING USE CASES

Just as users are different, *use cases* are different, and the innovator needs to understand them deeply.

Let's continue the automobile example. An important factor in the automobiles is how you wish to use the car: is it for commuting in a city where fuel economy is essential, driving in rougher terrain rural areas where a higher suspension and four-wheel drive might be necessary, or for doing heavier work such as construction or farming, in which case you might need a small truck or van.

Understanding and designing to a specific use case are vitally important to achieving excellence in design. A few more examples: in food, there is eating the main meal or having a snack; and there is having each at a specific time of day, such as breakfast, lunch, afternoon, dinner, or after dinner. And then, there is at-home consumption versus on-the-go or mobile. Very quickly, food innovation becomes a three-dimensional consumer use-case targeting exercise. Going onto the web, you might find a product named "Perfect Size," which is a portion-controlled chocolate cake for "empty nester" adults to be baked in an hour and eaten at home. Then, you might find "Perfect Size for One," which is a much smaller mix designed to be microwaved in just a minute at home for the Millennial rushing off to work or craving a quick snack at night.[1]

A technology example is IoT in healthcare for the elderly. Consider a venture that builds sensors and the software for beds, chairs, and floors – connected through a router – that serves as a health alert monitoring system for the elderly living at home. Detecting heart rates, movement, toilet flushes, and falls on the floor are all achievable with these sensors. The use cases here are health monitoring while sleeping, sitting in a chair, going to the toilet (too much), or falling.

The way to achieve insight is first, and foremost, to *fall in love with your user's problems*. Become an expert in their use cases. This includes their problems, fears, and frustrations in specific use cases. This understanding then focuses and motivates your innovations to improve the use case, create something significant, and quite literally put a smile on that user's face after they use your new product or service.

As we mentioned in an earlier chapter *design thinking* practitioners have changed some of the words. If someone says "jobs to be done," it is simply what the user is trying to get done in a specific use case. And user problems are called "pains," and the improvements you can make with your innovations are called "gains." Use cases: jobs to be done. Needs and frustrations: "pains." Better product or service features: "gains." Don't let the fancy words set you back. Listen to the target user carefully, focus on specific use cases, and use your creativity and skills to create a more pleasing experience for the user. You can be as good a designer as anyone else if you become the expert in your user.

Occasions is another word you might encounter, particularly in consumer products or services. It just means a use case. Consumer products companies prefer it to use cases because occasions also suggest a time of day and type of event. Breakfast is different from dinner; weekday cooking and eating are different from weekend activities; and a holiday party is different from a regular meal. A party is another occasion – a celebration, such as the one we hope you have after your team gets an A in the course!

FACTOR IN THE BUYER (WHEN S/HE IS NOT THE ACTUAL USER)

From the discussion above, you must identify specific opportunities according to different users and different use cases. Within each given Problem Space, there may be many different types of people who suffer or must contend with the issues contained in that Problem Space. Healthcare spans people of all age ranges, for example.

The user is often not the buyer. If you own a pet, you buy the pet food for your dog or cat. Or, when you use a particular software product in a company, someone in the IT department has decided in favor of that software over some other product. As an innovator, you need to understand these actual buyer needs and concerns just as much as the end-user's needs and concerns. You hope that the buyer's perceptions of the user's needs align those of users. Then, to please the buyers, you might also include additional features that in the case of software purchasing, include maintenance and training, as well as price.

For example, let's say that your Problem Space is sustainable home construction, such as that chosen by Kevin in Chapter 2. Your goal is to build green, energy- and cost-efficient homes for young, environmentally conscious professionals with young families. Our goal is to create sustainable, green materials, such as Kevin's roofing tiles. As Kevin's partners, we would segment buyers as different types of homeowners – according to the amount of money they earn or possess, and hence, the size and style of the house they can afford. Lower-income, mid-range, and luxury or premium housing solutions would come into our segmentation scheme. Then, based on our market and customer research – namely the size of the segment in terms of money spent on new homes and those segments with significant, underserved needs for sustainable home construction – we would designate an initial target market within the broader customer segmentation, such as premium home construction by affluent people willing to spend more for "green." Creating a more comprehensive segmentation of different end-users helps to make sure that you have considered all the major segment options before making the critical decision of your first target user and use case. Once we have the target user and use case in hand, innovation teams often perform a secondary behavioral segmentation. In this example, it would be to identify those homeowners who prioritize environmental concerns and those that don't. With this targeting, we can then dig into the specific problem areas that we will address for these users – to create sustainable, recycled building materials.

Now, let's use Kevin once again to see where the user is not the buyer. We could build sustainable roofing materials to be used on top of retail stores or apartment complexes. Or for small office buildings. Each of these market segments has its own architectural designs and purchasing preferences that influence the purchase of roofing materials. Moreover, the tenant does not make the decision. Instead, it is either the retail mall owner, the office building owner, or the apartment building owner. Further, there are other important stakeholders in the decision-making process: architects, builders, and roofing contractors in either new construction or replacement roof services. There might even be government officials in a geographical region who monitor energy efficiency standards for homes and buildings whose regulations we would need to understand. As an entrepreneur, there is often an ecosystem around the primary end-user that you need to explore and understand. Any one of these other stakeholders can either facilitate or become a roadblock to your innovation.

A glossary of customer-related terms

Glossaries are usually dull. Not this one! It is vital for successful innovation.

The word "customer" is used so freely for all businesses that we sometimes mean different things with that expression. You need to be specific, using specific terms to represent particular things or entities. Innovation *for* whom and for *what specific purpose*?

Here are operational definitions that should prove helpful.

The user	The user is that person or company using a new product, system, or service. When we drive a car or take a subway, we are the users of transportation; when we eat a tasty meal, we are delighted users of the food. Often, innovators (particularly in the software industry), call these the "end-users" of a product or service.
The use case	A use case is the what, when, where, and how often the user uses (or *experiences*) a new product or service. As an entrepreneur, you need to think about use cases carefully and select one or two for your innovation.
The end-user	In certain instances, the end-user can be different from "the user" because there are multiple different kinds of users in one use case or occasion. For example, take baby diapers. The end-user is the baby. The user is the parent changing the diapers. Easy on and off or change-me indicators are important needs for parents, whereas, for the baby, rash prevention, absorbency, and "no leak" are needed. Both are users, but the baby is the ultimate end-user. Now, if an older person happens to be wearing a diaper for incontinence, that person is both the end-user and the changer of the diaper! In the medical monitoring system example above, the patients – the elderly – are the users; a nurse might also be a user, or a physician, or the building manager, or IT manager who needs to install and maintain the system. They are all users in some shape or form – *and that is why it is clearer to refer to the patients themselves as the end-users of the system.*
The buyer	Often, buyers are also the users. But just as often, they are not. When you buy lunch for yourself, you are both the user and the buyer. When you buy a gift for someone else, food or otherwise, you are the buyer, and someone else is the user. In B2C ventures, age, gender, and other demographic factors can be used to segment both users and buyers, whether it be beer or cars. In B2B ventures, think about the software used by companies. As an employee, you are the user. But someone has decided to purchase and provide that particular brand or make of software for employees, be it an IT department manager or some other manager. Part of their job is to evaluate and buy the tools that other employees use. Therefore, buyers are the actual decision-makers for a purchase. It is the same for our diaper case: a baby will not decide which brand or quality of diapers to buy; it is the parent. It is these buyers who have the money. They may have their own specific concerns that you need to address.

Market segments Market segments are the aggregation of the users, buyers, and use cases within an identifiable portion of a larger industry. It is a higher-level grouping of specific people and activities for which economists and consultants gather data to show broader activity and future trends. For example, snacks are a definable segment in the food industry, drinks another, and frozen meals yet another. A quick search on the web will tell you the size of sales and growth rates and the competitors introducing new products into each one of these segments. In healthcare, in-patient surgical services are considered a different segment than rehabilitation or skilled nursing facilities that are provided after a patient is discharged from the hospital after surgery. Home healthcare is considered yet another market segment. Each one of these segments has sales or reimbursement revenue and a projected growth rate associated with it.

Consumer versus customer For most business-to-consumer (B2C) businesses, the consumer is the individual buyer of a product or service. However, the actual customer of the venture is often the store itself. When we go to a grocery store, the consumers are the shoppers walking down the aisles; the customer, on the other hand, is the retailer itself. As entrepreneurs, we have to convince the grocery store to remove someone else's product from the shelf and put our new product there instead. This often boils down to the entrepreneur convincing a buying manager. These buying managers – sometimes called merchandizing managers – are further divided into major categories, such as the dessert section versus the cheese section. These buying managers are the direct customers of any food or drink venture. The sell-in story has to be carefully crafted to meet their interests – which is how your new product will draw consumers into that part of the store to produce more revenue versus products in that aisle today.

Try to be as specific as possible when using these terms. Explain precisely what you mean to your audience. Do some actual field research to understand users, buyers, and major influencers for purchase decisions. Think of this as developing and communicating a clear picture of what users, buyers, and key influencers need or desire – and then meet these needs in your new product and service designs.

TWO SIMPLE TEMPLATES FOR USER/BUYER/USE CASE SEGMENTATION

We can now formalize these ideas into two simple frameworks: where you start in terms of a user focus for innovation and where you might expand as your innovation grows and your company scales. Take a look at Figure 5.1. It summarizes essential information for your initial target user group. Provide a name for that user group, information about age, gender, and life stage or status. For example, for a B2C chocolate venture, the primary user might be a Millennial female. Then state the primary use case for the innovation. Then, identify the target buyer if it is different than the user. For example, for gift chocolate, if we were to target a wedding occasion, the user would typically be the bride, and the buyer, her parents. Also shown in the Figure are other key stakeholders. In this example, you might specify wedding planners. They can have a big impact on the party favors that show up at weddings!

For B2B ventures, the sustainable home construction materials example also fits clearly into Figure 5.1. The user is the home buyer or owner; the buyer, the architect or home builder; and other important stakeholders, the local, state, or federal regulators and home inspectors. Moreover, new home construction versus repairs are two very different use cases, as is using

Target User	Specific Description Demographics, or dept/rank	Primary Use Case	Primary needs ("design drivers" for your venture)
•	• • •	•	• • • •

Primary Buyer (if different than user)	Specific Description Demographics, or dept/rank	Primary needs – "design drivers"
•	•	• • •

Other Important Stakeholders in the Buying Decision	Specific Description Demographics, or dept/rank	Their major concerns
•	•	• • •

Figure 5.1   The target user and buyer

a professional contractor versus going to Home Depot or Lowe's yourself to buy materials and install everything yourself. Each of these is rich in needs and opportunities for the innovator. In the real world, selling to an end-user versus a builder versus a retailer is very different – even for the same product or service.

With this initial focus in hand, we then think about the growth that might occur based on our first innovation over the two to three years. We might extend our innovation to either new types of users or new uses for current target users. This is expressed in Figure 5.2. Your initial target user is repeated on the first row. You have the choice of working on the same use case

User Group	Specific Description (Professional status, organization)	Primary Use Case (that you will address)	Relative Segment Size and Growth Rate (words, or numbers)	Your Priority

How do I find some people in each one to talk to?

Figure 5.2   Adjacent user groups

(for example, dinner meal solutions for single people versus households). Then, on the right of the figure is an important question: *how do I find people to talk to* in this customer group? This will be important in the chapters to follow when we want you to interview a dozen or more such target customers.

Figure 5.2 contains multiple rows. We want you to consider how you might expand from your first customer group, often called the beachhead, to other *adjacent* groups. Adjacent growth is reasonable, achievable growth, leveraging the things you are already good at in a business to new applications. Note that these different potential customer segments may have slightly different use cases than your first user group.

For example, in the case of food snacks, you might start with an afternoon snack and then expand to morning snacks. Or, if you are creating a robotics venture, it might start with warehouse applications and then move on to manufacturing assembly applications. Or your telehealth application might begin with hospital-based primary care applications, and then expand into home-health nursing applications, and later, to mental health counseling services. Each of these would be three distinct rows on the Figure 5.2.

You must then do some quick research on the web to find industry reports for each identified market segment, as well as the size and expected growth rate for that segment. After gathering these data and assessing your options, you then highlight your priority user segment and the reasons for that selection. This might be because the segment size is larger than others or that your background and skill set make a particular market segment the best first choice. The nice thing about applying Figure 5.2 to your project is that it shows the listener that you have considered a few different options and have landed on your top choice for good reason – and that you know where your venture might grow next.

To gather market segment information, look for industry studies, reports issued by industry trade associations, industry magazines, or government agencies in the U.S. or elsewhere – with some digging, you will find data on current spending in an industry and an existing or emerging market segment. The table shown in Figure 5.2 becomes a great way to summarize the dynamics of your business opportunity.

Careful user and use case segmentation also tends to reveal many new innovation opportunities that a team has not yet considered. In fact, developing Figure 5.2 sometimes leads teams to pivot from their original idea. You start in one market segment only to find that there is better opportunity in a closely adjacent segment. This is precisely what is occurring today for many medical innovators: they start with healthcare in the hospital as being the point of initial attack, only to realize that healthcare delivery outside the hospital is where better opportunity lies due to patient needs, healthcare provider demand, and venture capital.

As you develop innovative concepts for your chosen Problem Spaces, think a bit out of the box regarding new emerging users and use cases. For example, software and services for distance education in rural communities is a hot, emerging area for innovation, as is diagnostic image artificial intelligence (AI) in healthcare, or driverless transportation. In other words, one of the rows in your figure might be a small but emerging target user group or use case that is rapidly growing. For example, IoT – sensing and monitoring – is being applied to all sorts of new phenomena. At this point, keep your mind open. Identify a few adjacent market applications within your Problem Space and then consider how that sharpens or changes your initial focus.

CHOCOLATE INNOVATION AND THE CASE OF MY M&M'S

One of your authors was twenty years past his first startup and had started to write books as a professor. One of these was titled *The Power of Product Platforms*, which became popular with practitioners.[2] One such practitioner was John Helferich, the U.S. head of R&D at Mars, which makes M&M's, Snickers, Dove, Kind Bar, and Wrigley's gum.[3] Mars is one of the largest manufacturers in the world in three distinct categories: chocolate, pet food, and chewing gum.

Innovation starts in the hearts and minds of people. You must be committed to thinking on behalf of the user. Mars had many employees thinking about how to innovate on behalf of their consumers. John was one of them.

"Hello Professor, this is John. We would like you to visit Mars." When the realization that it was not a joke about visiting a distant planet, but a truly large company, the temptation was too hard to resist. A few weeks later, a driver was waiting at the airport. We headed out to a large Mars facility that was a center for chocolate design and one of the company's largest manufacturing plants.

Chocolate is a rich example of segmenting users, buyers, and use cases. In chocolate, women prefer chocolate over men, and their preferences indeed vary by age group. However, the actual buyers often are not these same women but their loved ones, often men as a gift for women. In the children's segment, kids are both the users and buyers, but usually, moms and dads buy the chocolate treats. At a deeper level, when someone buys chocolate for themselves, it tends to be as a snack. When consumers buy chocolate for someone else, it is a *gift*. *Snacking* and *gifting* are two entirely different use cases or occasions, exhibiting different motivations, shopping behaviors, price tolerances, and more specific use cases such as birthday parties, weddings, or romance.

John Helferich was the R&D V.P. responsible for creating chocolate innovations for these different users, buyers, and use cases. That morning, during a review session for the chocolate business, the author's job was to provide advice on the company's platform strategies. Mars was already highly proficient in producing different chocolate products for different people and occasions on the same machines and with common ingredients. It took only an hour for the author to say in effect, "This is outstanding. A few tweaks, perhaps, but nothing much for me to add." John then made the invitation to visit the chocolate lab to see some current innovation work. It was an opportunity too good to pass.

Neil Willcocks, at that time a mid-level Mars employee circa 2000 (and who eventually became the global head of Mars R&D for both chocolate and chewing gum), was the host. We walked back to the R&D "kitchen" to look at food and packaging ideas and prototypes. At one point, we met a team working on new technology programs, who proceeded to show us their favorite project: a modified ink-jet printer generating patterns on flat chocolate bars. And just not text, but bitmapped pictures. Neil had created a roadmap showing the customization possible for the candies and the packaging. This led to an exciting conversation. If the team could print on something round – and more specifically – on the blank side of M&M – we realized that it was not just a new product but a new business relative to Mars' core business. It was also a way to reach out to directly connect with consumers around the M&M's brand. Personalized M&M's candies, occasion-based, would be unique, ordered online, and drop-shipped directly to the consumer. The concept was later branded as My M&M's.

The team's user segmentation focused on different occasions where printed candies might make a poignant impact on consumers. This segmentation was essential. *Who, what, where, when, how, and for what occasion* drove the segmentation and customer discovery process.

For example, the team considered different chocolate gifting occasions for custom-printed M&M's. One occasion was a goodie bag for kids' birthday parties. Another significant occasion was wedding celebrations because customization was an obvious need and the occasion itself suited to bulk orders. Valentine's Day gifts for loved ones seemed another important occasion for individual orders. The team also had promotional chocolates for business conferences and corporate training on its roadmap. The possibilities for growth seemed limitless.

Next, look at Figure 5.3. Dads were seen as somewhat different than moms. Dads were often the primary buyers of chocolate for Halloween, and this behavior might extend to chocolate for birthday parties. Further, if it was a dad, he might be more of an impulse buyer who perceived My M&M's as unique and special for the occasion. All the other kids attending the birthday party might also ask their dads to buy the candies for their parties. (This actually occurred on a regular basis after My M&M's launched.)

Target User	Specific Description Demographics, or dept/rank	Primary Use Case	Primary needs ("design drivers" for your venture)
• Young kids	• Boys and girls • Under 12 years	• Birthday parties • Other celebrations	• Fun, fun, fun • Personalized for them, not off the shelf • Taste (sugary chocolate)

Target Buyer (if different than User)	Specific Description Demographics, or dept/rank	Primary needs – "design drivers"

• Dads #1
  (spend more)
• Moms, too
	• Young families
	• Middle income and higher
	• Values special occasions and
	  memories for and with kids
		• Must look great
		• Higher price means better and leads to impulse
		• Personalized messages and pictures
		• Last minute order, delivery to home

Other Important Stakeholders in the Buying Decision	Specific Description Demographics, or dept/rank	Their major concerns
• Moms if not the buyer • Other kids	• The other parent • Viral buzz marketing	• Moms: how much is dad spending on this treat? • Other kids: how can I make my own M&M's different and special

Figure 5.3   The target users and buyers for My M&M's

Now, look at Figure 5.4. It shows two additional target use cases: personal romance and wedding events. For romance, custom-printed candies in special packaging were a wonderful

User Group	Specific Description (Professional status, organization)	Primary Use Case (that you will address)	Relative Segment Size and Growth Rate (Words, or numbers)	MyM&M'S Priority	How do I find some people in each one to talk to?
Kids – and Parents	Under 12 years old	Birthday parties	Largest segment Growing steadily	#1	Mars Associates children Their friends Social network marketing
Adult women	18-65	Romance Valentine's Day	Large Growing steadily	#2	Mars Associates spouses Social network marketing M&M's stores
Grown-up daughters	Typically 20-35	Weddings	Small segment But bulk orders	#2	Mars Associates Wedding planners

Figure 5.4   Occasions for M&M's (use cases by users/buyers)

new Valentine's Day gift. And for weddings, pictures of the bride and groom for party favors were predicted to be, and later turned out to be, one of the largest occasions. The figure also shows the original identification of people to interviews as part of the customer discovery process. The team first approached fellow Mars associates, their friends, and some wedding planners.

The My M&M's team knew it had to complement its skills with external partners – a good lesson for any entrepreneur. For example, printing specific text and images on candies required a completely different printing process than that used for decades to put the single M on one side of the candy. A former student of your authors had left a large office printer manufacturer to become the head of R&D for a food printing company that designed piezo-electric printheads to print on foods. He became a supplier to Mars for these printheads. Mars used the same partnering approach to find a supplier for edible, smudge-proof ink. Nor was Mars in the business of drop-shipping products to households. For decades, it had shipped tons of traditional M&M's on trucks to regional distribution centers and from these to specific retail stores for the candy aisle or checkout counter. The team found a partner that was already very strong in direct-to-consumer fulfillment. (Plus, this partner's trucks were brown, the color of chocolate!)

Source: Mars, Inc. Reproduced with permission.

Figure 5.5   My M&M's branding

Step by step, the innovation team designed an ecosystem around its core product – which, in hindsight, was a premium service designed around a unique product. This is also the way that you, as prospective entrepreneurs, should think about designing *your business*. It saves valuable time and up-front financial investment. Plus, if you work with the correct partners, their contributions help make the venture first-rate. The team also found an interactive advertising agency that excelled in website design. Figures 5.5 and 5.6 show the results that emerged from this early stage of the work.

Entrepreneurs need to perform quick market tests to help refine and prove demand for their products or services. Mars performed an internal employee test of their children's birthday parties. The results were spectacular. My M&M's comprised the most incredible goodie bag that the kids had ever seen. When ten kids attended a birthday party and received My M&M's as a goodie bag gift, the moms and dads found themselves asked by their children to get My M&M's for their parties. My M&M's went viral among many of the young families working at Mars.

In another early test, the team produced bags containing some of the first white printed M&M's with simple complementary words designed for a middle school graduation party to be held on a cruise boat in the Boston Harbor. During a break from the music, the kids raced to the candies held in plastic glasses, realized what they were, and consumed them in seconds. "Look at these cool M&M's!" The candies disappeared so fast that the only possible conclusion by Neil and his team was, "I guess we're going to have to build a lot more printing machines!"

Source: Mars, Inc. Reproduced with permission.

Figure 5.6   The My M&M's web ordering experience

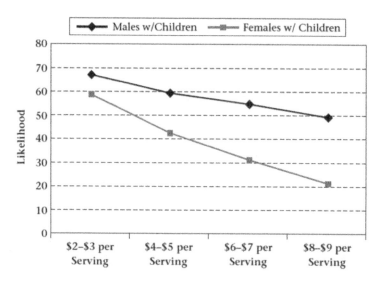

Source: Mars, Inc. Reproduced with permission.

Figure 5.7   Purchase intent of males with children versus females with children

The My M&M's team had to get a sense on pricing relative to traditional M&M's, which was approximately $3 a pound for flow-wrapped bagged candy. A specific type of marketing test called a conjoint study was conducted on 200 respondents, looking at feature/price tradeoffs. The sample included 100 young moms with children plus another 100 young dads with children. While both the moms and dads liked the My M&M's concept, after a certain price level, the moms, managing the family food budget, hit their limit. However, for those young dads, the higher prices did not significantly reduce purchase intent (see Figure 5.7). In fact, raising the price was later found to increase purchase intent, conveying an even more special gift for their children. In the months following the actual launch of My M&M's, the price worked its way to $30 a pound, approximately ten times the price of the traditional M&M's.

My M&M's is an innovation that remains fun and creative. It is also a clever innovation in how it leverages both the M&M's brand as well as the M&M's product itself, which is 99% of the printed My M&M's. It is also a great example of the power of segmenting target markets by users, buyers, and use cases. In fact, My M&M's can conceivably span all the life stages of a single consumer. Child birthday parties, graduations, weddings, job promotions, and retirements, plus the ongoing occasion of romance where chocolate has always been (and hopefully will always be) an expression of love from the giver to the receiver.

GENERALIZING FROM MY M&M'S TO YOUR PROJECT

Now, let's apply My M&M's to your innovation idea. Other students have before you, to good effect.

Over the years, we have seen students design new products and services that became excellent businesses. Typically, their work started with an idea for a Problem Space that they then made much more specific by targeting specific users and use cases. As their businesses grew, they expanded into adjacent users, buyers, and use cases. Kate has different flavors and carbonated beverages. Kevin does paving stones as well as roof tiles. Both are leverage their own common platforms created for the first product into additional products. It is a simple, yet powerful idea.

For example, we assume that most readers enjoy a nice glass of craft beer once in a while. While the beer industry has been growing at a slow rate of under 3% for decades, specific segments have enjoyed much higher growth, such as premium craft beer targeting Millennial males. Another growth segment of late is hard seltzer, growing at over 100% a year in the United States and that targets Millennial females. There are also flavored malt beers and non-alcoholic craft beers rising above the overall industry growth rate. Some years ago, we had one student who did market segmentation by age, gender, and by these basic product categories. She saw that young females were not well-served by the mainstream craft brewing industry. This student, Casey ended up being the lead developer for the Truly hard seltzer product from Sam Adams. It has been a huge hit, perhaps the most successful alcohol-containing beverage launch in the past decade. Casey was then promoted to guide beverage development for the entire company!

Or you can segment by geography. We had another student from Maine who was so inspired by the My M&M's story that he created a seafood direct-to-consumer gifting service, profiling the individual lobstermen and their lifestyle as the authentic character behind the gifting service. He and his brother, both lobstermen at the time, started a lobster distribution company in Maine, but then soon pivoted towards global seafood distribution. They realized that offshore markets presented a massive opportunity through airfreight. After running some tests, they began shipping lobsters and other prepared seafood products worldwide, having identified high-end seafood distributors and restaurants in Europe and Asia. They became the largest seafood export company in Maine and many years later, after incredibly hard work, sold their company for over $100 million! (See readyseafood.com).

Sometimes, innovators find it more beneficial to segment users and buyers by behaviors rather than purely demographic categories. For example, within a Millennial age group, some young men and women might be "daredevils" and more likely to buy an extreme sports innovation than the typical Millennial. Or, for some older men in certain categories, the age demographic does not matter as much as the psychographic behavior. For example, purchasers of sports cars such as the Mazda Miata are often men over fifty years of age, even though they do not need to drive fast or race cars. The best explanation is that these older men want to feel young again once behind the wheel.

Similarly, younger women who own dogs view that pet as the child they might have in the future – leading to the willingness to purchase the highest quality type of dog food at premium prices. The bottom line is that behaviors sometimes trump demographics for designing, positioning and branding innovations. Perhaps you should develop both a demographic and a behavioral segmentation or your target users – then see how each approach helps shape the design of your new product or service.

STEP 1: WHO ARE YOUR TARGET USERS AND BUYERS (IF DIFFERENT)? WHAT IS THE PRIMARY USE CASE?

We first want you to apply Figure 5.1 to your innovation idea. Remember, this framework represents the starting point, or beachhead, for your venture. We want you get even more specific about the target user, the target buyer, and the initial use case or occasion whose problems you will solve.

STEP 2: HOW MIGHT YOU GROW TO ADJACENT USERS AND USE CASES?

Next, think about Figure 5.2. This second framework shows your team's thinking about where your innovation might grow. That growth can occur in two ways: first, you can extend other adjacent use cases for your initial target user. Or, you can find different types of users who have the same essential use case.

An example would be if Kevin, from Chapter 2, who started making his recycled material roof tiles for households, decided to expand to retail malls, hotels, and other relatively small footprint buildings. Or, Kate has expanded from her initial focus on recovery drinks for athletes to health energy drinks for health-aware, environmentally conscious consumers, whether they are exercising heavily or not. Or, a venture can expand by addressing both new users and new use cases. An example of this would be how My M&M's started with kids' birthday parties and then expanded to couples who wanted personalized candy for their weddings or the corporate market needing company-branded candies for conferences and tradeshows.

Identifying two or three adjacent user groups and several next-step potential use cases takes careful thought and discussion. However, it is a good idea to understand where you wish to start and then, if matters go well, where you might grow. Perhaps more important, it might also get you to pivot to one of these adjacent segments as your initial target for this course. The adjacent market might be better in terms of size, growth, and user need. If that is the case, go back and redo your Figure 5.1.

Gathering data on market segment size and growth rates for Figures 5.1 and 5.2 should be reasonably straightforward. A little bit of digging on the web should get you all the information you require and help you fine-tune your segmentation approach. To gather this information, we ask that your team spend several more hours searching through the web for industry reports – either from government sources, trade associations, or articles in various publications. Keyword searches on "market size" and "growth rate" following the name of your Problem Space usually uncover many potential information sources. For example, a keyword search might be "market size growth healthy foods Millennial consumers," or "market size growth healthcare IoT for the home," or "market size growth solar energy rural communities." Be creative. An hour or two's search will reveal a wealth of information. Get data from free sources as much as possible.

For students at universities with large libraries, you might have access to a "research librarian" who can show you special industry reports to which the institution has subscribed. For electronics, for example, the Frost & Sullivan, Forrester Research, International Data Corporation (IDC), and the Gardner Group all have specialty reports on current and future trends, competitors, and market sizing for technology-intensive industries. The reference librarian should know these and others to help you understand market size, growth, and other vital factors that will help you prioritize market segments and specific applications. And remember, always say "thank you" to your reference librarian!

*** *** ***

A special comment for societally focused innovation teams: let's say you wish to create a virtual e-learning classroom for the rural poor. And since these users have little purchasing power, your solution is most likely to end up as a nonprofit organization seeking grants from local, national, and international foundations or government agencies. You must still think and act as if you were a startup, seeking to grow its user base *whether they are paying you or not*. In such cases, the foundation or government agency is the *buyer*. Customer segmentation – segmenting a market by users, buyers, and use cases – remains fundamentally important to any successful innovation, be it a for-profit or not-for-profit venture. Being a nonprofit venture does not mean being inefficient, either in the innovation process or in its go-to-market and operations management. Given the enormity of the problems facing society – healthcare, climate, clean water, transportation – governments will likely be essential channels for funding innovations and delivering them to citizens. And governments will turn to innovators such as you because the private sector tends to innovate much faster and more effectively than the public sector. Many government agencies around the world also have special set-aside grants for entrepreneurs because they see new ventures as the way to grow employment. The government official, as a buyer, will know a good idea when s/he sees it. Win that sponsorship with the insights gathered with the methods here. Later, you will have to learn the ins and outs required to sell into the government. These include procurement processes and budget cycles. Not easy, but with some work and patient, very doable.

NOTES

1. Meyer, M.H., Crane, F.G., and Lee, C. (2016). "Connecting Ethnography to the Business of Innovation." *Business Horizons*, 59(6), November, 699-711. It is a fun story.

2. Meyer, M.H., and Lehnerd, A. (1997). *The Power of Product Platforms*. New York: The Free Press. For those interested in a more current articulation of platform strategies and methods, see: Meyer, M.H., and Cassis, J. (2020). "Implementing Product Platforms in the Global Enterprise: Lessons from an LED Industry Leader." *Business Horizons*, 63(4), July-August, 421–434.

3. M&M's Brand, My M&M's, Snickers®, Dove®, and Kind® Healthy Snacks are registered trademarks of Mars, Incorporated or affiliates.

6
Gaining insight into user needs

THE PURPOSE OF THE CHAPTER

The previous chapter helped you segment your target users into different groups and to identify their use cases within your Problem Space. Now we move on to how to quickly and effectively understand specific user needs within these use cases. These needs become the design drivers for a particular product or service design concept. This chapter builds on the Customer Experience Maps and Mind Mapping that you did in Chapter 4 – and it sharpens your Customer Value Proposition. In the last chapter, we asked you to gather industry data on the web or through your university's reference librarian, this chapter will focus on end-user and buyer interviewing techniques and apply them to at least a dozen more individuals representing target users, buyers, and use cases. This is the essence of *user-centered design*.

LEARNING OBJECTIVES

We have three new methods to learn in this chapter. These are fundamental innovation skills that will serve you well whether you start your own company or take an innovation-related job (product management, engineering, IT, etc.) in a large company.

1. Learn methods for interviewing the users and buyers for your new product or service. Try to have a dozen in-depth interviews with target users, and if different, additional interviews with target buyers, using a structured interviewing guide that we will review in this chapter.
2. Identify both "perceived" and "latent" needs amongst your target users and how they change across an entire use case.
3. Create a persona for the target user, which reveals the most important characteristics and problems of that user, and then, the benefits that your innovation will provide and the major design points for your innovation. Then build a persona for the buyer, if s/he is different to the user.

With these insights, we then ask you to refine the first version of your Customer Value Proposition. As a result of your work in this chapter, your CVP should sharpen in its focus on user needs and benefits.

USER-CENTERED DESIGN TO IMPROVE THE USER'S EXPERIENCE

The innovator – either as an entrepreneur or corporate innovator – wants to create powerful products or services that dramatically *improve the user's experience*. And any given use case can actually contain more than one specific user experience. For example, Starbucks innovated the customer experience of going to a coffee shop by adding a comfortable, den-like environment and wireless connectivity to its excellent coffee products. The consumption environment and the taste of the coffee are distinct experiences that combine to create an overall, pleasing customer experience. Each is an important component – almost like a good engine works together with a pleasing interior and exterior design of car to create a happy customer. And the services flooding into connected cars will dramatically improve the driver's experience for certain use occasions – such as avoiding traffic jams or finding stores with certain types of products and promotions. The method is the same: target a specific type of user, get clear about his or her major use cases, learn the user's problems and frustrations in those use cases, and then think of ways to improve both specific and the overall user experience. This approach guides the innovator to create distinctive products and services that are pleasing and highly functional for intended users.

KARTHIK'S JOURNEY OF PERSONAL AND USER DISCOVERY

Let's consider the journey of Karthik Mahadevan (Figure 6.1), another of your authors' former students, who not only started a company with a clear social mission but, in the process, discovered his passions to help those in need and the fulfillment of innovating to that purpose.

Karthik took industrial and design thinking courses as a student in Chennai, India. Through these courses, he became enchanted with the process of product design and wanted to pursue a career in industrial and product design.

Karthik's father had been his inspiration. His father had grown up in an impoverished Indian family, escaped poverty through education and landed a job with a large company in Dubai. His father then returned home to India to start a new company designing and installing electrical grids. Belief in oneself and a strident faith that hard work brings success were the creed by which Karthik was raised. While in high school in India, Karthik realized that one of his core values was fundamentally *problem-solving*; and that to solve a problem well, the designer needed the skill of creating a robust *design* for

Source: Karthik Mahadevan. Used with permission.

Figure 6.1   Karthik Mahadevan

the solution to that problem. When presented with a problem, Karthik could not rest until he solved it. This meant being able to dig deep with target users and bring all the latest and best technology to bear in meeting the user's most essential needs.

Karthik followed his gut instinct for college, enrolling in an Industrial Engineering program at Guindy University in Chennai, India. He had two roommates – one was also studying product design, and the other, a software engineer. Together, these three friends started working on joint projects for their classes. They had fun and also learned to trust one another.

After graduation, Karthik took a job as an industrial engineer in a consulting company in India. His tasks seemed mundane, but it was a job, a salary, and good experience. However, he was somewhat frustrated. His bosses used his industrial engineering work only for incremental improvements to existing processes in client operations, often factories. The work often lacked the creativity that Karthik wanted to achieve in his problem-solving. Also important was that his consulting job offered little "skin in the game." You did a job and then moved on to the next, often with a new client.

Karthik came to realize that he wanted to create his own new products. At one point, he was watching videos of Steve Jobs that struck to the core. Karthik realized that he wanted "a career as a creator," to be independent and to create tangible things that helped real people with big problems that needed solving. In fact, in his mind, while the well-known design consultancy IDEO was indeed a great design firm, Apple was his inspiration. It made actual products, incredibly well designed, with both hardware and software, that were simple for users yet powerful. If you readers have not watched some of Steve Jobs' most popular videos, take a few minutes to do so now. You, too, will be inspired.

Compelled with this personal mission to be "a creator" and a "problem-solver," Karthik inventoried his professional skills and realized that industrial design by itself was not going to be sufficient. This was a crucial step in his journey of personal discovery. He wanted to learn how to design new things from the user's perspective, to improve the user's experience, and to innovate to make things possible that had not been possible before – *just like Steve Jobs*. He felt he needed to go to graduate school to learn additional skills.

This is where we met Karthik. He was enrolled in an intensive, experiential course titled "Clean Tech Ventures" at the Technical University in Delft, the Netherlands, the place where we met Kevin from our earlier chapter. TU Delft is a great design and engineering university. For a number of years, we had traveled to Delft to teach a graduate-level course in new venture creation, primarily for engineers. A dozen highly technical teams attended the course each offering with the hope to land next door in YES!Delft, a technology incubator that is amongst the best in Europe.

For one of his prior courses at Delft, Karthik had chosen as a project the design of technology to assist blind persons. It was very challenging from a technical sense, merging mobile technology with vision AI in image analysis and action. And it was and remains a significant "addressable market." Around the world, there are over 43 million visually impaired people with very little other than canes to help them navigate their environment.[1] It was a specific Problem Space begging for new solutions.

Karthik came into the class full of determination but not yet well-focused. Who should he speak with, how should he find blind people to talk with, how would he find and prioritize their use cases in daily life, and from all this, how might he then create a product – in this case, a mobile app offered as a service – that would be the basis of his own company? How could he monetize his solutions for the blind to make a reasonable living and build a company? These were basic, fundamental questions that many of you readers might have at this very moment! And like any other first-time entrepreneur, Karthik had many more questions than answers. However, in our view as teachers, he was amongst the hungriest learners of the lot. Quickly, Karthik became a laser-guided missile with the goal to build a mobile app to assist the blind in their activities of daily living. Let's see how he did it and use his example to illustrate the methods that Karthik learned and used himself to create his venture.

THE POWER OF UNDERSTANDING USE CASES

In the previous chapter, we emphasized identifying different potential customer groups and focusing on one for your innovation, based on sound reasoning. Now, with a chosen target user, you need to do the same thing for use cases. As we have learned, a use case is a specific activity in which your target user is engaged and where potentially your new product or service will substantially improve the user's experience.

For entrepreneurs starting companies, it is important to focus first on a single-use case, one that appears essential and that your instinct and initial work in earlier chapters tell you poses considerable challenges for users. Dig there first and find gold. Then, over time, you can expand to other use cases that are closely related or "adjacent" to the first, e.g. the adjacent growth areas we explored in the prior chapter.

For example, we saw in the My M&M's example that the team started with birthday parties for children, designing printed candies and packaging for that specific *occasion*. The My M&M's team then expanded to weddings with party favors, graduations, and the more general occasion of romance, which in many countries boils down to Valentine's Day, or its equivalent in countries around the world. Later on, the team expanded to B2B occasions such as hiring, promotions, retirements, and conferences. Now that you have identified your first target user group, think about the two or three related use cases. Again, pick one of these that seems best to continue your innovation journey.

Karthik faced many potential use cases. He spent considerable time with visually impaired people on the streets of Delft, using his goodwill and interest to make new friends in the vision-impaired community. It became clear that simply reading a street sign, bus or tram number to get to the university was a problem. Just imagine if you were blind and had to walk or take public transportation to school! Then, as Karthik spent more time with vision-impaired people, he observed a range of "activities of daily living": they had to go shopping and understand what they were buying and the price of items – and then pay for that item without being fooled by cashiers. Grabbing lunch was another important occasion. How many restaurants print a menu in Braille or have recorded item listings? This became another compelling use case to address. Getting dressed in the morning and choosing coordinated colors was another occasion that popped up, particularly for women. For a blind person, the entire day comprised many different use cases, all interesting, some probably more important than others. Karthik realized that building a mobile app with vision AI was what he wanted to do and that it could have a diverse, ever-expanding range of practical applications to help the vision-impaired.

Karthik had to start somewhere. He began with the use case of getting to school, building an app for it that was multi-lingual. He then proceeded to the shopping occasion. Menu ordering came next. As at the time of writing this book, Karthik and his team have developed software for a growing number of inspiring use cases.

Now, let's see Karthik's methods to learn specific needs and design his software.

JUMP INTO THE HEARTS AND MINDS OF YOUR USERS

With an initial, target use case in hand, the next step is to learn what users truly need. Many companies start because the entrepreneur/innovator has been "the user" or "the buyer" for the type of product or service s/he wants to create. Recognizing the critical flaws in existing products and services in that use case, feeling her/his own frustrations, the entrepreneur sees the gap and strives to create something hopefully a lot better.

Many of you reading this book may be examples of this type of innovator. You may be frustrated with what you are forced to use in your chosen Problem Space and have already thought deeply about the design and performance of a better solution. In fact, that might be your primary motivation for enrolling on this course.

For example, one of our closest friends and mentors, Al Lehnerd, was a senior manager at Black & Decker. Al had six kids. His wife left for a church retreat for an entire weekend, leaving Al alone with all of the kids for two days straight. After 48 hours of nonstop cleaning, which included plugging in his vacuum cleaner a dozen times, Al was left with a sore back and a burning desire to do something about it. He went to work on a Monday morning, and in just a few days, he and his team designed and prototyped a portable, rechargeable vacuum cleaner that did not have to be plugged into an electrical socket. This tool became known as the Dustbuster – a blockbuster success with consumers, with use cases in homes, automobiles, boats, and other such places. The point: the Dustbuster was born from Al's own frustration.

However, even if you are like Al and are a clever innovator, you still need to validate your idea with other users. Al did a lot of validation for the Dustbuster concept with different types of target users. Once he had some prototypes of the machine, he could not assume the broader market would consume *what he* personally liked and needed. An innovator needs to make sure the pain s/he thinks target users have is in fact their pain. If you are representative of the target user within your specific Problem Space, it should be pretty easy to start a conversation, commiserate, and learn more deeply from others. At this point, remember that *you are not selling anything*. You are there to learn as the precursor to the product or service design.

User-centered design methods will enable you to *uncover people's fears, frustrations, and concerns*, and from this begin to create next-generation solutions.

DOING THE INTERVIEWING: "FIELD RESEARCH"

Karthik began his fieldwork walking around the streets with a few select visually impaired users. He viewed them as his co-designers. You must now try to do the same, extending the initial customer discovery work you performed to determine your Problem Space to a much more detailed, granular level of detail.

Talking only over the telephone or through emails is not going to cut it. You've got to see their faces, their expressions, and their exasperations that emerge from deep-seated concerns. A nonverbal expression can tell you a lot as a designer. And the degree of severity of a problem is often best learned by a nonverbal or four-letter verbal expression, far better than a traditional market research survey!

If you cannot meet target users face to face due to distance or public health concerns, teleconferencing technologies such as Facetime, Zoom, Teams, Google Meets, or some other similar mechanism can come in quite handy.

However, the preferred way of doing this type of "ethnographic" field research is to observe the user in her/his place of use. That will mean different things for different use cases. For example, we once helped design a new type of energy-efficient replacement window for homeowners. Part of the solution was to make a window that was much easier to install for window installers. This could only be learned by going to construction sites to observe how they were installing windows. All the current windows required that construction people climb up ladders to install windows on the second or third floors. So, the team designed a window that could be much more simply and quickly installed *from the inside*. A relatively simple idea and not that hard to execute and that made a big difference to builders in terms of saving time and reducing the risk of injury. *Installing from the inside instead of the outside* is an excellent example of what we call *a latent need*. Also note that in this case, while the homeowner is the buyer, the builder is the actual "user" for window installation – showing why segmentation of users and buyers and learning their use cases is so essential for innovation.

This replacement window product took the market by storm in the home improvement market, including the Home Depot channel, because of the productivity benefit provided to installers or builders. Later, the team then created an entirely new window design using recycled wood and plastic with an extrusion process that melted composite pellets for the window frame and sashes instead of cutting and fastening different pieces of wood. If you have a spare moment, look up Renewal by Andersen. It substantially increased the company's revenue. In fact, Andersen disrupted its own product category of traditional wood windows to be part of a greener society.

WHAT IS A REASONABLE NUMBER OF INTERVIEWS FOR CONCEPT DEVELOPMENT?

How many homeowners or builders did this company have to interview to get these insights? Thousands? No. Hundreds? Also no. Try a dozen target users in three successive rounds of customer interviewing: 1) for initial needs discovery, 2) to then show early prototypes to learn more needs and preferences, and 3) to show improved prototypes to solidify the design of a minimum viable product. It is the quality of user research and needs discovery that matters here, much more than the quantity. Finding truly representative users and buyers and having deep conversations with them is the priority at this stage of the innovation process.

Karthik went on commuting, shopping, and dining excursions with blind people about every other day over the course of six months. This translated into twelve to fifteen target user interviews each month. He and other members of his team have continued these immersions ever since. Even during the pandemic-related lockdowns in the Netherlands, they used digital channels. Customer discovery with rapid cycles of interviewing and applications development for specific use cases are part of the DNA of Karthik's company, combined with its social mission. He later surveyed 100-200 users when he needed more quantitative data for packaging and pricing decisions.

Conventional marketing science tells us that a sample of a hundred or more is essential to do any serious statistics to get "reliable" results. Here, however, we are more concerned with deep insights than statistics. Deep insights rarely come from a one- or two-page survey. Instead, such insights come from thoughtful observation and conversation with target users and buyers.

Working with colleagues at our university, we once studied a large number of "design firms" – companies that serve as innovation experts for large corporations. It showed that nearly 80% of those firms preferred in-depth interviewing with ten or fewer target users for a specific design. *That's ten user immersions or fewer* by well-known design firms such as IDEO, Continuum, and Frog. The reasons are two-fold: first, after a while, after talking to ten to twelve users, you might not learn much more that is new for early design and development. Second, time and money are typically in limited supply, particularly for entrepreneurs. Learn what you need to know and get on with the process of building the prototype and then, improve it. Once you launch a business and its products or services to living, breathing customers, the feedback on current designs and much needed new features will come pouring in! You just need to keep your eyes and ears open. User-centred design is really *user-inspired design.*[2]

This approach is the essence of lean innovation: learn deeply, learn fast, design and prototype, show users your ideas, and keep learning until you achieve the design of your first, minimally viable product or service.

Speaking to just six customers is probably not sufficient when you are just getting started on a new design. We can push the limit to be extra rigorous to ten to twelve in-depth conversations. Think of three rounds of a dozen users and/or buyers each to play it safe: the first round for initial discovery; the second round to run your product or service concept and initial design by a mixture of the same and some additional target users; and the third round to show another dozen or so users your actual prototypes. In Chapter 12, we will also learn how to do a final Reality Check that is a survey where we recommend at least 30 user-respondents for a classic type of "concept test." But for now, we focus on the in-depth immersions with target users and buyers.

This number of in-depth conversations with users and buyers is reasonable for this initial design stage – and this course. And rather than have a hard limit, perhaps it is best to keep trying to speak with additional users and buyers until you find yourself not learning anything more.

For users and buyers in B2B contexts – institutional or corporate users and buyers – getting a dozen of these individuals for each of these three stages might be very difficult. For example, getting an hour with even six CIOs, building managers, or large hospital administrators will challenge most new innovators. Ask your teacher for guidance – we give our B2B students a goal of six interviews for each of the three phases in early design. You will also probably need help from your teacher and other mentors close to your university to get access to such business users. LinkedIn searches are another great source of contacts. Search on a specific industry, look for graduates of your school, and then send them a connect message saying that you are a student looking to gain insight into their area of work and request a time to talk for 30–40 minutes. LinkedIn is well-suited for this type of B2B customer discovery. And the tip of the day: *always ask an interviewee if s/he has someone else* that they think you should speak with about your innovation idea.

Karthik tried different approaches to finding target users and professional blind-person associations with whom to speak, ranging from cold calling to asking acquaintances for introductions. Both approaches worked with varying degrees of success. When speaking to potential business partners, he also found it helpful to understand the organization structure first in order to find the right people to approach.

INTERVIEW TARGET USERS IN THEIR PLACES OF USE AND PURCHASE

Once you've identified target users and buyers, how will you approach them for information and insights? We suggest the following: do not ask them to visit you or meet in a neutral space such as a café. Instead, go to their place of activity – be it a place of leisure, family activities, or work, depending on your innovation idea. Half of the insights you gain will probably come from simply observing users in the appropriate setting and seeing them respond to specific situations. And yes, a café might be just fine if you are making products of coffee snacks and beverages, or mobile work tools, or apps. Having worked in the coffee industry ourselves, there is an amazing amount of mobile and laptop computing and communications by professionals working in a Starbucks or an equivalent setting. This makes field research in a café for those Problem Spaces appropriate.

Karthik went with vision-impaired persons on their commutes, shopping excursions, cafés, and into their homes. Their needs became readily apparent. He visited these users several times to show wireframes and other prototyping concepts.

It would be best if you innovated in this way, too. What sort of authentic experiences could you either directly participate or observe with users and buyers? How might you do this for a pure software product or mobile application? If your innovation team is focused on a new food or drink, where can you innovate with your target customers? Think, and then, *just do it.*

EFFECTIVE CONVERSATIONS WITH TARGET USERS

Always ground yourself in the idea of improving the user's experience. Your mission is to discover what people like, what they need, and what frustrates them.

If at all possible, we want you to observe users first and talk second. This combination of observation and conversation, preferably in the place of purchase and the place of use, is called *ethnography*. This term comes from the anthropologists that explored the traditional cultures of remote tribes. Perhaps the most famous anthropologist is Margaret Mead, who believed that the environment in which people are raised causes most cultural and behavioral differences amongst people – not family genes. She went to the South Pacific and Southeast Asia to observe and test her theories with indigenous, remote island populations.[3]

Following in Mead's footsteps, product designers believe the best way to learn about user needs and frustrations is not to send a survey to hundreds of target users, but rather, immerse with far fewer, for intense periods of time. This leads to our recommendation of three rounds of a dozen users for your projects.

Simply observing the customer's activities for an hour or so should reveal a wealth of opportunities. We also think you will love doing this if you put yourself into the mindset of being open to new things, listening to other people's ideas, and connecting the dots of the users' needs and their social or work environment for new product or service innovation. You've got to be in the proper mindset – get a good night's sleep before, set aside the stress of other homework for a while, and jump into this innovator's journey of needs discovery.

We never cease to be amazed at the inconvenience, poor quality, or simple nonperformance put up with by users across nearly all categories of products and services. Seeing that, with your own eyes, will be the source of your best innovations. Look for frowns, sighs, and other signs of displeasure – as well as smiles, laughs, and other signs of the opposite. Are users sitting down or on the go? Are they alone or with other people? Look for what the user is doing *with other people* or *other systems* in their places of use. There may well be opportunities to improve teamwork or multi-person collaboration within a product or service area. And, if you are in the B2B systems domain, you will have to learn about the other systems with which your system must work. Designing this type of interoperability upfront into a solution makes life so much more convenient for both users and buyers.

Once you begin a conversation with a user, please try to listen more than you talk. *You are not selling anything yet.* This is so important. Let us repeat it: *you are not selling anything yet*. Resist the temptation. This is the biggest mistake that entrepreneurs and innovators make when starting a new project – you are there to learn, not sell. If you start selling at this point, you will significantly diminish if not ruin your chances of learning anything new. You must focus your conversations on the user and buyer and her/his problems. The selling comes later.

PREPARE A DISCUSSION GUIDE

Next comes a structured interview or conversation guide for these user and buyer interviews. First, forget the preconceived notions of a highly structured questionnaire. It is far too early in your innovation development cycle for a large survey study. Think about a few open-ended questions. And if possible, even before getting into detailed conversation, try to observe your users as they purchase a product or service before putting it to use. Ethnography and conversation in the act of using or doing will reveal great nuggets of needs and frustrations with current solutions.

You need to be prepared. You should know the types of information that you want – information that will help you focus your product and service development, the pricing, the marketing messages, and the route to market.

A structured interview guide helps. Take a look at Figure 6.2. It contains eight questions that will provide tremendous insight from interviewees.

A Discussion Guide with Target Users

1. How do you define the activity or problem? (*Teach me how I should think about the activity or problem area. It is probably bigger than how I define it now.*)

2. What do you use now in terms of products or services in this activity? (*Teach me the current competitive set.*)

3. Where or from whom do you buy products or services? What is good about that channel? What is not so good? (*Teach me the realities of the channels or the preferred routes to market.*)

4. How satisfied are you with your current products or services that you use in this activity? What is your greatest source of dissatisfaction or frustration with using these? (*Please tell me who you think is the best and the worst!*) What are your workarounds? (*I would love to see them!*)

5. Who is responsible for the buying decision? Is it you or someone else? (*Can you help me speak with them also?*) How is the buying decision made? Who and what are the key influencers? (*You should be writing down notes because this is where most entrepreneurs slip up!*)

6. What are the criteria used when evaluating alternatives? Is there a clear set of metrics as part of those criteria? (*Can you teach me how you currently evaluate current products and services.*)

7. How much do you spend each month or year on products or services within this activity? (*Tell me if you think you are getting your money's worth, either by your facial expression or in words.*)

8. What would be the ideal solution for you? How would *you* measure its value to you? (*Let me know what you think will be better than anything on the market today, and how customers would make their buying decisions.*)

Figure 6.2   A discussion guide with target users

Please read through these questions and think about how you might tailor them for your project. The italicized sentences in parentheses after each question are the types of information you want to gather. Karthik took questions such as these in our class and prepared his own personalized interview guidelines. After several interviews, he found himself not needing a reference question sheet. It just began to flow naturally. It will for you, too. Karthik used a combination of the interview questions shown in Figure 6.2, plus ideas from other design courses he took at Delft, including the approach from a guidebook written by Rob Fitzpatrick, called *The Mom Test*.[4]

The combination of observation and in-depth questioning will make you very smart about the needs, preferences, and purchase behaviors of your users and buyers. It takes empathy, a certain curiousness about your user's problems, and a sincere desire to try to solve those problems. A user will pick up on this sincerity and want to help you, sometimes spending more time than you initially planned. *Be compassionate with your target users; fall in love with their problems; be their innovative solutions provider.* It can be the great thrill of this class project and perhaps more if you start your own company.

After each interview, reflect and take notes after each user and buyer interaction. This is essential. If you are talking to people in a shopping mall, for example, grab a cup of coffee at a café and review your notes, highlighting key points. Sometimes this is best done with a team-mate, seeing and hearing interviewees with two sets of eyes and ears. Plus, two sets of hands for note-taking is helpful. Shared learning is exciting and fun.

If you have a particularly fantastic interview, ask the interviewee if he or she might consider having you take a video on your cellphone of that person recapping some of their key points. Also, take a video of the surroundings – the place of purchase and perhaps the place of use. Some of these video clips will prove powerful telling the story about the user's problems and the benefits you can bring to the user later on. Taking a video obviously does not work in all settings. Just try your best.

When it comes to the detailed interview questions shown in Figure 6.2, you need to remember to:

- **Position and conduct these discussions as conversations, not formal interviews**. The user is the teacher and you are the student. This means detaching yourself from the solution for the moment – even if you are the most intelligent person in the room and think you know five times more than the person with whom you are speaking.

- **Use open-ended questions** – that is, questions that cannot be answered with "yes" or "no." You can see that none of the questions in Figure 6.2 can be answered "yes" or "no."

- **Asking about the ideal solution**: Asking the user about his or her ideal solution only comes later in the structured interview guides. You don't ask them this first. You need to establish the overall context of use and the competitive environment first. Only then will the customer's ideal solution make the most sense.

- **Always offer genuine thanks**, both before and at the end of the conversation. If you meet ten target customers, the chances are that three or four of those individuals may want to participate in trying a prototype of the new product or service. Or, if the "customer" is a store manager, he or she might become a test channel partner. Treat all of these people as partners. They may help you in the future. Let them know how much you value their insights.

- **Try to get additional leads.** Ask the interviewee if they know someone else that might be interested in speaking with you.

- **Try to go into the place of use and the place of purchase to observe activities and talk about them.** As noted above, a great way to achieve concentrated interaction with a user or buyer is to ask if you can join them the targeted use case – such as when the user is shopping, exercising, cooking, working, using or fixing machines, or searching for certain types of information on the web. You can ask the questions in the interview guide as you join her/him in this activity.

Above all else – here, let the interviewee be your teacher. It is up to you to decide if they provide valuable insights or not, but go into these sessions with eyes and ears wide open and your thinking cap turned full on.

As noted, buyers can often be different than users. When they are, you need to interview representative buyers as well. This applies to both consumer products and B2B products, and to services of either type. The same discussion guide can be repurposed to speak with *buyers*. As a rule of thumb, if you are going to talk to a total of thirty individuals for your project, several dozen should be the end-users and at least six should be buyers.

But there are always exceptions to this rule of thumb. For example, it may be that your users cannot talk! If you are designing pet food, all you can do is speak to pet owners. Moreover, the actual buyer for your company is the pet food store owner or website. So, you need to think about all three beings: the pet (for nutrition, volume, and taste), the pet owner (for nutrition, cost, and messaging), and the store owner to differentiate from existing pet foods and break onto the shelf. In this case, spending an hour with two or three pet food store owners will be worth its weight in gold. Pick a slow time to try this, which tends to be mornings.

Or, you might be designing for a situation with multiple stakeholders. Any hospital product or system might touch the doctor or nurse, as well as the patient. It might also impact the IT staff in the hospital. And, of course, those individuals responsible for procurement are impor-tant to interview as well. That might mean the Chief Financial Officer (CFO), the Medical Director, or the head of administration and operations. Like other corporations, hospitals are giant, multi-headed user, buyer, and influencer organizations. Your journey of buyer needs discovery may take you in multiple paths. What is for sure is that nothing gets purchased without the approval of different administrators in a large healthcare provider. Their needs and preferences are just as important as those of the physician or the patient.

Work with your teacher to scope your user and buyer discovery. No entrepreneur completes the totality of her/his field research in a month or even two months. Instead, this is your first deep pass at discovering needs. You want to achieve a sufficient number of high-quality user and buyer interviews to determine the requirements that will yield the most crucial design drivers for your new product or service. Agree on that number amongst your team and with your teacher – and then, using the methods in this chapter, aim for quality over sheer quantity.

LADDERING INTERVIEWEES: THE POWER OF "WHY?"

As you work your way down the interview questions, you will invariably branch from certain questions into deeper, more specific conversations. When that happens, here is a critical inter-viewing tip: when a user tells you that something is important or a problem, try to follow it up with, "Why is that important?" or "Why is that a problem?" This makes cursory, high-level interviewing become "in-depth interviewing." This technique can lead to deeper, more mean-ingful insights.

This approach is simple yet powerful. The user says, "I have this problem." You then ask, "why?" Then, the interviewee gives you the reason. Then, you try to ask, *why is that* so impor-tant? And if it makes sense, ask *why* even a third time. This approach gets down to the most profound drivers for a perceived need or a latent frustration – and if you can uncover that need or frustration, you will be able to design a solution that is all the more useful.

For example, turn to one of your teammates and ask why they are getting their current college degree. The first answer might be, "I want to learn new things." You might then ask, "Why is that important to you?" The response might be, "I feel that without this education, I won't be able to advance to the next step in my career." You might then ask, "Why is this important?" And your friend might say, "I want to be successful." And then you might ask, "What does success mean?" which leads to a much deeper conversation such as how to balance career success and contribute to societal needs for personal fulfillment and happiness.

There are, of course, much simpler laddering examples. A friend of ours designed a mouse-trap with a much less forceful spring that still breaks the poor little mouse's neck but does not hurt the user's finger should the trap shut by accident while setting. Fear for fingers is the need; a less powerful spring mechanism the solution; both of which became clear after a two-step laddering: "What are the concerns you have setting this mousetrap?" "It can accidentally trip." "Why is that important?" "I don't want to hurt my fingers!" From this, we achieve a clear design driver to create a mousetrap that kills the mouse but won't hurt the fingers or the snout of your pet dog or cat!

In your fieldwork, please try to ladder your users. Ask "Why" whenever you can, and have some fun with it.

FINDING DEEPER INSIGHTS FROM THE INTERVIEWS: LOOK FOR PERCEIVED AND LATENT NEEDS

Now we get even more specific about types of user needs. When you do your observation and interviewing of target users and buyers, realize that not all customer needs are of the same priority for the innovator. Some are more important – or more strategic – than others.

Here is a good approach for prioritizing needs. There are (a) perceived needs and (b) latent needs. A perceived need is one that users and buyers already recognize and, in many cases, have a fair idea of how it can be addressed: "I need it to drive faster!" "I need it to last longer!" "I need it to cost less!" Performance, quality, and price tend to be the "big three" perceived needs. All competitors in a target market segment can understand this with standard customer research. In the mousetrap example, "killing the mouse" is the perceived need – there are many mousetrap products on the market that purport to get the job done. On the other hand, "Not hurting my fingers" is a classic latent need. Other than the cruel sticky pad traps where the mouse dehydrates to death, there is no "not hurt the fingers" yet still effective mousetrap on the market. (Look up "The Intruder Better Mousetrap" on YouTube, if you dare!)

Both types of needs – perceived and latent – are typically lumped together as the user's needs, against which you innovate to create real benefits for the user. But for us, however, the differences between perceived and latent needs are so important that they should not be lumped together! As an innovator, you must understand the user's perceived needs, *but you must also do more. You need to find those latent needs.* A latent need is a fear or frustration that the *user doesn't know how to solve.* The latent need may be expressed with a quick phrase, some type of physical expression such as a sigh or clenched fist, or even a swear word. Part of that frustration is that the user knows the problem but has not found a solution for it in the market and cannot even imagine how it might be solved.[5] Later on, when you present that same user with a solution to that intractable problem, s/he says, "Great! That's perfect!" You have put a smile on that user's face. Then hopefully, they will become an actual customer and also tell other prospective customers just how great your new product or service is for that specific problem.

Finding and solving latent needs is one of the most important secret weapons for the innovator: work hard to find and validate the latent needs of target users in particular use cases, and then be clever in solving those needs. The result is a new product or service with function and price that screams "value" to the user. Think Apple in terms of seamless integration between phones, iPods, laptops, and workstations; Tesla, in terms of electric, self-driving and speedy vehicles; or fast-growing, popular food products. Enterprise customers say the same thing about their favorite piece of software, such as Zoom, which makes work-from-home achievable, more scalable and fully featured than its market predecessor, Skype. These innovations all addressed important latent needs when they were first introduced.

Like these examples, finding one or two latent needs and addressing them clearly puts you on the path to success. Understanding perceived needs is still very important but consider meeting these perceived needs as the price of entering an existing product or service category. This might include the speed of delivering a product or service, how quick a machine works, or the quality of a food or drink. Perceived needs are what one might call "table stakes" for a poker game; you need them to sit at the table. But understanding and solving latent needs are what will win the game. Therefore, you need to design and deliver both types of needs – perceived and latent – in your new product or service.

Figure 6.3 provides a general framework for thinking about perceived and latent needs, as illustrated by a modern automobile. Tesla electric cars, for example, get tremendous acceleration, have great suspension, and boast comfortable, luxurious interiors – all *in addition* to being electric vehicles with self-driving capability. A Tesla meets both sets of needs for the affluent yet energy-conscious car buyer.

In Karthik's case, just about everything he learned from blind users was a latent need. Yes, some apps could "speak" printed text in different languages. However, none were using intensive vision intelligence to automatically read text and numbers, distinguish colors, or recognize specific faces in a manner readily available to the typical user. Karthik's set of use cases presented what we call a "target-rich" environment for innovation, ripe with needs and problems to solve. He then staged the delivery of functionality in his app to solve these latent needs in subsequent releases: reading a bus number, shopping, ordering a meal, recognizing a friend, and so forth. When a company has quarterly release cycles, as do many software companies, there are plenty of moments to delight your users further and make new news.

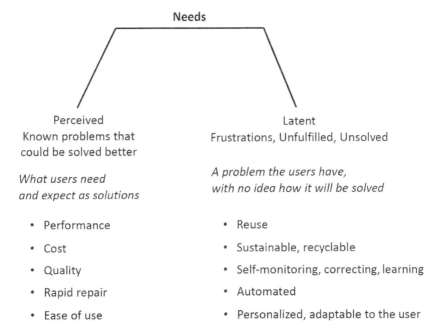

Figure 6.3 Find and categorize perceived and latent needs

As shown in Figure 6.3, latent needs are often found in the following categories or functions:

- **Reuse.** This is a growing concern and source of frustration in industries. In software, we see it in market leaders such as Microsoft and Oracle (where reusable chunks of code and data across multiple products or web services are the name of the game). In consumer products, companies such as Starbucks are actively experimenting with having consumers employ reusable tumblers or returnable plastic cups.

- **Sustainability.** This is also an important latent need, particularly amongst younger customers and the industries that serve them. Once consumers have finished using a product, they are increasingly frustrated that they have to throw the product or packaging in a garbage bin. For example, in many U.S. cities and towns, one must pay a $20 fee to dispose of an old refrigerator, air conditioner, TV set, or computer monitor. Some ventures have flourished by recycling used equipment or replenishing it (e.g. inkjet and laser printer cartridge refills). We have watched one of our student ventures, Pure Solutions Management, grow to provide environmentally safe, organic pesticides to residential and commercial properties. Sustainability is a powerful driver for entrepreneurship and innovation.

- **Self-learning or machine learning.** These are products, systems, or IT-enabled services that continuously learn from the data and environment in and around them to create more precise, more customized decision-making or operation. An example might be a driverless truck that adjusts its motion to the speed and intensity of the traffic around it or a climate monitoring system that continuously learns and improves its predictive ability based on the environmental data flowing into it from various sensors. For example, a modern system for controlling the temperature of chilled cases inside a grocery store will adjust set points based on the temperature both inside and outside the building. AI and ML (machine learning) remain mainly in the category of making the unexpected possible – solving classic latent needs.

- **Automation.** Automation has been a compelling latent need in industry beginning when Henry Ford developed highly automated assembly lines for automobile production in the early 1900's, bringing the cost per unit of the Model T down to the point where his factory workers could afford buy their own car. Ever since, automation has become a focus of both manufacturing and information technology innovations, be it in the robotics placed into assembly lines, automated workflows in IT, and some public transportation systems. Automation is often referred to as "straight through processing" in financial services (for approving loans, handling stock transactions, underwriting insurance, and many other areas). And now it is coming into the home. You can see this in the robotic vacuum cleaners offered by iRobot, Samsung, and others, and in the smart home control systems for entertainment, climate control, and security. Using computer intelligence to reduce or eliminate human error is a profound innovation driver, entering new domains such as driverless vehicles and medical diagnoses.

- **Personalization.** In a world of mass-produced products and services, many customers appreciate – and will pay extra for – items tailored to their specific needs. Few suppliers know how to address this need. Those that do can differentiate themselves. Dell rose from obscurity, in part, thanks to its ability to use flexible manufacturing to customize and quickly deliver PCs. We also saw this at play in My M&M's. And many people believe that the future of healthcare is personalized medicine where drugs are tuned to the individual patient's genetics.

Any one of these types of latent need can be a powerful driver for your own innovations.

Also, as technologies mature, features that were once considered answers to latent needs tend to become more commonplace in products or services, and therefore become part of table-stakes design as perceived needs. Several decades ago, precise GPS or cell-enabled location services were considered unique and life-saving; today, location services continue to save lives but are found in a wide range of devices, including our cellphones. The latent need has evolved into a perceived need over time.

From a commercialization point of view, finding and solving a powerful latent need allows the entrepreneur to differentiate – and that allows charging a price premium for her/his service. This is all relative – for example, if you are in a category where an expensive app is $10 a month, a standard app is $5, and a very basic app is free – well, even if you have an app loaded with solutions for latent needs, $10 may be the premium price.

Finding a latent need and solving it should be one of the litmus tests for developing your innovation idea. It is the best way to ensure that you won't have a "me too" product or service. And if you find two or three latent needs, you might save several for the next release or generation of your product or service. This will delight your customers and keep your competitors guessing as to what's next up your sleeve.

UNDERSTAND THE FULL USE CASE: LOOK AT THE BEFORE, DURING, AND AFTER

Use cases involve the element of time. A use case is an activity with a clearly defined process. This provides an interesting structure: *before the primary use, during the use,* and *after the use.* And though "during" might be the main event for competitors in your category, you can uncover powerful latent needs in the *before* and *after* as well. Try to find the perceived and latent needs in each step of the user case or process.

For example, an amateur astronomer takes his equipment to a backyard viewing location, aligns the telescope's mounting with the celestial pole, and sets out his star charts, red flashlight, and other accessories. S/he may also have to drag out a long electrical extension cord. This process may take ten minutes, and it occurs *before* any stargazing activity can begin. The *during* phase involves finding the desired celestial objects in the sky, including some calculations and searching, examining them under different magnifications and with varying filters of light, and perhaps some photography. The *after* part of this astronomer's use case involves bringing in and storing his equipment, logging his observations in a notebook, and possibly working with digital images created during viewing.

It's easy to be so fixated on the *during* part of a customer's use case that the *before* and *after* parts get overlooked – though each may be equally important for the customer and serve as the basis of a differentiated product or service solution. Using our backyard astronomer's experience as an example, equipment makers have been highly innovative in making the *during* activity easy and enjoyable. A new generation of computer-guided telescopes points directly to a deep-sky object selected by the user from a handheld menu, eliminating the need to work with charts, make calculations, and fumble around in the dark. The *before* is served by downloading maps of the universe for specific observation, and the *after* with recording and note-taking through mobile apps. And of course, designers have eliminated the electrical cord, making powerful telescopes running on batteries, with WiFi connectivity to cellphone apps.

Identifying and then designing to the *before, during,* and *after* of specific use cases can be a compelling discipline, For example:

- **Consumable Products:** Returning to gift chocolate, giving chocolate for Valentine's Day is a specific use case for which you might want particular flavors, colors, and even a "rush service" because you only remembered Valentine's Day a few days before! There might be a different use case for weddings – where you want to buy hundreds of dollars of unique, customized chocolates with the bride's picture on the packaging or the chocolates themselves. Or, for Mother's Day. The *before* is going to a website to see a selection that suits the consumer's need quickly; the *during* is the actual delivery of the chocolate to the loved one, with pleasant taste and strong product performance (e.g. the taste, richness, and texture of the chocolate); and then the *after*, maybe a web-based service for capturing pictures and expressions for your chocolate fans' Facebook page. Understanding and designing to the full use case helps create an enjoyable, distinctive experience for the intended user (which in this example are two people, the consumer or user and the buyer).

- **Software/Systems:** As we have suggested before, monitoring patients with sensors in various use cases is one of the exciting frontiers of healthcare delivery. The hospital is moving into the home. This presents a vast array of innovation opportunities for entrepreneurs. Monitoring systems to help the elderly live independently in their homes. The *before* is understanding personal medical history so that the monitoring system can be tuned to issue alerts for each individual; the *during* is the monitoring itself through small, wireless sensors fixed into furniture and bathroom fixtures; and the *after* comprises responses by nurses. The entire system addresses the latent need to assist the elderly in their homes, with specific sensors and software for particular conditions and *occasions* within the more extensive use case. An exciting project!

  For enterprise software companies, an important *before* is how to quickly integrate a specific software application into a company's larger database and security infrastructure so that it can start working (the *during*). Then, once it is working, the data and alerts it feeds to decision-makers or other computer systems become the *after*.

- **Services:** Financial preparedness and planning is an excellent example of designing to full use cases. Nearly all professional financial services firms work towards specific use cases and offer solutions tuned for them. These use cases tend to follow *life events* for users. Attending college is one such event of which you readers are all too familiar. A tax-friendly college savings plan is the service designed for it. Retirement is another, and there are all sorts of investment planning approaches and products designed specifically for that time. And then sadly, there is death, and for it, there also exist planning and products delivered as a service for burials (the after) and generational gifting (the before).

A service that achieves scale in terms of the number of customers is likely to have been designed in a highly structured way, addressing perceived and latent needs for specific use cases or occasions, just as if the service itself was a product.[6] Consider Uber, Airbnb, or Peleton. Ask yourself, what are the use cases for each one of these services? How have these companies designed specific solution components for the *before, during,* and *after* of each use case with their respective apps or streaming services? What is *clever* about their designs, and what is not so bright? For example, how does Uber or Airbnb make it easy to find a ride or a place to stay and then pay for it? How do these companies respond if something does not go right, *after* the ride or overnight stay? Or, how does Peleton satisfy the latent need of "boredom" in the at-home workout routine and make its spin classes exciting? The answers to these questions are not complex – the work comes in determining the most critical perceived and latent needs and then executing on the software and service design to address these needs in simple yet powerful ways.

Good design, therefore, applies to any product or service, or software embedded as part of the product or service. It requires understanding the whole use case and the perceived and latent needs along each step of the way. Figure 6.4 is a template that we want you to apply to your project idea, first to document what you have learned after interviewing ten target users, and then later, as a way of communicating the primary design drivers for your new product or service. You can see the before, during, and after arrayed at the top. We would like you to change these words to capture time periods within your target use case. Then, based on your interviews, put down bullet points or short expressions of the perceived or latent needs for each step. These will lead to high-level design points for your new product or service.

Tesla is a good way to think about the template. The "before" is planning a trip. The "during" is the actual driving experience. The "after" is when the driver return homes. For each one of these activity states, Telsa has innovated. It has excellent trip planning data services, powerful electric motors for rapid acceleration and battery systems for long range driving; and automatic updating of systems software upon driving back into the garage. Within each activity state, innovation addresses perceived and latent needs. For example, the electric motors provide speed and effective fuel economy to address an obvious perceived need; no-touch

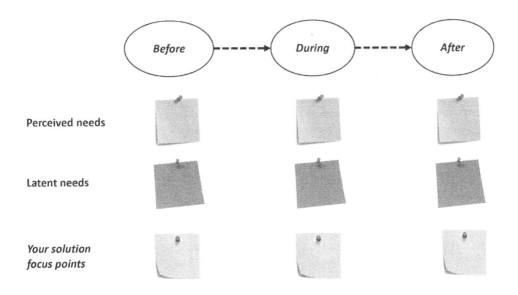

Find Perceived and Latent Needs Across the Entire Use Case

Use sticky notes on a whiteboard or a spreadsheet before committing anything to PowerPoint
Create this after your first set of user interviews.

Figure 6.4   Find perceived and latent needs across the entire use case

Karthik's Application of the Use Case Mapping Template

	Going to Shop	**Shopping**	**Paying**
Percieved needs	• Safe navigation • Obstacle detection • Wayfinding	• Finding products	• Paying the right cash amount
Latent needs	• Contextual information of what's happening around them (including things that might be dangerous)	• Knowing about additional information (discounts or promotions) • Ability to shop quickly	• Being sure products are being properly scanned and you're not being cheated
The solution focus points	• Reading street signs and information on public transport	• Reading product labels • Reading signs in the shop	• Identifying bank notes (if paying in cash)

Source: Karthik Mahadevan. Used with permission.

Figure 6.5   Karthik's application of the use case mapping template

driving and parking meet the latent needs of persons with failing eyesight, and perhaps someday, will become regular practice for all drivers.

Karthik used observational, semi-unstructured methods to gather insights but then was very systematic about capturing these insights into forms such as that above. Figure 6.5 is his representation of a vision-impaired person shopping in a grocery store.

DEVELOP A PERSONA OF THE TARGET USER AND BUYER

We can integrate and summarize the insights from users and buyers into a specific form called the "persona." A "persona" is a profile of the target user, and if the user is not the buyer, then a separate persona for the buyer, too. Developing crisp, powerful personas of target users and buyers is common practice in the design community, and investors and executives now often expect these in pitch decks.

Included in a persona are the target user's demographics, needs, attitudes, behaviors, and purchase preferences. When we say "user," we mean the customer group that will be the focus of your venture – the group derived from your segmentation work in earlier chapters. You might include a picture or video of a single individual in the persona, but that single picture or clip must be clearly representative of the larger group.

The User Persona

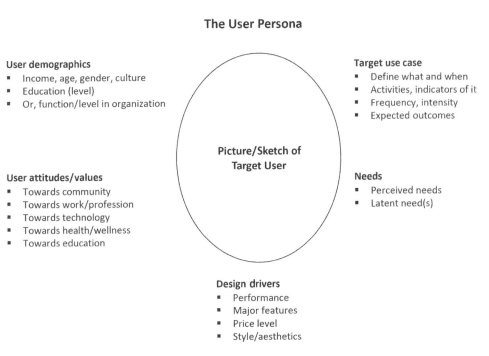

User demographics
- Income, age, gender, culture
- Education (level)
- Or, function/level in organization

User attitudes/values
- Towards community
- Towards work/profession
- Towards technology
- Towards health/wellness
- Towards education

Picture/Sketch of Target User

Target use case
- Define what and when
- Activities, indicators of it
- Frequency, intensity
- Expected outcomes

Needs
- Perceived needs
- Latent need(s)

Design drivers
- Performance
- Major features
- Price level
- Style/aesthetics

Figure 6.6   The user persona

Figure 6.6 shows a template for the user persona. With the user's permission, cellphone-recorded videos make PowerPoint personas all the more persuasive and powerful.

We define each of the significant areas in the persona as follows:

- *A picture* that is representative of the target user. This makes your innovation story come to life.

- *Who they are, e.g. the consumer or industrial demographics of the target user.* This can be age, gender, and ethnicity, or industry niche, geography, size of a company, position, and level of responsibility of the person in the company.

- *Their attitudes and values.* These are the cognitive value or belief systems of users and buyers. An example might be a young male's attitude towards driving versus mom driving the kids to school versus professional commuters. In a corporate or enterprise setting, the attitude of mature IT managers might be one of risk management with proven technologies, whereas younger IT managers are more willing to try new technologies or "open systems" software.

- *Define the target user case in terms of significant activities and expected outcomes.* This provides the focus of your innovations for the user. Be clear. For example, using a car to drive to work is a different use case than weekend errands, which is different than weekend fun and exploration. What are the significant activities that lie within your target use case?

- *The perceived and latent needs in the use case.* A persona contains a few select words or phrases for a user's or buyer's needs and frustrations. For perceived needs, use the major types of performance, quality, and cost expectations; for latent needs – well, this becomes some of the magic in your new product or service. Only use a few select words on this template – you can explain the bullet points when presenting to your audience.

- *The primary design drivers for the new product or service.* A design driver is a feature or function that you must have in your innovation to satisfy the target user and put a smile on his or her face. Or, in the case of automation, the "user" might be another machine or system within a larger computer or industrial process. In this case, imagine that the device or system is a person that can smile or frown. Do the same thing: what is needed to put a smile on its face?

Buyers may be different than users. Figure 6.7 is a variation on the prior template for a buyer persona. For example, diapers are for the baby but are purchased by the parent. You would create a persona for the baby and a persona for the parent, and perhaps even different buyer personas for the Mom versus the Dad. Innovators often overlook buyer research and don't develop specific buyer personas. That comes back to haunt them later. Think of it this way: if the user is not the buyer, who will pay for the new product or service? Aren't they equally crucial in terms of design?

For example, consider B2B systems and services. Employees use software that has been purchased by decision-makers somewhere else in the company. The users want certain features to meet their own performance criteria and needs and would love to be surprised with

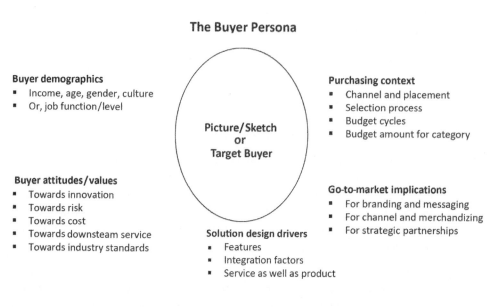

The Buyer Persona

Buyer demographics
- Income, age, gender, culture
- Or, job function/level

Purchasing context
- Channel and placement
- Selection process
- Budget cycles
- Budget amount for category

Picture/Sketch
or
Target Buyer

Buyer attitudes/values
- Towards innovation
- Towards risk
- Towards cost
- Towards downsteam service
- Towards industry standards

Go-to-market implications
- For branding and messaging
- For channel and merchandizing
- For strategic partnerships

Solution design drivers
- Features
- Integration factors
- Service as well as product

Supplement with insightful quotes

Figure 6.7   The buyer persona

some new, unexpected functionality. An IT procurement manager is probably thinking about "good enough" in function but more deeply concerned about software and vendor reliability, cybersecurity, licensing or subscription costs, and upgrade policies, as well as any sort of costly systems integration.

Importantly, for those of you considering B2B sales, the buyer persona must show what you have learned about any specific buying process. This might include a request for proposal, pilot programs, and a calendared buying cycle. For example, if you are designing a new public health system or transportation system, you must learn the processes and metrics for decision-making. Your user might be the patient or citizen, but your buyer will be the public health official or a transportation manager. These types of government workers have *budgets* set every year, and within them, general areas or specific programs for spending. As the entrepreneur, you've got to know where and how you fit – and bring this into the buyer persona.

A closer look at Figure 6.7 shows elements of the persona specific to buyers. These include the purchasing context, such as the type of channel and location in the channel (such as a store), and the selection or purchasing process, which is often complex in enterprise buying. Also, you should try to learn the buying calendar for B2B sales, and the budget amount for your category of product or service on an annual basis. This information should come from talking to the right sorts of people using the discussion guide described earlier.

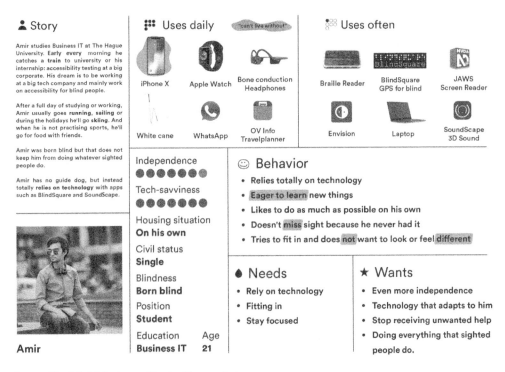

Source: Karthik Mahadevan. Used with permission.

Figure 6.8   Karthik's user persona for the visually impaired user: the student

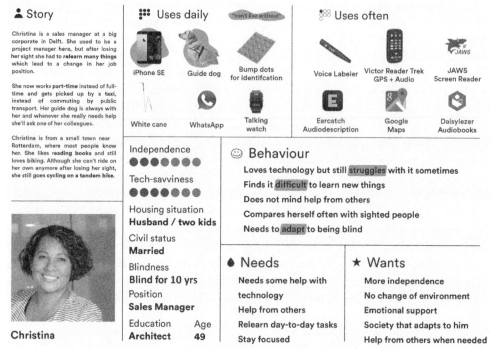

Source: Karthik Mahadevan. Used with permission.

Figure 6.9   Karthik's user persona for the visually impaired user: the professional

As an example of the template application, take a look at two personas for two different types of Karthik's target users: the student and the professional, Figures 6.8 and 6.9 respectively. A tremendous amount of work went into developing the insights for these personas, as you can tell by the detail in Karthik's figures. And as these exhibits show, personas can clearly communicate user insights. That is what you want to achieve in your personas.

AN EPILOGUE (AS OF JANUARY 2022) TO KARTHIK'S JOURNEY OF USER DISCOVERY

Karthik stayed in touch with one of his college roommates from the university in India who had taken a job as a programmer at a large software development company. This roommate was also named Karthik, and like Karthik #1, Karthik #2 was highly skilled in his own work, in this case, programming. They became partners, one doing design and the other coding. And the team expanded, as shown in Figure 6.10, where the two Karthiks bookend each side of the team.

As Karthik #1 continued intense user research and design in his New Ventures class at Delft, Karthik #2 was programming at night, still in India. The basic architecture was that of a mobile app, with voice commands, image capture, and processing on the cellphone's CPU, and then

Source: Karthik Mahadevan. Used with permission.

Figure 6.10   The Envision team with Karthik #1 and #2 on each side

Hear what you see.
Different use cases for Envision AI

Source: Karthik Mahadevan. Used with permission.

Figure 6.11   Hear what you see. Different use cases for Envision AI

accessing and building image databases in the Cloud. The Karthiks named their company Envision with the brand message *Hear What You See*.

While Karthik #1 was exploring use cases and designing the functionality, Karthik #2 was developing both the core infrastructure and specific applications for those use cases. It is a great example of a Cloud-based data service, with libraries of an increasing array of objects, languages, and actions; it is also a powerful example of *machine learning*. The system becomes increasingly familiar and accurate with the user's voice for commands. And, based on the power of the "crowd" in its user base, the app became increasingly intelligent about an ever-growing array of physical objects. The user points her/his cellphone camera at the object, issues a voice command, and the image processing and action begins. Quickly, within a matter of a second or two, the system responds with a voice response for the vision-impaired person. Given the global community of vision-impaired persons, the app had to operate in many different languages, for voice commands, reading text or numbers, and speaking back to the user. Over several years, that number of languages has expanded to about twenty!

As the core functionality improved, the Karthiks incorporated a broader array of use cases. Figure 6.11 shows a few of these. The first on the left is shopping in a grocery store, hearing the system say the prices that one would ordinarily see. The second image is reading mail and other correspondence, such as bank statements. Another illustration is reading a standard menu card. Then yet another, actually recognizing the person in front of you (with a bit of training) and even detecting if she is smiling or not. If a person gets lost, s/he can use Envision AI to capture an image of the surroundings, use geolocation services to precisely map the spot, and call a friend for further assistance. Getting dressed in the morning with color matching combinations is another use case.

Importantly, when a new object comes along through the app, the system registers that object and begins building its intelligence about it within its internal data structure that includes shape, construct, size, and even color. There is no question that the Karthiks have built rather remarkable software that enables "hearing" an ever-greater range of activities in daily living.

The company was officially launched in 2018, moved into the Yes!Delft incubator in the Netherlands. Karthik #2 quit his job in India and moved to the Netherlands. Working lean, the co-founders started bringing in programming and support staff, often as interns and later as paid employees. They began selling the app on the Apple and Google marketplace for a $2 per month subscription fee or a lifetime $90 fee. And then, in March 2019, the company achieved a breakthrough by winning the Google Play award. Soon after, Envision received a seed investment of approximately $300,000 from an early-stage impact investing firm based in the Netherlands, and more recently, an approximate $2 million Series A investment.

In 2020, the Karthiks decided to tackle the latent need for hands-free operation. This is focused on the somewhat older target user, whose specific persona is shown in Figure 6.9, an older individual who is not as tech saavy as the Millennial. Hands-free became a latent need for the Karthik's to address. Look at Figure 6.12 for the result. Partnering with Google, they loaded Envision AI onto the Google Glass Enterprise Edition, which bundled together sales in the range of $3000 per Glass – expensive, yes, but considering that a visually impaired person will continuously use these glasses during her/his waking hours, of high value. With an expanding

Source: Karthik Mahadevan. Used with permission.

Figure 6.12 Envision glasses

user base, seed capital, impressive technology, and Google as a strategic partner, Envision is moving forward to reach millions of vision-impaired persons whose lives it wishes to improve. It is on-trend and a wonderful example of a high-tech, AI machine learning solution with a societal mission. Consider further that Envision started as an original concept in a class, championed by an individual with a personal passion for user discovery and design, and who subsequently built a team of like-minded people with different but complementary skills. *If Karthik did this, perhaps you can, too.*

Reader exercises

Now you've got some work to do – the fun type – but work, nonetheless. The only way to truly understand user needs – and therefore to design the solutions to serve users – is to enter the worlds of the users and buyers. Do not expect this research to be something that you can put off until two days before your class meeting when presentations are due. It takes time to plan your attack, conduct the discussions, and synthesize the results. Reaching out to target users does not come naturally to some first-time innovators, but put on your social hats and view this as an opportunity to meet new people, learn about their problems, and then help them.

STEP 1: HIT THE STREETS (OR ZOOM)

Your fieldwork for this chapter is to observe and talk to target customers. Shoot for ten highly representative target users in this first round of interviewing, and then subsequent rounds of ten users to first show your initial designs, and the hopefully to show actual prototypes next. No need at this point to speak to more than ten users and perhaps a few buyers for initial needs discovery: we want quality more than quantity. Also, if you have an excellent interview with a target user, please remember to ask if that person might know of two or three additional persons with whom it would be good to speak. This is particularly important for B2B-type ventures where you cannot simply find new users walking down the street. Modify the discussion guide in Figure 6.2 to have the questions that best match your innovation and target users. Identify perceived and latent needs using Figure 6.3, and map these across the entire use case using the template in Figure 6.4. Use these templates to guide your research and communicate what you have learned. Also, keep track of the number of end-users and buyers with whom you speak. Your teachers will want to know that number.

If possible, we want you to observe and talk to target users not just in their *place of use* but in their *place of purchase*. However, both venues must be safe for you to visit – in terms of personal safety. Try not to meet a complete stranger alone in a remote place for the first time. People are now so comfortable with Zoom that it is a close second best to being there yourself. But then again, it is hard to develop deep trust with someone you have never met before over Zoom, and you cannot read body language or subtle expressions. Seeing how someone shops for a product is incredibly revealing. You learn how they make decisions, consider current competitors, how much they buy, when they buy, and what they feel comfortable paying on that purchase occasion. The same applies to a B2B venture wishing to design a new industrial product, enterprise software, or service. Speaking to users and buyers in their own context can make all the difference. Conduct the interview in a café, a store, an office, or wherever your innovation takes you. And consider working with a team member as the safest way to proceed and to get two sets of eyes and ears forming learnings from the same interview.

STEP 2: CREATE PERSONAS FOR THE TARGET USER AND BUYER (IF DIFFERENT)

How well do you know your target user, and perhaps if different, your target buyer? Prove it by developing a user profile and the buyer (if different) by completing the templates in Figures 6.6 and 6.7. Don't forget to photograph or find representative pictures of the target user and buyer. Apply your field research to build a story around them about who they are, what they do, and what they need.

STEP 3: PREPARE AS A TEAM FOR A MAJOR REPORT-OUT TO THE REST OF THE CLASS

Your teacher will set a time for all the teams in class to share their user and buyer research results. You should prepare the various templates in this chapter and tell the class how many people you spoke to as well as how and where this occurred. Use pictures and videos from the ethnography to provide even further context and authenticity to your presentation. You might even try role acting to show the types of latent needs experienced by your target users. Also, please return to your Customer Value Proposition (Figure 4.10) and sharpen the rows for "the solution for" and "provide the benefits", which are the user needs you have uncovered and the value to the user in solving them.

*** *** ***

In learning the methods of this chapter, you now have the foundational elements for creating an impactful innovation. You have the tools to understand the needs, fears, and frustrations of target users and buyers. This is powerful stuff. You have also learned how to do this systematically through structuring conversations. The goal is to deliver concrete insights, map use cases by activity steps as well as the perceived and latent needs along the way, and summarize all that you have learned with personas. This is what professional designers do. Apply these methods well, and you can consider yourself a true designer! As we have said before, *fall in love with your users' problems*, which means understanding these problems deeply, and then innovating to solve them in a way that puts smiles on the user's face. It's common sense, but essential for effective, mindful innovation. It is generally known as *design thinking*.

In the next chapter, we will learn how to take user insights and transform them into well-architected products or services, just as Karthik did, and Kevin and Kate before him. But first, please get to work on the reader exercises!

NOTES

1. See https://www.orbis.org.

2. Meyer, M.H., and Marion, T. (2010). "Innovating for Effectiveness: Lessons from Design Firms." *Research-Technology Management*, 53(5) (September–October), 21–28.

3. Mead, M. (2003). *Sex and Temperament in Three Primitive Societies* (1st perennial edition). New York: Perennial/HarperCollins.

4. Fitzpatrick, R. (2013). *The Mom Test: How to Talk to Customers & Learn if Your Business is a Good Idea When Everyone is Lying to You.* Robfitz Ltd.

5. Meyer, M.H. (2007). *The Fast Path to Corporate Growth.* New York: Oxford University Press.

6. Meyer, M.H., and DeTore, A.D. (1999). "Product Development for Services." *Academy of Management Executive*, 13(3), 64-76.

7

Product and service design

THE PURPOSE OF THE CHAPTER

Now that you have developed an insight into your target user and buyer needs within a specific use case, it is time to design the new product or service. This is where we create a concept sketch followed by a structured design of a new product, system, or service that is used as the foundation for all further development. To begin the process of bringing that architecture to life, we will then learn the method called *composite design*. It is used to decide which parts of the design you should build yourself and where you can find other components already made and readily available to complete the design. This approach helps make your initial development efforts fast and effective.

LEARNING OBJECTIVES

After reading this chapter you should be able to:

1. Create a concept sketch for your new product or service.
2. Design a product line or service architecture.
3. Show the design drivers from your user research to be delivered by the major parts or subsystems of your product or service.
4. Decide how to implement that functionality using a technique called composite design.
5. Step beyond the internal workings of the product or service to consider the overall styling and packaging that users see, or the GUI (graphical user interface), for how the user interacts with the system or service.
6. Develop your next wave of user research to show your more structured product or service concept to another round of ten target users or buyers.

These are intended to be sequential steps. Create a concept sketch first, define architecture next, then assign design drivers to specific subsystems, then decide how first to implement those subsystems, and assess the resulting product or service as it is used across the entire use case.

At the end of these six steps, your team will be ready to start building prototypes. This might be a wireframe and data structures for some new software mobile or otherwise, a 3D-printed shape for a new consumer product, or a computer-aided design (CAD) for an industrial part, or a few safely prepared new food creations or drinks! Once again, we want you to show your prototypes to another ten or so users. Prototyping will be the focus of the next chapter.

ACHIEVING ELEGANCE IN THE DESIGN OF NEW PRODUCTS AND SERVICES

Before proceeding to our design steps, let us first establish the underlying mindset.

Customers recognize elegance in design when they see or use a product or a new service. For a product, its appearance is pleasing and in keeping with its function. It is easy to use and serves its purpose without complication. If it has user controls, its purpose and operations are readily apparent and self-instructive. Form and function have a seamless unity. If you think about your favorite products, such as an Apple laptop or iPhone, the fusion of form and function, of simplicity yet power, is apparent. Or, a Tesla uses voice commands to control so much of the vehicle, and yet accelerates faster than most cars on the planet. You cannot help but think that "this is a well-designed vehicle." You also see this in your favorite web-based services, such as Uber or Lyft. The app's user interfaces are intuitive and easy to use right out of the gate for first-time users. Yet, the functionality they provide is tremendous when compared to calling a taxi company of old for a ride.

In *The Design of Everyday Things*, Donald A. Norman explains that well-designed objects are easy to interpret and understand. In contrast, poorly designed objects can be difficult and frustrating to use, preventing the normal process of interpretation and understanding.[1]

Engineers recognize design elegance, focusing on inner and outer product dimensions: the appropriateness of the materials, the economy of components, and the ease with which different parts or materials fit and work together. Manufacturing managers, too, know design elegance when they see a physical product design that requires a minimum number of parts and assembly steps and whose quality can be automatically tested with other machines and computers at the back end of an assembly process. For software, designers strive for user interfaces that are Apple-like, which means intuitive yet allowing access to all of the deeper functionality that the software provides.

In sum, well-designed products and services achieve elegance in both form and function. They do what they are supposed to do and appear to the user to do so with ease. We like to think of this as products or services that are *efficacious* and pleasing to the user.

Achieving this fusion requires thinking beyond just the engineering, programming, or the chemistry necessary for a new product or service. Beyond the pure function of the innovation, you must pay attention to the user's emotional and cognitive perceptions and feelings for it.

For example, we loved our old Mazda Miata not just because it zipped around traffic, but also because of its exterior and interior styling. We liked driving it, and if truth be told, wanted to be seen driving it. Other types of target users feel the same way about their BMWs or Land Rovers. The Miata gave us a sense of freedom and self-enjoyment, *to feel young again*, at a very reasonable price. Our colleague's BMW does the same for him, but in a different way that better suits his emotional and functional needs and taste. In this sense, vehicles are more than just transportation on four or two wheels; successful vehicles create unique experiences and

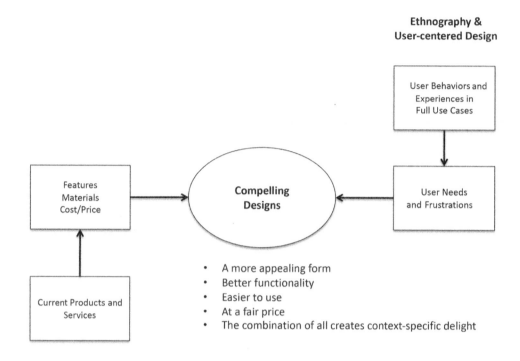

Figure 7.1   Appealing to the functional and the emotional

allow their users to form emotional connections. This is what you want as a designer for your products or services.

The innovator must dig deep into his or her ethnography to find those points where an emotional connection can be forged. Part of this is the aesthetics or appearance of the product or service, supported by the brand name and messaging. And if a product or service performs much better than anything else on the market, users will fall in love with it as well. For example, your authors feel this way about their favorite fly fishing rods. Most premium rods look a lot alike, but the best ones outcast the others by a wide margin. "I love this fly rod" is the result.

Emotion-connecting form and function-delivering features blend to make an innovation that is compelling to the user. Take a look at Figure 7.1. It shows on the left side the general process of functional engineering. This involves looking at existing products or services in the marketplace, seeing how they are made and what they do, and then improving them with new technology and better functionality. Sometimes this engineering-focused process leads to disruptive, market-moving innovation – but more often, only incremental innovation is produced. On the right side of the figure are the processes we have been learning in previous chapters – the ethnographic process that can make the difference between just a me-too product and another that is exceptionally pleasing to the user. A design that moves the market is then the synthesis of these two disciplines: breaking down the functional and technical components of a product or service category to understand what works and how to do it better, and then, to understand users' emotional and cognitive needs, and design to address these as well.

Blending these two approaches often means getting people good at each approach to join your team, to respect one another, and then work together to serve your customers. Just think about Apple once again. They always seem to do both: excellent engineering combined with user-centered design to bring their target users generation after generation of pleasurable technologies. There has always been more than one person doing it, *more than a single Steve Jobs*. Apple has outstanding technologists who work with equally outstanding designers to create products such as the iPhone or MacBook, or successful services, such as AppleCare and the Genius Bar. Apple's executives provide the necessary focus and leadership for these teams.

Take a moment to consider: "How does this thinking – the synthesis of good engineering with a deep understanding of user needs – apply to the innovation I wish to create?" Before you leave this thought, write down two or three ways where you might tackle a significant user need or frustration with a clever application of a physical or software technology, or a good ingredient, or some type of styling or packaging. Which of these ideas are "function" and which are primarily "form"? These thoughts might be the way to achieve product or service innovations that your users will cherish.

IT'S THE BENEFITS OF THE TECHNOLOGY THAT MATTERS, NOT THE TECHNOLOGY ITSELF

Another essential principle is to keep your eye on the tangible benefits you want to provide to the user. This means thinking not only about the functions and features of a new product or service, but about the benefits of these functions and features. *What will be the tangible benefits and impact on the lives and experiences of your target users?* Think about these benefits first, and only then, the best way to deliver those benefits.

Your authors have had many experiences designing new products and services across a broad spectrum of industries. Some of these have been real hits; others considerably less so. From this experience, the difference between a great innovation and a just-okay one is not in the specific functionality of what the product or service itself does but the impact of that functionality on the work and lives of the end-user. Think impact, not just function.

For example, an LED light in an office with an occupancy sensor is much more than the LED, the sensor, and the communications subsystems in the new light itself. Instead, it can be a way to tell if someone has entered an office or a conference room, and perhaps in the future, *who* has entered the room! Just imagine the benefits of tracking visitors or finding a conference room for a quick meeting. Or, as another example, think about Boeing's 787 airplane, known as the Dreamliner. This plane uses very sophisticated composite materials for key parts of the frame and wings that are stronger but lighter compared with traditional metals. This allows the aircraft to be flown at substantially lower fuel costs, which for its target customers – the airline companies – is as important as the seating, entertainment systems, or interior climate control technology. All these innovations make a difference – a big difference – for their intended users in specific use cases. Do this for your innovations, too.

For example, you can have an extremely powerful motor in a car that can hit 160 mph, but if the effective speed limit is capped at half that amount on most highways, then that maximum speed doesn't make all that much of a difference. You might want to focus on other types of functionality. On the other hand, if you design the software for a self-driving car, suddenly groceries can be more cheaply delivered, or your elderly relatives driven safely home from a friend's house after dark. Clear benefits for specific use cases come from the innovation. Achieving that impact is what makes an innovator feel good about his or her work.

Another essential idea: Sometimes the benefits a user needs can be best delivered through a service, rather than a product, or through a combination of both a product and a service. For example, our former students created an environmentally safe fertilizing and pest control service for the suburbs of New England (see Figure 7.2). For the first years of their business, they sourced bio-friendly chemicals from nontraditional suppliers. Then, after a while, they created their own proprietary bio-friendly fertilizing and pest control mixes, using it as part of their service. More recently, these entrepreneurs started selling that new material – called Progaea – to other landscaping businesses and retailers.

The properties of that material provide the "function." All the while, their focus has been on excellent customer service to keep their clients, their children, and their pets *safe*. This service is the "form" or packaging around the product.

With this mindset – providing both form and function, combining technical engineering with cognitive user understanding, and a dedicated focus on delivering tangible benefits to target users – let us proceed to specific methods for elegant, efficacious design and apply them to your efforts.

STEP 1: CREATE A CONCEPT SKETCH OR STORYBOARD FOR A NEW PRODUCT OR SERVICE

A concept sketch communicates your design vision to your target users, your teammates, your teachers, and, later to your investors. Appealing images are important here! It is an iterative process, done best over a cup of coffee with your teammates, where each pass sharpens the vision. And you don't have to be an excellent sketch artist (although being a terrible artist doesn't help the cause). If you can't draw, find a friend who can. Or use a computer.

Please, take some time and put creative energy into these concept sketches. Think about every part of your first sketch and consider how you might make each part better and more pleasing to the target user. And do not be afraid to think out of the box – be the clever, creative innovator that your users need.

A concept sketch reveals a team's design vision for its innovation. For example, Starbucks had the design vision of a retro café. Such design visions drive functional considerations – such as the types of "hand-crafted" drinks brewed at Starbucks – and form or packaging considerations – where the cafés themselves feature wood, warm pastel colors, lounge chairs, and tables. Your sketch can also be of a process or service in which the user is engaged. It helps bring

Brian and Trevor
Cousins and Co-Founders of Pure Solutions

"Growing up in New England, our fondest memories are of being outdoors. As both cousins and best friends, we started Pure Solutions to protect what was important to us–our family, our friends, and the environment."

– Brian and Trevor, Cousins and Co-Founders of Pure Solutions & Pureganix.

PROGAEA® Natural, Botanical Pest Control Products

PROGAEA® by Pure Solutions is a family of botanical pest control products utilizing proprietary botanical extracts and oils to provide safer, environmentally sustainable methods for outdoor services such as tick, mosquito, and deer control.

Source: Pure Solutions, Inc. Used with permission.

Figure 7.2   Pure Solutions: Brian and Trevor, Founders, and developers of PROGAEA™

the service to be provided to life. Each step is beautifully and elegantly designed. Or, process innovation might be embedded in software that is hidden from most users, but which makes a larger process happen much more smoothly. Ventures in the mobile, digital payments arena are precisely that. Their concept sketches show a "before" and "after" process diagram in which their software eliminates, quickens, and otherwise facilitates a much better transaction episode for the end-user.

Design sketches can often start as extreme or somewhat radical, but eventually get moderated due to the realities of the marketplace and suppliers. We have seen truly wild concept sketches that end up as special yet "normalized" products and services. However, the initial wild concept sketch became the "North Star" that motivated the development team to create something different and unique. This is the time to be bold!

For example, let's start with concept sketches for a standalone product, in this case, a vehicle. Figure 7.3 shows the concept sketch made by designers for the automobile manufacturer Honda for a new SUV concept, called the Model X. Its target consumer was the young sub-30-year-old male whose use cases were not traditional commuting, but rather, hauling bicycles, surf boards, and partying at the beach, living the life of what Honda called "endless summer." The concept was commercialized as an SUV called the Element, one of the company's first crossover vehicle designs. Whether you love it or hate it, the Element is a unique design! The original concept sketch was very hip and extreme, and called "a brain cage on wheels." Note the large wheels, the funky styling (compared to Honda's CR-V, for example), and the nontraditional pillarless, open swinging doors (perfect for hauling gear or partying at the beach). These features cost Honda more money to tool on the manufacturing floor. But to its credit, Honda stayed true to its design vision.

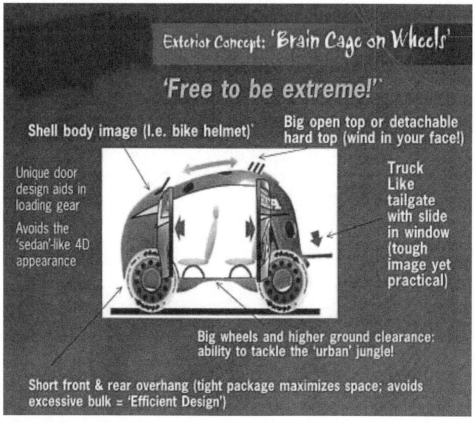

Source: Reproduced with permission of Honda.

Figure 7.3   A brain cage on wheels

The Honda team also developed a different concept sketch for the Model X interior, titled "The Freedom Zone," which placed a premium on cargo space and flexibility in using it. Figure 7.4 shows the concept sketch for flexible seating. The design center for Honda was located in Southern California. It is therefore no surprise that the design team took its inspiration for the interior concept from a beach lifeguard station, where young men and women stored various gear.[2] To bring the interior concept to life, Honda's engineers created a new paradigm for flexible seating (the ability to fold seating any which way desired by the user). This approach appeared later in many other vehicles, such as the HR-V, the CR-V, and the Odyssey. This, along with a no-carpet hose-it-down interior and a poppable moon-roof at the posterior (to

 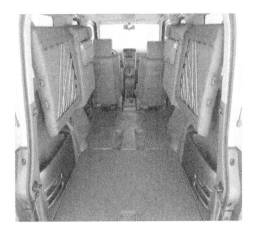

Source: Reproduced with permission of Honda.

Figure 7.4   The freedom zone

carry bookshelves or other tall items during apartment move-in/move-out), became the hall-marks of this fun, utilitarian SUV targeting the young driver.

Often, concept visioning also shows how products, apps, or other software are employed with a more extensive process or service. In such cases, the concept sketch is different than just a product sketch. Instead, it is more of a process flow diagram that shows how things change or evolve over the entire use case. This is often called *storyboarding* the service or process.

As a personal practice session, take just two minutes to draw a storyboard for getting a taxi on a busy city street during rush hour. Then, take five minutes to storyboard Uber's service. The process steps go from ordering a ride, waiting for the ride, taking the ride, paying for the ride, and providing feedback. It is vastly different (and better) than a traditional taxi service. And that is why Uber, Lyft, and others have been so appealing to the general public.

Let's consider several more examples. The first example is a meal solutions company that creates complete meal solutions for individuals who do not want to go shopping and do not know how to cook the ingredients needed or prepare and cook those ingredients. A company called HelloFresh, started in 2012 in Berlin, Germany, focused with this Problem Space. By the end of 2020, it had over five million customers in numerous countries around the world, with a strong focus on Millennials. The combination of young consumers not knowing really how to cook and the pandemic that started in 2020 fueled the company's growth. The consumer subscribes to different meal plans. Then, the ingredients arrive at the person's door once a week. You put everything into the refrigerator and then cook individual meals following precise instructions. The consumer gets a tasty, healthy meal and, in the process, perhaps impresses the kids or a new friend. The storyboard traverses the entire use case: decide what to order, then order, then refrigerate, prepare, and enjoy, and cycle back to reordering. We could have just drawn a box with food ingredients and instructions on the inside – but that would be boring and do little to describe the use case and the experience we wish to create for that use case. Hence, we create a storyboard that includes the physical product.

Another example of storyboarding is the mobile app storyboard shown in Figure 7.5, a concept sketch for a new service to share parking spaces between one car driver leaving a space and another looking for a space. Imagine that the driver about to leave offers to wait for the next car driver to arrive to take the parking spot. For this service, the arriving driver deposits a small fee to the departing driver through a financial intermediary. All this is achieved through an app with location services and a criminal background check to ensure that no one is waiting for a thief or hijacker to show up!

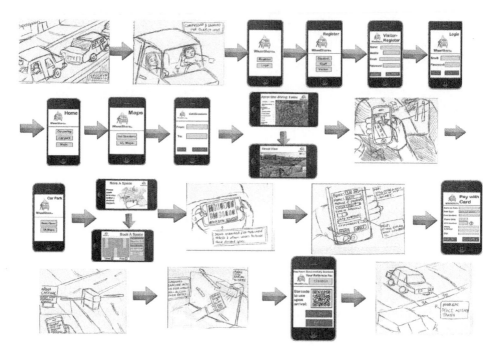

Figure 7.5   A concept sketch for a parking space-sharing app

As you can see, just like the meal solutions example, the storyboard shows an ideal, improved process flow.

Designing mobile apps as standalone or as part of a more extensive service lends itself particularly well to storyboarding. First, get yourself a free, highly-reviewed wireframing tool. Then, based on your process or service vision, create a simple initial wireframe for that step, adding a few comments to the wireframe at each step in the overall process. Capturing the screen images and arraying them along the entire use case becomes your storyboard. This might serve as the bones of a future MVP.

Let's illustrate this by continuing with a storyboard for the elderly patient monitoring system described in prior chapters. The concept sketch is an IoT system. By IoT, we mean a combination of sensors that monitor and create alerts within workflow management software in the Cloud. The software then manages and organizes responses to medical episodes and tracks how quickly healthcare providers respond to specific events.

Let's call the elderly user Charlotte. At present, Charlotte might be wearing a button on her wrist or as a pendant around her neck that she presses when feeling very ill. Our innovation might be to have various sensors that detect medical problems, based on a continuous comparison of Charlotte's activities against her medical record stored in the Cloud (see Figure 7.6). This might be an elevated heart rate, or, when the bed sensor determines that she has not risen from bed in the morning, an alert is automatically sent to a nursing station or call center. Or, if there is a significant thud detected on the floor, the call center is alerted once again to check on Charlotte's status. All of these potential problem areas become part of your design vision for a new subscription service for the elderly.

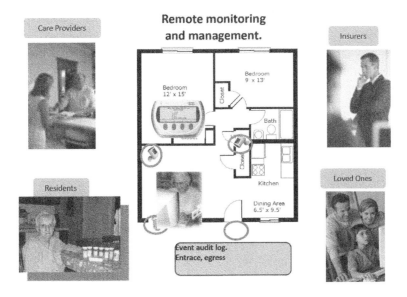

Figure 7.6   Medical monitoring for independent living by the elderly

In fact, a good number of the Problem Spaces delineated in the second chapter of this book are already being addressed in one form or another by an IoT type solution.

Process sketching for concept creation is important. Sketch your vision, show it to your teammates to create an even better storyboard, and then show it to your teachers and mentors. Eventually, you will want to show your concept sketch to another round of target users and buyers to see what *they* think.

STEP 2: DEFINE THE PRODUCT OR SERVICE ARCHITECTURE

This is the next step to bring your idea to life.

We are going to share an "engineered" solutions approach to product and service design. By "engineered," we do not mean that it is just for engineers, or computer scientists, or chemists. Instead, it simply means that we will take a structured, modular approach towards building a new product or service.

The first step is to define *an architecture* for the new product or service with different parts or chunks of functionality that comprise the overall solution. We refer to these chunks of functionality as *subsystems* within a more extensive system, which is the overall product or service. For example, the patient monitoring system for the elderly is the total product or service, but within it is a subsystem that measures things (with specific sensors for beds, chairs, floors, and toilets), and then, the workflow software for handling alerts and responses, plus the database system underneath the workflow software. Or in the Honda example, the SUV is the total product comprised of the major subsystems that include the power train (motor, transmission, exhaust); the chassis, which is the underlying structure plus suspension and even the tires; the interior "cab," which includes the seating, entertainment, and other comfort and safety systems; the driver controls, including the steering, pedals, and connected driving services); and last, the exterior frame comprising the exterior styling, the doors, exterior lights, and rooftop skylights or other accessories. In other words, to create an architecture for a product or service, or even better, a product line or suite of services, we organize the larger product or service into its logical parts.

Next, from our work in prior chapters, we have already found the specific *design drivers* that users need in terms of function and appearance. Once we have a product or service architecture, we can assign particular subsystems as the best place to implement specific design drivers. For example, real-time alerts for heart problems require a specific sensor in the bed, plus workflow management in the software that alerts other people that a problem has occurred. Or, *acceleration* is the job of the motor, taking a corner sharply at high speed is the job of the chassis; or, driving your elderly mom to the store *without you doing the driving* is the job of the driver controls and navigation subsystems. Make the organization of subsystems and the design drivers attached to those subsystems as clear and intuitive as possible.

This combination of the subsystem and the user need creates a clear focus for what each particular subsystem in the product or service is supposed to accomplish. It is only after taking this step that we then decide how to implement that functionality. In a food product, that means a recipe and ingredients to achieve taste or healthiness; in an electronics product, we have to select the CPU, communications, the power supply, and software for each primary subsystem to deliver its functionality. Even the chair upon which you might be sitting has specific designs and materials for the seat, the back support, and the height adjustment mechanism. If it is a good chair, the team that designed it thought carefully about its architecture, its subsystems, and the design drivers for each subsystem, and then how to implement that functionality, whether for the office environment, the home office, or the dorm!

Now, let's define a product architecture. And then, a service architecture. Both types of architecture designs require *modularity*, like Lego, where different parts or pieces can be assembled with standard interfaces to allow users to create or do what they expect and need.

General description:

Primary purpose / goals from the user's perspective:

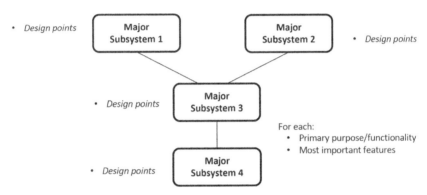

Figure 7.7   The layered architecture template

Figure 7.7 shows the product architecture template. You can see several subsystems, arranged like layers of technology, with bullet points labeled as *design points* next to each subsystem. This is a simple framework that helps organize the implementation of an innovative idea. We place a higher-level description of the product and its primary purpose at the top of the template. This helps keep the overriding goals of the design in mind as we dig further into the architecture below.

To illustrate this, let's consider single-serve coffee. In Figure 7.8, you will see a representation of Keurig's coffee machine and K-Cup architecture. Keurig Dr. Pepper is a large, successful U.S.-based beverage company. Its largest single product line is its single-serve brewing machines coupled with hundreds of different branded K-Cups. Some of these are from the original Keurig brand – Green Mountain Coffee – and others from partners that include Dunkin', Starbucks, and Peets. Each has its flavors and intensities, offering choice and variety to the consumer – and for Keurig, all of them work just as well on the same format brewer. On the left side of Figure 7.8 is the architecture of the brewer, and on the right side, the architecture of the K-Cup. Then, each architecture is implemented in different ways to provide the necessary functionality, and variety or scalability for that subsystem. For the brewer, this might mean a latte-making machine versus the traditional black coffee-making machine. For the

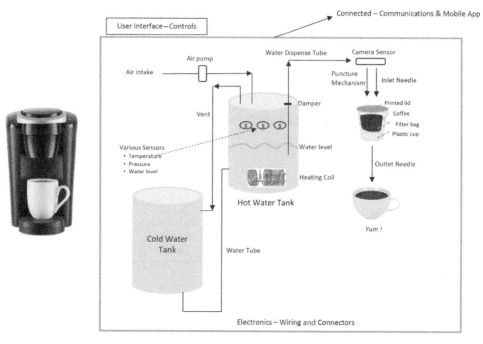

Source: Developed and used with permission from Bob McCall.

Figure 7.8   The Keurig product architecture

K-Cups, this is simply different types and amounts of coffee placed within the cup itself. More disruptive innovation might be to make the K-Cup itself largely recyclable, something that the company has been working on diligently for a number of years and testing in the market today.

Keurig has a very clever product architecture design that delivers both base level functionality plus a wide range of variety on top of it. This helps achieve recurring revenue, e.g. the money consumers spend buying additional K-Cups. Think about how your product architecture can power your venture's business model. In the Keurig example, if the standard markup on the cost of making the brewer is twice that of its Cost of Goods Sold, the markup on the coffee and container materials in the K-Cups is considerably higher, e.g. 10 cents to produce versus 60 cents per cup retail price. The company's business model is powered by its product design.

FOR SOFTWARE PRODUCTS OR APPS, SPECIFY THE SOFTWARE STACK AS ITS ARCHITECTURE

If you are working on a software product, there will be layers of technology that you should specify, using Figure 7.9 as a guide. These are the primary underlying subsystems that nearly all software has in one form or another, e.g. "the engine under the hood." Figure 7.9 is just Figure 7.7 with different labels and additional layering for the core subsystems. Data feeds from other machines or databases on a network are typically shown at the bottom, the database management system in the middle, the logic or knowledge management right above the data (now often called AI or ML/machine learning), the GUI and reporting subsystems near the top, and a Cloud server at the very top or surrounding everything – with its own security layer. Many of these subsystems used external tools, private or open source. For example, MySQL is often used for database management, Wireframe.cc for GUI, and Azure or AWS for Cloud delivery with sign-on security. If your project for this course involves software, take a shot at Figure 7.9. Keep your figure high level so that you can focus on your top priority design goals.

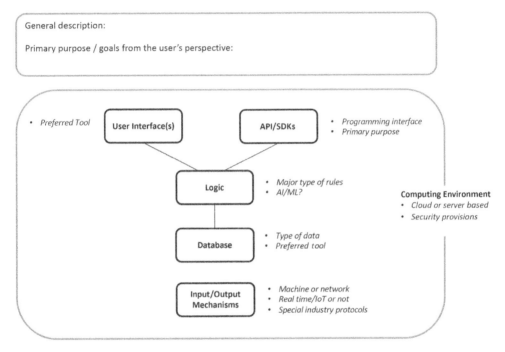

Figure 7.9   A layered architecture for software

DEFINING ARCHITECTURE FOR A SERVICE INNOVATION

Now, let's consider the architecture of a service. Whereas for products, we can get a lot done in just one single template, services innovation requires two. The first of these is a *process flow diagram* for the service.

The process flow diagram follows the storyboard framework described above. But this time, the specific steps are explicitly labeled, and for each step, the information inputs, activities, and outcomes of each step identified as simple bullet points. This means defining the specific activities that occur in the service as a series of steps. This template is shown in Figure 7.10.

Having defined the current process steps, you then look for opportunities to eliminate unnecessary steps, improve current steps, or add additional steps to make the process

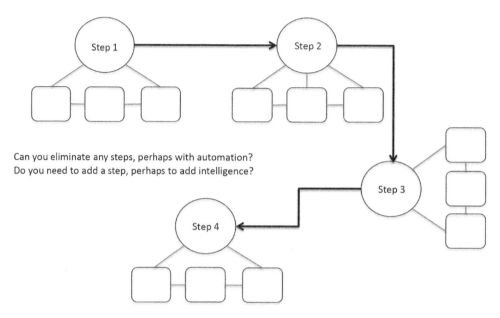

Figure 7.10   The process diagram template

smoother and better. Eliminating a step in a service can be done with automation, be it between computers or a mobile app. Improving a step can be done by understanding more precisely what a user needs in that service, perhaps through data analysis and personalization. Adding a step might be providing better analytics for the overall process, including a specific process step for machine learning on existing process activities and data. A service or process redesign often has new feedback loops from later stage steps into earlier ones – to make those earlier steps more precise or intelligent. For example, an equipment repair service might analyze the failure points in customers' current installations to better train and equip its field service support staff.

The second template for service and process innovation is shown in Figure 7.11. Here, we focus on what users need and how you wish to innovate for each significant step or subsystem of the service. You can see that the service also has its major subsystems, arrayed as rows in a table. The columns then show the strategy to innovate and improve each major subsystem or part of the service. This services innovation grid is the equivalent of the architecture of a product, but in this case, we use a slightly different format for specifying the major chunks of functionality for a service. For each row or major process step:

- Give the process step a name, perhaps directly from the prior template.

- What are users' current problems in that step? These are the design drivers from your user research.

- How are current service providers addressing these problems today, if at all?

- How do you plan to innovate within that step to solve the user's problems?

- And last, what are the data needed to measure outcomes? Define measures of effectiveness, efficiency, and quality, for the specific subsystems and for the overall service or process, as well as the source(s) for these data.

Measuring such outcomes is very important for continuous improvement.

When combined, these two templates will help your team determine how it wishes to improve the lives of the target user and how you plan to do it. Moreover, like the product architecture template, these two services innovation templates are excellent communication vehicles for conveying your plans to your classmates, teachers, and perhaps later, investors.

Now, let's illustrate these two figures with an example. We will stick with coffee.

As we noted earlier, students in our classes have done projects for Dunkin' because the company is headquartered close to Boston. Some of these projects have focused on improving the Dunkin' mobile ordering app and changing the in-store order and pick-up process. Dunkin' has been experimenting with new model stores in recent years with high throughput, double lane drive-through take-out designs. These service innovations are important for Dunkin' store owners because most of their sales occur during the morning commuting hours. Losing any significant percentage of that business hurts, either because of an in-store ordering line that is too long, a parking lot that is too full, or a drive-through lane moving at a snail's pace. Speed and simplicity are king, backed by a limited menu designed for speed in preparation and value for the consumer. Figure 7.12 shows what can be considered Dunkin's view on how the consumer orders a cup of coffee. And Figure 7.13 is how one of our student teams innovated to improve that process.

The Process "Step or Subsystem"	The Problems (Perceived or latent)	The Traditional Approach	YOUR INNOVATIVE APPROACH	Data Needed to Measure
Step 1				
Step 2				
Step 3				
Etc ...				Quality Cost Time cycle User satisfaction

Figure 7.11   The process or service innovation template

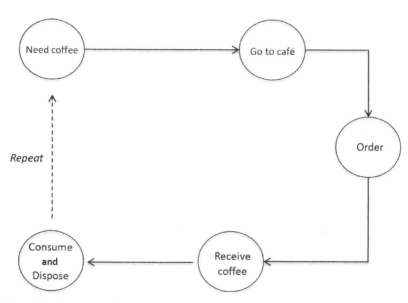

Figure 7.12   Getting a cup of coffee

The Process "Step"	The Problems (Perceived or latent)	The Traditional Approach	OUR INNOVATIVE APPROACH	Data Needed to Measure
Step 1 Realize the need	• Need a cup of coffee • Ad hoc	• All ad hoc	• Scheduled, adjustable • Mobile app orders	• Customer repeats per week • Mobile app pre-orders
Step 2 Go to the café	• Limit parking spots • Slow drive-through lines during rush hour	• Wait for a free spot and wait in the drive-through line	• Home delivery of fresh, hot coffee	• Drive-aways • Orders per hour by day of week
Step 3 Order coffee and pay	• Long waiting lines in store • Digging out credit card • Handling credit cards: virus/germs	• Make them wait! • POS Register: Cash and credit card • Less mobile apps	• Mobile app: favorite orders • Mobile payment • Store tag linked to debit account	• % food w/ drinks • % mobile payments
Step 4 Receive coffee	• Too hot, or too cold • Too much milk or too much sugar • Someone else's order	• Muddle through	• Name-printed labels for identification	• Cycle time from order to pickup
Step 5 Consume and dispose	• Too much milk or too much sugar • Someone else's order	• Ask for it to be fixed • Fill up the trash bins	• Recyclable materials	• % recyclable content • Cost of materials
Total process		**Total measures**	• Orders per hour per day • Types of orders – single versus bundled • Mobile app enabled orders • Revenue, operating costs, operating profit	

Figure 7.13   Improving the ordering and take-out process in Dunkin'

Starbucks, while in the same business as Dunkin', is very different in its service design. Starbucks has become the high-end coffee café for friends and business people to meet and work. They order their coffee and sit down for conversations. Around universities, Starbucks also serves an intense student study occasion. Both long conversations and studying are hard to find in the typical Dunkin' store. Accordingly, Starbucks as a service not only features more richly flavored coffees and lattes, but more comfortable seating, tables, and desks suited for studying and one-on-one meetings. The primary theme is that of a retro West Coast café with wooden interior furnishings. Electric plugs, phone charging mats, and featured music are also part of the store experience. While Dunkin' is product-focused, Starbucks is experience-focused, and both are successful in their respective service designs and branding strategies.

Next time you go into a Starbucks, observe its service design. Do the same at Dunkin'. Each is well-designed but in different ways.

DECIDING HOW TO IMPLEMENT SUBSYSTEM FUNCTIONALITY: THE BEAUTY OF COMPOSITE DESIGN

With an architecture and design drivers in hand for both products and services, we can now begin to decide how to implement a specific functionality required in each major subsystem in the product or service architecture. For some subsystems, you will do all the recipe development or engineering yourself, and for other subsystems, use outside suppliers. For example, if you are developing a mobile app or a data intensive service of some sort, you will probably want to use either the Amazon or Microsoft Cloud service rather than buy and build your own web hosting services.

Take a look at Figure 7.14, the composite design template. It shows the different subsystems from the product architecture template or the major process steps from your definition of a new service. Then, for each row, you define the method by which the desired functionality can be achieved. Is it hardware, software, chemistry, or recipe, or packaging that you design and implement, or is it something readily and best obtained from an external supplier? Given the skills needed and the limited cash on hand, most entrepreneurs do not try to do everything themselves, for either a new product or a new service. This is true for R&D, manufacturing, and logistics or shipping. Even in a mobile app, entrepreneurs such as Karthik focused on design and very specific points of engineering, and then used commercially available software tools and services to complete the product. And you recall, rather than invent their own heads-up displays, he piggybacked on top of Google Glasses.

The way to use Figure 7.14 is to create a table where the rows are each significant subsystem in your product or service architecture. Then, look at how existing competitors in your product or service category implement these specific subsystems to achieve their current level of functionality. Then, think about how you want to implement that subsystem – whether it be through using existing technology or developing something rather unique and special. Typically, experienced innovators try to use existing technologies where readily available and then add value to them through additional engineering or service delivery. This makes development fast but effective, better than recreating the wheel for every single subsystem. Few

Look at several competitive solutions and see how they implement the desired functionality, then decide your own approach, subsystem by subsystem.

Product Subsystem or Service Step	Implementation options as seen in existing competitors or related products/services	Your preferred approach
	• •	
	• •	
	• •	
	• •	
	• •	

Figure 7.14   The composite design template

entrepreneurs have the cash on hand to hire the dozens of engineers or build the manufacturing capability needed to launch a new product or service. It is best to get the innovation into the market quickly and then learn from actual users how to improve it and the various services needed around it.

We call this approach "composite design."[3] It is the combination of using existing and newly developed technologies. The resulting product or service is "the composite" of both in-house and external technologies, product components, and services. The approach can increase the technical feasibility of what you are trying to prototype simply because you are using full functioning best-in-class components from the outside world.

It is also important that whatever you design works when it is integrated into its environment or context of use. If your design, for example, is working in an environment of high moisture, you need waterproof housing – just as Apple made its new iPhones survivable with an accidental fall into the shower. Or software that can read and write the most popular database formats. Or a healthcare service that can be delivered remotely if a pandemic should sweep through the country.

To illustrate the composite design method, consider the Snakelight. Look it up on Amazon. You will see a flashlight with a flexible, shape-retaining neck that allows the flashlight to be wrapped around a pipe for hands-free, portable lighting. One of our mentors, Alvin Lehnerd, designed it many years ago when he was trying to fix some plumbing in his basement and needed two hands to apply glue and fit sections of PVC piping. Like many do-it-yourself plumbers, to illuminate the setting he had to stick the end of a dirty, foul-tasting plastic flashlight into mouth. His thoughts went to how to avoid having to do this. His Black and Decker team sketched the architecture – bulb, the lens over the bulb, batteries, contact points and connective wiring, the on–off switch, and the outer plastic housing. And then they thought: What if the architecture was modularized, split apart a bit, and instead of having a fixed housing around everything, what if the bulb and lens remained on one end of the design, the battery housing on the other, and the "neck" was redesigned to feature flexible plastic that could be wrapped around a pipe for hands-free operation? Then, by simply putting one slightly smaller diameter of the plastic neck inside another, the flashlight neck would retain its given shape so that it would remain wrapped around a pipe to illuminate the user's point of focus. Hence the name, a Snakelight. Its composite design is shown in Figure 7.15. All this design work was done quickly. Since its launch, Black and Dekker has sold millions of these ingenious flashlights, based on Alvin's insight into the target user, the use case, and the latent needs driven into the subsystem called "the neck." Some designs are timeless because they solve long-lived problems so very well.

The Snakelight ™

Subsystem or Service Step	Implementation options as seen in existing competitors or related products/services	Snakelight approach
Bulb and lens	• Different bulb sizes (low light to bright) • Different light colors (white, red, etc.)	• Brighter on spectrum • One color
Neck	• Fixed rigid housing to store batteries	• Flexible neck. Two layers of plastic • Batteries stored in stem of housing
Power supply	• Alkaline • Rechargable – fixed or replacement	• Alkaline or rechargeable • No fixed rechargeable pack
Switches	• On/off • Variable – strobe	• On/off
Housing	• Plastic • Waterproof	• Not waterproof

Figure 7.15 The composite design for the Snakelight™

The process of breaking a product or service down into its component subsystems and then deciding what to use for each particular subsystem should seem fairly obvious. What is not so obvious to the first-time entrepreneur is that you don't have to invent something new for every single subsystem! You can take what already works for some systems and then innovate for others, combine them through well-designed interfaces – and voila, you have a better product or service! The final design is the composite of different existing and new technologies or components within a specific architecture.

Composite design is a straightforward method once you have defined the product or service architecture. And it works for software well. For example, developers often try to create mobile versions of applications software already running on large computers. To do this, they replace the GUI, add security layers for data access, and then tap into existing databases from the older application. For example, SAP (the dominant enterprise accounting and inventory software in industry) has both its Mobile versus SAP Enterprise versions – they both hit the same company, user, manufacturing, and other related databases using the SAP Cloud Platform.

There are exceptions, of course. A new drug typically involves applying a new molecule – new chemistry – to cure a specific disease. It's hard to split a molecule up – although biotech companies sometimes try to do this by adding different chemistries to core molecules to create new therapeutic applications. These drug derivatives are often called co-adjuvants.

Composite design works for service innovators as well. A simple example is that you might want to create a new website focused on bringing healthy new products to parents of young children. The underpinnings of this new Etail business might be Shopify and a media server with customer testimonials for specific products. There is no need to reinvent the wheel for the eCommerce solution or the media server. This way, you can focus on product selection, content development, and marketing, and use another external supplier such as Hubspot for the latter.

Or, as another example, let's say that you want to create a service to help students store their belongings over the summer and quickly expand your service to multiple universities in different locations. One approach is to raise tens of millions of dollars and build climate-controlled, secure warehouses in other cities. Or, you might explore a reseller's agreement with a large, national storage company to provide the infrastructure needed. There are several of these that cover the entire U.S. This way, you could focus on the web app, the marketing of the service, and helping customers get their belongings to warehouse. You could even provide a premium service to help students pack, box, and ship to the warehouses, and at the end of the summer, ship and unpack. You might partner with local moving companies to do this work and feature reusable containers from other partners. In other words, as the service provider, you are the hub of a service network, owning the brand, the website, the customers, and control the flow of money, making a single, seamless concierge service for the target user. This is composite design, no less than that for the Snakelight.

As yet another successful example, two former students founded a venture named CrystalKnows, which provides AI software for email messaging that scrapes social networks to create personality profiles for the "receivers" of an intended message. The software then tunes the wording and phrasing of the email message to be more impactful for that receiver. The composite design has the company's own, proprietary special natural language processing algorithms. However, it relies on content from existing social networks, accessed through the application programming interfaces (APIs) from LinkedIn and other social networks. Many software-enabled services that are data-intensive tap into commercially available databases. *This is composite design, too.*

Whatever your application – product, service, an integrated system – apply composite design to your architecture framework to create a rapid, powerful implementation strategy. *What subsystems do you wish to build yourself; what others can you buy, license, or use for free from external sources?* Then think, how much more quickly might you get to an MVP using this approach rather than building everything from scratch. The chances are that you will get to market much more rapidly. Also, a composite design approach usually means that you will have to borrow or raise less money from investors than you would otherwise need to hire engineers or chemists.

To be successful with composite design, you need to study and understand the industry ecosystem around you – to learn about the components, data, and services provided by other companies or organizations in your field of work. You will have to do this anyway when you have to build a business plan later based on the innovations created in this course, so you might as well start that process now. An hour on the web with some reasonable searches for free industry reports, trends, and players provides a great running start.

DESIGN THE STYLING OR GUI, AND THE PACKAGING

Styling and packaging are typically left as the last step of the design process. In fact, most books on innovation and design ignore packaging altogether. It shouldn't be that way. In many cases, it is at least as important as the core product or service. The packaging is what the buyer sees first on the shelf in a grocery store. Or, an automobile shopper first sees the styling of the exterior of a vehicle. And even in a service, users will see the user interface of the software by which the service is accessed or the styling and trained attitude of the persons delivering that service. Packaging, broadly defined, is very important.

Figure 7.16 is a template to define the packaging for your product or service. On the left is a picture or sketch of your packaging concept for the physical product, an actual package design, or an exterior design. For a mobile app, this is the GUI. For a service, perhaps also a GUI or how you wish service delivery persons to appear, be it in professional attire or a colored uniform, or if you are an apparel venture, wearing the venture's clothes. Then, on the right side are two boxes: one for form (or style) and the other for function. Functional packaging might be a package that chills or heats the food or beverage or has solar cells integrated into the exterior to produce power.

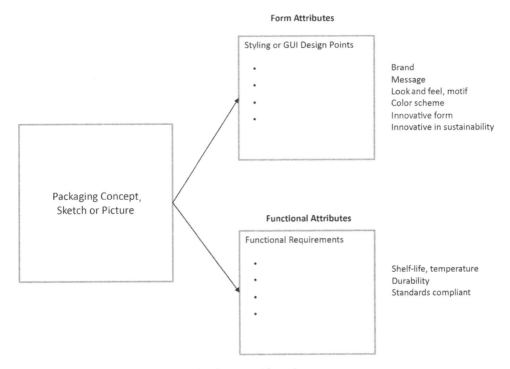

Form Attributes

Styling or GUI Design Points

- •
- •
- •
- •

Brand
Message
Look and feel, motif
Color scheme
Innovative form
Innovative in sustainability

Packaging Concept,
Sketch or Picture

Functional Attributes

Functional Requirements

- •
- •
- •
- •

Shelf-life, temperature
Durability
Standards compliant

Figure 7.16   Packaging design, for form and function

Let's first consider packaging from the perspective of form or style. As mentioned above, form means a lot to car buyers. Car designers often call this the *styling* of the vehicle. It is a crucial design driver together with aerodynamics and crush resistance for the exterior subsystem or outside frame of the vehicle. A Tesla *looks* sleek as well as runs fast and clean. In Chapter 5, the My M&M's case is another excellent example: the shell's custom printed text and images *are the styling*. Otherwise, the product is just a traditional M&M in different colors. And rather than just have the same old brown flow-wrap packaging for M&M's, the custom printed candies are shipped in see-through bags or wedding and other party "favors." At one point, the company had $200 crystal bases sent along with the candies to make that "lasting impression" for a loved one on Valentine's Day.

As part of styling, the packaging or exterior of a product, or the website and marketing collateral is also a primary place to create *branding*. This includes the product or service name, your company's logo, and the messaging around the offering. If it is food-related, one would show product images that suggest great taste and quality of ingredients. Logo and brand names are essential for everything – products, services, or connected systems sold as services.

Styling or appearance is tremendously important for software, be it a mobile app or software running on the Cloud for an enterprise application. The "packaging" for software is the GUI. As noted above, you should include the GUI as a key subsystem in your architecture diagram, but we can be even more specific here. Any software used by a human must be easy to use and straightforward, intuitive in getting it to do things, but also powerful in the doing. The end-user should be able to achieve or access all the functionality in the software without high levels of stress or training. The screen cannot be too busy or overloaded with buttons or menu systems. Please take a careful look at your favorite mobile app or enterprise software GUI, and then try to emulate it for your design. There are many fine examples of elegant software. In the education world, Canvas is supplanting Blackboard as a learning management system primarily because it has a straightforward, more intuitive interface.

The packaging of a service can also take on a physical, shaped form. Consider the lobby design of a high-end hotel versus one that is inexpensive. That lobby is as much packaging as the styling of a Porsche. Or, styling might be the color of the uniforms of employees or equipment deployed to provide that service. United Parcel Service is often referred to as "Brown," the theme for its delivery personnel's clothes, UPS trucks, and even some of its buildings. Designing a new experience – a fresh *feel* for the user – invariably involves packaging. Plus, you must try to *stand out* visually in what is typically a sea of noise of competing products, software, or services for any consumer-facing product.

Next, there is a second box in Figure 7.16 that represents packaging *for function*. For example, a new food snack typically requires foil packaging materials to provide a moisture barrier to extend shelf life. Functional packaging also includes recyclable packaging. Reusable, recyclable, or even biodegradable packaging is becoming a must-have for Millennial consumers. Some drink-innovating students are now using aluminum cans instead of plastic bottles because aluminum is more recyclable. True biodegradable plastics will be available in the years ahead. *Sustainable packaging is becoming mainstream.*

Packaging can also have the vital function to *protect*. Electronics and medical equipment need packaging that can protect the equipment. This means being drop safe. Packaging is also getting much "smarter." For example, different types of drugs need to be kept at a specific temperature. Packaging of the future will monitor temperature as well as location. Anti-theft might be another feature you require. Some cannabis delivery services are already working on tamper-proof, theft-proof packaging. Software apps now have identity management built directly into the user interface – we consider this part of the packaging, too. Once again, Apple's FaceID capability is rather exceptional in its correctness and convenience.

In all of this, you must keep costs and the retail or user price in mind. Your target user/buyer may not wish to pay the extra money required to achieve that styling or its function. Mars uses inexpensive flow-wrap for many of its products because items sell for under $1. In contrast, Gillette uses beautiful, hard-shelled protective packaging that adds considerably to its costs, perhaps 25% of the total cost of goods, including razors and blades. When one sells each cartridge for approximately $5, there is the margin to spend more on higher-quality packaging.

Finally, packaging for consumer products needs to account for shelf presence. Do you want them just thrown on the shelf – or do you prefer some type of shelf packaging or hangers where the product is in a vertical standing position to increase consumer awareness and appeal? This is often called *secondary packaging*. This includes the boxes or "shippers" in which the product is sent and displayed in the store.

Innovation in these packaging dimensions, form and function, is important and can capture the consumer's interest. Packaging design will also be considered carefully by a retailer if that is the intended channel. Packaging and shelf appearance must "sing."

We ask you now to think creatively about the packaging designs for your products or services. How can you make this packaging or the software user interfaces special relative to what exists in the market today? Are there innovation opportunities in either the form or the function to make the overall product or service more functional, smarter, or simply much more appealing to the target user? How will your innovation stand out in the sea of noise so often present in a mature, crowded marketplace filled with other existing and new products or services? This is not an easy question, but for your innovation to be a commercial success, it is a question that cannot be avoided.

Reader exercises

These should be amongst the most fun exercises in the book.

STEP 1: SKETCH AND STORYBOARD YOUR CONCEPT

Refer to Figures 7.4, 7.5, 7.6, and 7.7 for examples. First, sketch the core product or service. For a product, this is the product design and perhaps its place of use (such as a baking tool sketched into the kitchen). For a service, it is a representation of the workflow or process. And for software, a representative GUI. You can show how the product, service, or software transforms across the use case in a storyboard.

STEP 2: DEVELOP THE PRODUCT OR SERVICE ARCHITECTURE

Refer to Figure 7.7 for a product. Think of the Snakelight example. For software products/apps, refer to Figure 7.9. Or, for services innovations, apply Figure 7.10 to create a process flow diagram that shows the inputs, activities, and outputs for each significant step in the service, just as if it was a subsystem in a product. If you sketch how the process exists today and then identify those steps that might be eliminated through automation or just common sense, this will help your readers better understand the impact of your thinking. Then, Figure 7.11 complements 7.10 with a higher-level services innovation strategy. The data needed to measure the speed, cost, and quality of your subsystem innovations become important design drivers for building the necessary software to support the delivery of the service.

If you are working on a software product that has a fundamental impact on the underlying use case – how a user does something – you should probably also draw a process flow diagram (Figure 7.10). This drawing shows the typical user process before your innovation. Then, mark up that process diagram to show how you have improved that process. For example, a driverless control system for a car is a new subsystem, but it also fundamentally enhances the use case for an older person going shopping. It would be good to sketch out "the before" and "after" for a new software or system design.

STEP 3: DESIGN THE STYLING AND PACKAGING OR USER INTERFACE FOR YOUR PRODUCT OR SERVICE

Refer to Figure 7.16. The tips that we have are to:

- Design for form first, including styling, the logo, and the brand message.
- Then design for functional packaging, including recyclability, protection or shelf life, and any "smart" features that would be of great value for your target users or buyers (e.g. location, temperature, etc.).

STEP 4: SHOW AND TELL

By completing the steps above, you will have a wonderful set of graphic illustrations for your product or service. It would now be advantageous to find another ten or so target users or buyers to get their feedback on your designs. Bring your discussion guide with you in case it is someone you have not interviewed before, and can gather yet another set of customer interview data on those questions, in addition to getting feedback on your designs.

You will find that as your concepts take shape and form, such conversations will become even more exciting. Things have progressed from "what is your problem" to "we think this may be our solution." Have fun with this. Make it an experience that you will remember. Also, please return to your Customer Value Proposition (Figure 4.10) and give it another quick read, sharpening any row where you can. Then improve the integrated concept statement at the bottom.

NOTES

1.   Norman, D. (2013). *The Design of Everyday Things: Revised and Expanded Edition*. New York: Basic Books.

2.   For a more detailed description of the Element's design and development, see: Meyer, M.H. (2008). "Perspectives: How Honda Innovates." *The Journal of Product Innovation Management*, 25(3), May, 261-271.

3.   Ackoff, R. L., Magidson, J., & Addison, H. J. (2006). *Idealized design*. Pearson Education Incorporated; Meyer, M.H., and Lehnerd, A. (1997). *The Power of Product Platforms*. New York: The Free Press.

8
Competitive analysis, positioning, and branding

THE PURPOSE OF THE CHAPTER

This chapter provides methods to assess your new product or service concepts relative to current competitors to ensure differentiation and distinctiveness. Through this process, you will also sharpen your designs to more clearly separate them from the competition. With competitive positioning differentiated, you can then think about how to brand new products to convey and message an innovation's special place amongst the crowd.

Branding includes the name of the product or service, the short, powerful message following that name, and other exciting elements by which an entrepreneur builds a brand image around her/his product or service. These visual cues include the colors used on the website and the images of people and places that suggest a meaningful experience, rather than just a functional product. This part is fun, creative, and often as critical as the design of the product or service itself. Interestingly, an innovator can reintegrate branding back into the product or service design, typically as an overall design language that unifies form and function as you might see in a sleek, all electric car or the customer service "Easy Button" in Staples. That's when the magic happens.

LEARNING OBJECTIVES

After reading this chapter you should be able to:

1. Perform a detailed competitive analysis.
2. Develop a precise positioning relative to competitors, based on functional, emotional, and even social dimensions from the eyes of target users.
3. Develop a brand name and the messages to support it.

PAUSE AND TAKE A DEEP BREATH: ARE YOU READY TO PROCEED FORWARD?

In reaching this point in the book, you have achieved many significant milestones. You have:

- Defined your Problem Space and the specific problem to be solved.

- Created a team to tackle the problem, based on shared values as well as natural and learned skills.

- Ideated a solution for them – be it a new product or service – based on some initial field interviews, and from this, defined your initial Customer Value Proposition.

- More crisply defined your target users and buyers.

- Discovered their perceived and latent needs across an entire use case through intensive field interviewing.

- Translated those needs into an attractive, useful new product or service design based on an underlying product or service architecture.

That's a lot! If you've learned and applied the methods, you already have received your money's worth from this book.

If you know in your heart that you could make your product or service concept much more impactful, *please* return to the previous chapter and take yet another spin. Refinement is essential. *Everyone pivots.*

If needed, talk with your teacher. Develop a realistic schedule for course completion that still meets the semester timeline. This might mean doing the prior chapter and this one in parallel. *Entrepreneurs do two things at once all the time!* Now onto competitive analysis, positioning, and branding.

LET'S MEET… JOSH AND MANNY!

Let's meet two more entrepreneurs, Josh and Manny. We love these two guys and are rooting for their success. They are two athletic "bros" who grew up in adjacent towns, became friends, and whose favorite drink was *chocolate milk*. That's right: chocolate milk. The picture of the two friends in Figure 8.1 tells it all: two young men who still love their chocolate milk.

There was a significant problem, however. Both became lactose intolerant as teenagers. Lactose is the sugar – a carbohydrate – found naturally in milk (humans and cows alike). Humans are typically born with an enzyme called lactase that breaks down the lactose sugar to be painlessly digested. Unfortunately, a significant percentage of people start producing less lactase upon puberty. This reduced ability to properly digest lactose causes lactose intolerance … it is not a pretty picture. Symptoms may include stomach pain, bloating, diarrhea, gas, and nausea, starting after ingesting dairy products such as milk or ice cream. For Manny and Josh, this was a disaster. Forget Coke, Pepsi, or flavored waters. Instead, their favorite drink

Source: Josh Belinsky. Used with permission.

Figure 8.1 Josh and Manny: co-founders of Slate Milk, Inc.

was chocolate milk – especially chilled after an intense workout. Suddenly, however, it was off-limits!

Thus began the seed of a promising new venture. Many years later, they realized if they could make rich-tasting, all-natural chocolate milk that was lactose-free, branded for people of all ages, with significantly reduced sugar content relative to other chocolate milk, plus more environmentally friendly, they just might have a competitively differentiated product.

THE IMPORTANCE OF COMPETITIVE POSITIONING

Every innovator and their venture need to have a clear competitive advantage in the eyes of their target users. This becomes part of your selling proposition to users and/or buyers. If you are selling to a larger retailer or a corporate intermediary or reseller, your positioning will also be one of the first things they will want to know. Your pitch must come in 15 seconds, be grounded in your industry, and ring true to the listener. "How are you different?" they will think and ask. You must have a decisive answer.

This means how your new offerings – either products or services – provide more value than those of close competitors. You may decide to price your offerings higher than anyone else, but then you should also *do a lot more than anyone else*. In contrast, a venture can choose to be a price leader (charge less), perhaps based on less expensive materials or supply chain efficiencies. But then again, your product or service cannot be a piece of junk. Otherwise, comments to that effect will quick appear on social media – not a great way to launch a new company.

Figure 8.2 shows a continuum of price–performance for products, in this case, drinks. In general, your innovation and the company behind it can pursue a few broad choices regarding competitive advantage: cost advantage or non-cost-differentiation advantage. Products or services need to be positioned on this continuum because this affects customer perception of

	Low/No Cost	Moderate Cost	High Cost
Product (Drinks)	Generic Tap Water	"Product" Bottled water – Evian, Dasani, Aquafina Iced Tea	"Branded" Acqua di Cristallo Energy Drinks – Bang
Systems (Productivity Suites)	Google Apps Apple Apps	Microsoft Office	Salesforce
Services	Intuit Turbo Tax Do-it-yourself	HR Block	Accounting Firms

Figure 8.2   The competitive continuum

value and price. Think about beer. There are the traditional mass-market, inexpensive beers that don't necessarily taste bad but don't set the world on fire. Then, there are the craft beers, many of which are truly outstanding and often twice the price of traditional mass-produced beers.

An inexpensive product or service does not have to be poorly performing. Instead, it can provide solid functionality but be less costly. The way this tends to be achieved is by being produced at a lower cost or sacrificing profit. Many such value-focused products or services try to give the target user 80% or more of what the broader market wants, at 20% or 30% less price relative to feature-rich, premium-priced offerings. Many successful businesses have been created with this type of competitive positioning. Dunkin' versus Starbucks. Honda versus BMW. A community health clinic versus a much larger, multi-service hospital.

The clever ways in which lower-cost suppliers achieve such costs are worth studying and considering for any venture. For example, Uber tends to be significantly less expensive than a traditional taxi because Uber does not have to buy taxi cars; it has a sharing economy business model where the drivers own their own vehicles. Depending on the time of day within its pricing model, an Uber ride can be considerably less expensive than a traditional taxi. At the same time, the process for using and paying for an Uber ride is straightforward via its mobile app. Similarly, Airbnb is less expensive than the typical hotel – yet easy to book and pay with its app. The typical Airbnb lodging will not equal a three-star hotel but is often just as good if not better than a one- or two-star hotel. Both Airbnb and Uber offer great value to their target users – and that is why both have grown so explosively.

A genuinely differentiated product or service shines in the eyes of the target user. It simply does more, does it better, or does it faster. Such premium products or services have a styling and brand image superior to the middle-of-the-road or low-end alternatives. Such products and services exist all around you. Think of the unique restaurant that you might go to once or twice a year for a special occasion. Or consider the newest Apple MacBook or iPhone, which sell at a price premium relative to other laptops or cellphones. These are products that not only function great but look great. Such products or services develop a *cache* or *élan* that sets them apart. This translates into sales.

The authors see the same thing for public services in South Korea. Taking a train ride is an experience completely different than in America. Passengers book and change seats with ease through a mobile app to get specific seat assignments; a train stewardess stands at the front for boarding and egress, dressed in uniform, wearing thin gloves, and *bows* as a sign of respect to passengers. The WiFi zips as fast as the bullet train, which itself glides on a suspended chassis. And the coach class seat feels like first-class for the American rider. It is a differentiated end-to-end experience relative to most other national and private rail systems.

There is functional or performance differentiation and then, cost differentiation. These are typically seen as two very different strategies. For functional or performance differentiation, there are three primary conditions for success:

- The functional point of difference that is the basis of the competitive advantage must be genuine. This is the speed and effective fuel economy of Tesla, or the knowledgeable call center staff of a retail services firm such as Fidelity Investments.

- Target users or buyers must perceive that functional differentiation as meaningful and valuable. While great marketing can make mediocre products look superior, sooner or later, the truth comes out.

- Third, the functional competitive advantage should not be easily copied by competitors, whether it is by the sheer difficulty of achieving that functionality or by some type of patent protection on that point of differentiation.

For a company to have a sustained cost advantage, it must have a clear, scalable way to achieve lower prices:

- It must have significantly lower costs in materials or software tools and then, the cost of assembling them to make the finished product or service. This is often achieved by a unique, highly efficient method of production or service delivery.

- Second, the cost advantage can come from a more efficient distribution method, such as the digital transmission of a book rather than printing and mailing a copy. Or an online store rather than a physical store.

- Third, a company can drive down costs through scale, which means making and selling a very high volume relative to competitors. This approach means making so much of a product or delivering so much of a particular service that the machines or computers used for production can produce each unit at a lower unit cost.

Amazon is an example of implementing all three approaches to achieving cost advantage.

Functional or performance advantage is typically well within an entrepreneur's reach because s/he can innovate her/his way to a unique, feature-rich offering that directly solves a vital problem for target users. Cost advantage is harder. For a physical product, the startup typically cannot raise the capital needed to build a high-volume production operation to start. Instead, it needs to find a contract manufacturer with its own highly efficient operations. For software apps, that contract manufacturer tends to be Amazon Web Services or Microsoft Azure. They have such a significant scale that the cost of computer processing and data delivery is low. The presence of such external "manufacturers" makes it possible for a venture to deliver reasonably priced products and services in a way that could not be imagined twenty years ago.

Differentiation is classically a function of performance and price. The higher the price, the more the features and functions; the lower the price, the fewer features and functions, and the differentiating factor is just price. Yet, there are exceptions.

For example, the online jewelry retailer Blue Nile provides a premium service with certified diamonds, pearls, and gold, using a highly trained and pleasant call center staff. From our experience, this call center staff are as knowledgeable as any salesperson in a jewelry store, and the shipping of purchased jewelry is safe, insured, and rapid. Blue Nile charges less than other retailers because it has replaced the bricks-and-mortar store with a direct-to-consumer web and call center model. As a result, it differentiates on the quality of its overall service. Lower pricing is just the icing on the cake and draws first-time customers.

There are many other examples. One of the world's best also comes from South Korea. It is a home delivery service called Coupang that has direct contracts with farmers, beef producers, and mariculture or fishing operations. The vegetable, beef, fish, and eggs delivered by Coupang can be of *higher quality yet lesser cost* than shopping at the local grocery store. Its direct sourcing strategy and logistics capability are its keys to success, special even when compared to Amazon.

You must decide on a basic competitive positioning strategy: do you want to be a higher-priced, fully featured product or service, or a moderately featured product provided at a low relative price? Or, is your competitive strategy going to be like Coupang or Blue Nile – high performance yet low price, and still figure out a way to be profitable? Importantly, being stuck in the middle of the price–performance spectrum tends not to work, e.g., mid-level features and medium price. This leaves the innovator without a clear differentiating factor either in performance or price. Large traditional competitors might compete in the middle and have much deeper pockets for branding and promotion.

STEP 1: COMPETITIVE ANALYSIS ON FEATURES AND PRICE

The first step is to make a detailed competitive assessment of your new product or service design relative to direct competitors.

Figure 8.3 shows a general template for competitive analysis. The process is relatively simple. You need to jump onto the web or go to a store to look at the major competitors in the market for your type of product or service, app, or IoT type system. The template shows columns for major competitors running across the top and different functions or features running down the side. This competitive matrix reveals how your idea will stack up to existing competitors, even in its concept stage. From this, you might see that you are missing an essential set of features needed to be competitive or dial-up a particular feature to be even more differentiated.

Within Figure 8.3, try to gather specific information in terms of features and objective measures of performance for those features. For example, acceleration for a new car design is best stated in the seconds needed to reach 60mph. For food, calories per serving or grams of sugar per serving. Software may be the exception. Here, words will often work better than measures,

	Company A	Company B	Company C	Your Product or Service
Primary target user				
Functions and Features				
Dimension 1				
Dimension 2				
Dimension 3				
Dimension 4				
Overall				
Quality				
Price				

Figure 8.3   Competitive analysis on features and price

such as a better GUI or greater data security, the ability to incorporate real-time data feeds, and a special algorithm that provides X% accuracy in image analysis.

Important: You must never say to your friends, teachers, or later on, investors, that you don't have any competitors. Only a true visionary such as Steve Jobs or Elon Musk might be able to say such a thing – but truth be told, they always stated they had competitors. For example, Steve Jobs was mindful of the IBM PC, and automobiles such as the Nissan Leaf existed well before Tesla. By developing a detailed competitive matrix, the innovators can decide where to focus their energy to create a more powerfully differentiated product.

Therefore, to state "I don't have any competitors" comes off as simply naïve or lazy. Even if current competitors have products or services that are 50 years old, they are still competitors in the eyes of your users. And in software, sometimes the real competitor is a "home-grown" system or application. If that is the case for your new software product, put it down as "home-grown" in your matrix. Learn what the home-grown software does well or poorly from your user and buyer interviews, and capture this in the template.

Gathering competitive information is so much easier today than in the past. You can quickly do Google searches at no cost, find competitors, learn their product or service portfolios, see their claims about performance, and often get their pricing. Marketing and channel strategies are also often revealed. To add to this information are product and service reviews provided by independent industry writers and end-users. For more exploratory fields in science and technology, students can attend virtual conferences and tradeshows for little cost. This is often a good way to see the latest technologies, products, and services.

For some types of innovation projects, you can visit a store where competitors' products are on display right next to other products. Store visits with this competitive mindset are fun to do! Use the "student project" card to talk to salespeople and ask them why they prefer selling one company's products or services more than other companies' offerings. Learning competitive differentiation from an experienced salesperson can be powerful. Often, you might see that it is less to do with the performance of the product, but instead, with the commission paid to the salesperson for selling one product versus another.

Take notes during your web or store searches. Begin to dimensionalize the significant categories of features such as ingredients in or absent in food, speed and warranties for any machine, and the claims or marketing messages after each brand name. Also, look at pricing. Do higher prices support premium positioning? Are lower prices associated with basic or "value" products or services? This might also be reflected in how a consumer product appears on a shelf: the most expensive are displayed at the highest level, moderately high-priced at eye level, mid-range products at stomach level, and the discount or value offerings on lower shelves.

SLATE'S COMPETITIVE ANALYSIS MATRIX

Let's use Josh and Manny to illustrate these concepts. Their company is called Slate Milk. You might go to its website to take a quick tour.

As high school athletes, Josh and Manny were careful about what they ate and drank. They preferred chocolate milk for its muscle recovery function, knowing that it had more electrolytes than Gatorade, plus all that fabulous taste. So when they became lactose intolerant, they started drinking the chocolate milk called Lactaid, from Hood, Inc., which is cow's milk with lactase enzyme added to it before it's packaged to help break down the lactose. Manny and Josh would bring mugs of Lactaid Chocolate Milk to school, where their friends would make fun of them as "nut-cases" for drinking so much chocolate milk. But as they got older and went to college, Lactaid wasn't the most "hip" thing to drink. The brand itself announced to the world that anyone drinking it had a "weak stomach," even though recent estimates state that 65% of all Americans, as but one country example, are lactose intolerant. Within this segment, it is known that Asian and African Americans have a high rate relative to others.

These two friends then went to the same university (Northeastern) and remained close post-graduation. Both had the entrepreneurial itch. Manny started a software company that helped consumer product brands market their products through campus advocates. His startup became a popular job-posting board for students wanting to earn extra money "repping" brands on college campuses. Josh also ventured into startups as an early salesperson with several companies. While still in college, Josh joined a food startup that created a line of coffee-infused snack bars. From this, he learned about co-manufacturers and other supply chain factors. He also learned about developing a recipe for a food product, food safety regulations, and the needs and concerns of retailers to place a new product on shelf, including slotting fees, merchandising, and in-store communication.

After about three years of working in these various companies, the two friends were hanging out and bemoaning the vagaries of their respective industries. Then, they discussed starting a business together.

That moment of "Aha" was that night, precisely 11:30 pm on October 5, 2017. Manny sent Josh a presentation to create chocolate milk that wasn't just for kids. Josh told Manny he was insane to want to start a milk company as neither of them knew anything about milk. But then, Josh recognized the large market opportunity. A big market, a clear consumer need, and a product category that they both loved.

Six months later, they had developed the initial product concept, started organizing their supply chain, and worked through the Northeastern incubator to develop a business plan to raise money. First, however, there were several specific challenges that Manny and Josh had to tackle:

- Chocolate milk has a brand image that it's only to be consumed by kids, not adults.

- The chocolate milk brands on the shelf had way too much sugar (24 grams per cup of regular milk), which is not healthful for anyone (in terms of diabetes and other diseases).

- As stated above, for many people (again, most adult Americans), drinking regular chocolate milk causes a bellyache, and sometimes diarrhea.

- Milk production can be very wasteful and not environmentally friendly. Chocolate milk, like most other milk, spoils relatively quickly, often being thrown out before it's entirely consumed. In addition, dairy farms use a lot of water to sustain their herd and crops. And the packaging of milk is often in plastic bottles, which are rarely fully recycled.

The first two problems are examples of perceived needs; the last two, latent needs. They spoke with dozens of consumers in grocery stores and other venues. Even though they had been life-long chocolate milk enthusiasts, "we learned a lot," Josh said, "and we learned much that was new." Interview venues included the aisles of the store where they wanted their products to be displayed. The two entrepreneurs thought about how to achieve an eye level display, and the type of packaging that would stand out on the shelf against other milk products as well as other premium specialty drinks. By 2020, aluminum was becoming the preferred packaging for new beverages. Manny and Josh felt that dark brown colors had to be on the can to suggest the product inside, and the name itself had to connate a particular vision. The name "Slate" was simple, easy to pronounce, and most importantly, aspired to change the way consumers thought about chocolate milk. Their goal was to give chocolate milk a "clean slate." Also, they realized that the name was transferrable to other products should they want to disrupt other stale categories in the future.

Most important, Manny and Josh realized that if they removed the lactose in some manner from natural cow's milk, and since lactose is a sugar, their lactose-free product would have a significantly lower amount of sugar than both regular white milk and chocolate milk (where the big brands like Lactaid typically only added lactase instead of removing any lactose).

Figure 8.4 shows the result, Slate's first three product stock-keeping units (SKUs – the standard way of referring to a specific product from a manufacturer): "classic chocolate," "dark chocolate," and "espresso chocolate." Notice the cans – slim and a bit tall, a contemporary design with simple, clear branding on the front, with different shades of brown to reflect the different SKUs.

Next, let's take a look at their competitive matrix, as shown in Figure 8.5. The matrix highlights Slate versus two primary competitors, circa 2020: TruMoo and Lactaid. Note that TruMoo is one of America's top milk brands focused on children, and claims to be high protein and non-GMO, even though the dairy cattle are typically fed corn from genetically engineered corn seeds. Lactaid is the traditional lactose-free leading brand from Hood, Inc., and uses the same ingredient (enzyme) found in Lactaid tablets for oral ingestion.

Josh and Manny's competitive differentiation of Slate is on the right-side column: first, no lactose; second, 75% lower sugar (because the lactose sugar has been removed);

Source: Josh Belinsky. Used with permission.

Figure 8.4   Slate's first three products

third, no use of carrageenan (a seaweed-derived thickening and preservative commonly used in drinks, but which has been associated with intestinal tract inflammation); fourth, a longer shelf life relative to competitors (very important for both retailers and consumers); fifth, rich chocolate and coffee flavors; and sixth, more environmentally friendly aluminum packaging. All these points of differentiation were of high importance to their target consumers, Millennials that stretched into those thirtyish and fortyish Ys and Xers. Josh and Manny had a long list of competitive differentiators – it would be needed to get buy-in from major retailers.

At the time of writing, the product was only several years old. The two partners did this competitive analysis *before* their concept was fully brought to life. When they took a look at their analysis, they realized there would be vast amounts of work to fine-tune the recipe and

	TruMoo	Lactaid	Slate
Target user	• Kids	• Adults	• Millennials as primary, plus all others
Type/source of milk	• Use large farms across the country	• Use Hood's milk and other large milk producers	• Ultrafiltration – filters out lactose and some water (use the water back on family farms, H_2O neutral by 2025) • 30 family farms – Animal Welfare Association (AWA) compliant
Formulas/Flavors	• Variety of flavors	• One flavor • Lactase added	• Not just multiple flavors, added boosts • Coffee (dual functionality with caffeine + protein)
Health benefits	• 11g of protein per 11oz • 32g of sugar per 11oz • Not lactose free • Uses carrageenan	• 11g of protein per 11oz • 33g of sugar per 11oz • Not lactose free • Uses carrageenan	• 75% less sugar (9g) and 50% more protein (17g) than regular chocolate milk • 100% lactose free • Non-GMO, All-natural, No carrageenan
Packaging	• Plastic and paperboard • Brand targets mothers and children, loud colors with cows and splashes of milk • Spoils quickly	• Plastic and paperboard • Brand targets mothers and children, loud colors with cows and splashes of milk • Spoils quickly	• Aluminum cans, no plastic • Simple brand, inclusive • Year shelf-life, prevents waste
Price point	• Low price	• Mid price	• Premium price

Figure 8.5   Slate's competitive analysis

build the supply chain, but were confident that this work would lead to a truly distinctive product – and therefore, was well worth the effort.

What was that work? Think about four significant effort buckets: product development (recipe and packaging); the supply and processing of the milk itself, plus the flavorings; selling to retailers; and raising money to fund the business. From their prior work experience (harkening back to our second chapter on natural and learned skills), Manny and Josh were natural-born sellers and had honed their sales skills in jobs before Slate. And they both had learned the ins and outs of financing ventures from their prior startups. Recipe, packaging, and the supply chain were areas they would just have to dig into and learn.

Fortunately, they found other companies highly experienced in these areas. And while the two founders lived in Boston, they found partners in New York State. The first of these was a specialty formulation team that took on the challenge of blending ultra-filtered milk with a variety of ingredients and cocoa powders to make the three different SKUs that tasted delicious and hit the nutrition requirements of low sugar and high protein. Second, and which became a barrier to entry in its own right, they found a large dairy cooperative located in Upstate New York that raised cattle on hormone-free feed, guided by "cow nutritionists" serving member farms. This same cooperative purchased its own equipment for ultra-filtration, passing the milk through a set of ultra-fine membranes to remove virtually all of the lactose sugar and some of the water from the milk itself. Then, they had milk tankers with the ultra-filtered milk sent to a large bottler, also in New York State. This bottler also helped source the aluminum cans, blended the ingredients, and completed the shelf-stable canning process. Convincing this large bottler to work with a startup was a big challenge and took over a year of negotiation.

In sum, the combination of the recipe lab, the dairy cooperative, and the bottler/canner became Manny and Josh's solution set for production. This is a good lesson for other entrepreneurs: search for competent external partners that can lessen the initial capital investment needed to start and scale the business. With this composite design, Josh and Manny could focus on sales, marketing, and finance.

STEP 2: DEFINE COMPETITIVE POSITIONING

The competitive analysis matrix leads to competitive positioning. In turn, competitive positioning becomes the basis for pricing, channel selection, placement within the channel (often called merchandising). Positioning also impacts the choice of a brand name and the messaging. This is particularly important for any type of consumer product or service, where "premium," "gold," or "indulgent" are often found near the brand names of premium-positioned offerings.

Figure 8.6 shows three approaches to competitive positioning. The first, and the most common, is *functional* positioning – for example, what the product or service does relative to competitors. Words such *as speed, accuracy, efficiency* are often used for dimensions in functional positioning. The second approach is *emotional* positioning. This approach can be compelling for consumer products or services positions on how target users should feel along meaningful cognitive dimensions. *Safety, fun, exciting, contemporary* are all examples of words used to dimensionalize emotional positioning. Minecraft, Doom, and Witcher are examples of computer games with exciting, fun positioning, where Volvo has traditionally designed and marketed its products to emphasize safety over aggressive styling. The third approach is *social* positioning. This, too, can be extremely powerful for certain types of products or services. Words such as community-based, shared, or sustainable might help position an innovation on a societal basis. For example, Facebook is community, relative to the *New York Times*, which prides and markets itself on objective information.

Throughout previous chapters, we have focused a lot on the functional aspects of design. Our approach has been to determine what target users need, both in terms of their perceived and latent needs, and then frame those needs as design drivers and implement them as capabilities within specific subsystems in the overall product or service architecture. Figure 8.6 also shows that within functional positioning, you can also position along two dimensions of performance. Volvo: safety and elegance; Tesla: "green" and speed. It is crucial to plan your innovations to be better than current products or services on the market; these positioning grids – often called *perceptual maps* by marketing professionals – show how target users perceive a group of similar products or services relative to one another.

Materials innovations often hit multiple areas of specific, tangible benefits. For example, we mentored a materials scientist who created a substitute for traditional concrete. His chemistry has numerous advantages: (a) it cures more evenly in the presence of high moisture levels, (b) it cures considerably faster than traditional concrete, and (c) it is made from alternative materials and industrial by-products. Today, this concrete substitute is being used to repair concrete docks in heavily used ports. Materials innovation is hitting many different fields of applications: iron-free shirts or athletic pads that automatically inflate upon impact.

Creating an emotional positioning for an innovation requires a different mindset. Abandon the notion that consumers base their purchase decisions solely on features, functions, and price. The world is full of very successful and meaningful emotional brands. For example, men in North America have loved their John Deere ride-on-top lawn mowers because using them provides the personal feeling and emotional connection to the heritage of farming – even though it's just for mowing the lawn (and plenty of women drive these as well.) The same thing with sports cars – rapid acceleration with a slight growl from the engine, a tight cornering suspension, and leather-appointed interiors. The emotion: "Young again." Or the individual buying a Jeep Wrangler rather than purchase a commuter's SUV.

Similarly, many women have an emotional, passionate connection with their favorite clothes designers and brands. Women's cosmetics are about personal self-indulgence and "feeling good about oneself," as well as the functional dimensions of skin beauty and, increasingly, skin health. The design of chocolate treats for women has that same emotional connection of affordable indulgence with warmth and style.

The third dimension of positioning focuses on perceived and actual societal benefits for users. Our experience is that purchase decisions by Millennials and Gen Ys are strongly affected by their perception of societal factors. The majority of younger people rightly "care" about society and the environment – living healthily and consuming responsibly, protecting the environment, and improving social awareness of the problems of the disadvantaged. This broader care is reflected in their purchase decisions. Interestingly, there is an entirely new class

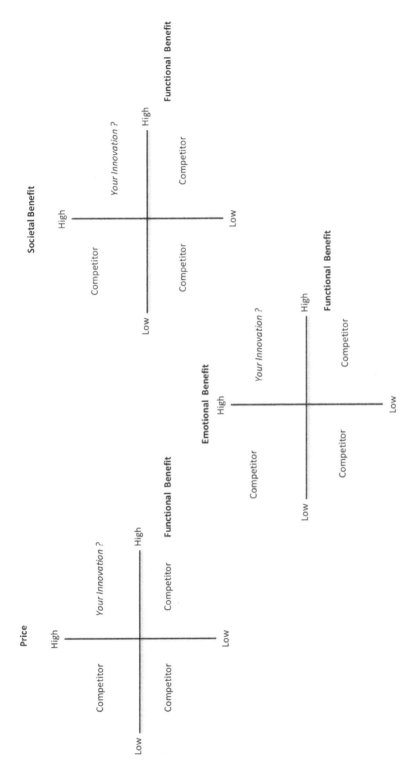

Figure 8.6 Three types of competitive positioning: perceptual maps in the eyes of users

of materials and components where the innovator does not have to make a tradeoff between performance and societal good. As we saw in the Pure Solutions venture earlier, fertilizers and pesticides can be manufactured from biodegradable and human and pet-friendly organic materials. Or, many governments have committed themselves to all-electric or hydrogen car sales in the future. *Good for society and the environment has become good business.*

Excellence in these three positioning dimensions – functional, emotional, and societal – *are not mutually exclusive.* One might argue that industry leaders in consumer categories need to excel in all three dimensions of positioning. Patagonia achieves this with high-performance outdoor apparel and perhaps industry's most sustainable supply chain, making the vast majority of its products with recycled materials and minimalist packaging. Lululemon and Apple are other examples that hit high scores in all three functional, emotional, and societal dimensions. These companies have planned their innovation strategies to yield specific types of functional, emotional, and societal benefits, resulting in competitive positioning that is then supported with outstanding products, software, and services.

As an innovator and prospective entrepreneur, you should consider developing all three dimensions of positioning for your product or service concept. Features, design, messaging, and positioning all go hand-in-hand. Think about not just what your product or service does, but how it "feels" to the user and contributes to societal and environmental causes. We hope that your passion for your chosen Problem Space persists when you get to these downstream activities.

On the right side of Figure 8.7 is a second important positioning concept: *breaking a tension.* The classic example is food, contrasting health and taste. Traditionally, food manufacturers have loaded their products with sugars and fats – *because sugar and fats taste good.* Healthier profile food products have had fewer ingredients, without all the sugar and fats, but most consumers perceived these more natural products as less tasty. And these products have traditionally been confined to retail outfits such as Whole Foods or Sprouts. Now, of course, an increasing percentage of packaged foods in mainstream grocery stores are healthy and tasty, resulting in careful, purposeful food design and recipe development. Plant-based substitutes for beef-based products are a clear example.

Before Beyond Meat entered its way into Dunkin' or McDonald's, a mid-sized manufacturer named Pinnacle Foods acquired and scaled a soy-based meat substitute Canadian company into the United States, branded as Gardein. It took courage and foresight on the part of the CEO to do this in a company known for legacy brands such as Hungry-Man beef dinners. We remember eating Gardein's meatless Italian meatballs – we were greatly impressed by the wonderful taste, breaking the tension between health and taste. And the use of beet juice to make plant burgers *look like* beef burgers added a third dimension of *appearance.* Now owned by Conagra, Gardein's sales continue to grow.

Think about the tradeoffs that users have had to make in your product or service category. List the different dimensions of functional benefits (or performance) on one side of a piece of paper, and then all the drawbacks, such as price or convenience, on the other. Then, how might you turn those drawbacks from negative into positive aspects? How can you break a tension in your product or service category?

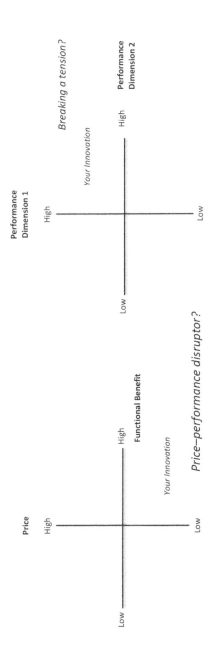

Figure 8.7 Price–performance and multi-performance dimensions analyses

For example, Apple created the Genius Bar in its stores. Imagine the worst aspect of owning a new computer – repair or training – becoming a convenient and perhaps even an enjoyable activity. This did not happen by accident. Apple designed its customer service functions carefully. This included a specific selection of support personnel working in the Genius Bar, its support and reservations systems, and the logistics of repairing damaged computers or phones, all deployed in scale to stores. As a result, Apple's stores grew to be the highest revenue-producing retail stores across *all industries* on a sales per square foot basis – and continue to hold that position. The power of innovating *bad experiences into good* ones cannot be underestimated. Try to break a tension within your Problem Space.

Before reading on, take a few minutes to consider this by sketching a few different competitive positioning maps for your new product or service idea.

SLATE'S COMPETITIVE POSITIONING

Manny and Josh wanted to "over-deliver" on functional benefits. This included zero lactose through ultra-filtration and the addition of the lactase enzyme, 75% less sugar than a comparable product, no carrageenan, environmentally friendly, shelf-stable, and with rich flavors (including coffee). Premium performance and premium price was their strategy.

They also wanted to create an emotional brand, harkening back to a time for consumers when they were young and viewed chocolate milk as an everyday treat, and a time when there was less worry in the world and more simple goodness. The sleek, simple packaging of the product supported the idea of simple goodness. Simple goodness remains a powerful concept sweeping across many food categories.

Figure 8.8 shows a competitive positioning for Slate in two ways: price–performance and on two dimensions of performance. It looks simple, but that simplicity was based on an intense period of thinking and competitive analysis, which *continues* as Slate scales across North America.

STEP 3: CREATE A BRAND STRATEGY

The next step is to develop a branding strategy that complements the competitive positioning. The important, fun stuff!

Branding includes the name of the product or service, the messaging behind the name, and the logos, color schemes, and visuals displayed on the web, packaging, advertising, and other media. As a product line expands with multiple elements, or even different product lines or services, the *brand architecture* extends to all of them.

You must continue to be mindful of your target users and buyers. How will they respond to the names and messaging that you use for your products and services? How can you test some options with them in your next round of interviews? And does your branding strategy help tell the story about your products, services, and company?

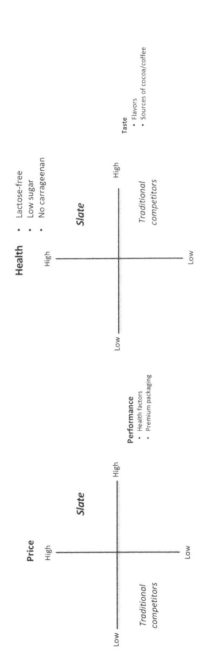

Figure 8.8   Slate's competitive positioning

CREATING A BRAND ARCHITECTURE FOR YOUR PRODUCT OR SERVICE

A brand is much more than a company name or logo. A venture's brand is the total experience created for users and buyers. Think of all the various "touchpoints" through which a user may interact with your company and your offerings: first, they hear and then learn about them, be it on the web or in a retail environment or from a magazine; next, they decide to buy it, on their own or from a salesperson directly selling it to them; and then next, the user might have to learn how to use the product or service; and only then do they experience its use. These are all critical touchpoints where you want to create and build a powerful brand as well as a positive experience.

Brands get *expressed* in the company, product and service names, in logos, signs, symbols, designs, and in messaging for different media. Branding is a combination of all these elements, plus more, such as company uniforms, company interior furniture and styling, web content, and even business cards. This branding helps a user connect to the product or service. In its own way, the brand name and messaging should provide assurance, satisfaction, and other forms of value to the user. Think about your cell phone: the product supports the brand with both its features and styling. Some elements of the total brand experience can be spoken or written, while other elements contain certain symbols that are strictly visual. For example, Apple's logo is fun, playful, and anti-establishment, even though Apple is at times the most valuable company in the world. The key elements that support that brand framework – the ones that matter most – are:

- *The logo and imagery that accompanies your company name.* They will appear on your website, business cards, letterhead, brochures, and other sorts of marketing material. In this early planning stage, it is not necessary to have a finished logo in hand. But you will need one once you start selling. As most entrepreneurs are not graphic artists them-selves, designing a logo is something you should probably outsource to professionals.

- *Product or service names.* There is an art to naming products or services well. And it rarely comes after the first try. It involves intense discussions with your team, friends you trust, and prospective customers. Signify, a leader in connected street lighting, has named its newest generation of connected street lights "BrightSites" and the software connecting them "Interact." The lamppost filled with 5G and sensor technology is no longer just a light – *it is a connected light.*

- *Product or service messaging.* This is often in the form of one to three words placed right under a company name and product or service names. This tells new customers in a concise word burst the key benefits or purposes of the product or service. For Staples, that tagline is "Easy." While there is no magic recipe for product or service brand name messaging, think of the possible taglines that would connect to the target user's signifi-cant functional, emotional, and social needs – and then try different messages with actual target users. *See what resonates most with them.* For example, Patagonia's statement on its website was "Environmental Justice is Social Justice," which connects its green supply chain and nature advocacy programs with precise emotional and societal positioning. "Advocacy" is one of its top-level menu picks on its website. The company sells apparel, but clearly, its mission is to impact the environment and society positively. To support this, another critical company message is "We are in business to save the planet." That is powerful. Patagonia backs up its statements with products and programs.

- *Unique feature naming and messaging.* Think about short, powerful, meaningful word combinations that lend zip to the marketing of a new product or service. Emphasize superior functionality. For example, certain insurance companies in the United States offer a "Safe Driver Insurance Plan" that rewards accident-free drivers with discounts on car insurance premiums.

- *Websites and social media.* Websites are so ubiquitous that we often forget that they are the primary portals for customers to learn about and interact with a company. The website itself is a branding statement, an essential part of the overall brand architecture. It cannot be an afterthought.

- *Community building.* Word-of-mouth grass-roots market development can be accelerated with web influencers and more general community building. Facebook, Instagram, YouTube, Twitter, TikTok, and other social platforms must now be part of a branding strategy. Customer reviews and forums for new products or services build community. Companies now retain *lead influencers* of marketing agencies that provide access to and manage such persons to advocate for a new product or service launch. Again, look for a few great examples in your category of products or services. Learn from them.

- *Events or activities.* These are face to face or virtual events providing opportunities to interact directly with the target user. Often companies launch their products or services at special events, attending themselves or hiring *brand ambassadors.* Farmers' markets, sporting events, and music festivals are examples.

These branding strategies are not new. Many excellent, classic examples remain vital today. Harley-Davidson sponsors events for its riders in countries around the world. For decades, it has been masterful at competitive positioning and branding – combining excellent motorcycle performance with marketing that celebrates the great American lifestyle of open roads and free spirit. The styling of the motorbikes, the bike, and apparel accessories all combine to reinforce the brand strategy. The result is impactful emotional positioning: riding a Harley-Davidson makes the rider *feel free*. It tries to build a *community* of enthusiastic users who become advocates to new prospective customers. Its branding strategy is far from a superficial sales pitch; instead, there is sincerity and belief in the messaging and these messages are strongly supported by its products and programs.Ultimately, a brand experience results not just from what you say, but from what other users say based on the features and functions delivered, and then, their willingness to spread the positive word within their respective communities.

Figure 8.9 is a third branding template to apply to your project in this chapter. It represents the significant elements of a *brand architecture*. At the top is the brand name, sometimes called the brand umbrella. For example, there is FedEx, with subbrands for specific services being FedEx Express, FedEx Ground, FedEx Freight, FedEx Logistics (integrated supply chain

Target user: _____	Brand name	•
	Logo and other marks	• •

	Message(s) following with the brand
	  – Functional positioning
	  – Emotional positioning
	  – Social positioning
		•
		•

	Product or service subbrand names (and Ingredient/Component names)	• • •
	Imagery, colors, other visual cues for website, packaging, displays	• • •
	Community-building strategies, including web and events	• • •

Use follow-on slides where appropriate for visuals, community-building events, etc.

Figure 8.9   The product or service branding strategy template

management), FedEx Office (document preparation and related services), and FedEx Services (a variety of back-office functions handled for clients). The same brand-subbrand naming convention exists in Uber, with UberX, Uber Pool, Uber XL, Uber Black, Uber Green, and Uber Eats. The Uber brand is at the front, followed by meaningful brand name extensions.

Picking names can be difficult. Rarely do you get it right the first time. That's the fun of it, however. Try for obvious choices, and then keep plugging away if names, trademarks, and URLs are already taken. This can be quickly checked by typing the name into a web search engine. You can also check with the U.S. Patent and Trademark Office, www.uspto.gov, or its equivalents in Europe and Asia for specific trademarks. Finally, there are a few pointers for naming new products or services:

- As noted, the company name needs to be available, not "taken" by someone else. Also, investigate URLs. With numerous URL suffixes available (.net, .co, biz, etc.) there are options beyond .com.

- Names for companies, products, and services should be distinctive, but they should also fit the venture's image and mission.

- Product and service names should suggest key benefits, either functional, emotional, or social. Pure Solutions, described in Chapter 7, is an example of a brand that captures a company's core mission. Look at the websites of creative companies in your industry to find examples of the powerful brand names.The name should be easy to pronounce and remember (with the exception, perhaps, of venturing in the life sciences where brand names are based on a conventional structure of word syllables, called *stems*, which convey information about the chemical structure, action, or indication of the drug.)

- And equally important, go that extra mile to try to connect your product and service names to your emotional and societal positioning.

SLATE'S BRANDING STRATEGY

Josh and Manny thought long and hard about their branding strategy. Chocolate milk could be called a hundred different names, but what would be a name that conveyed their creative, new approach? They talked about many names but ultimately decided that they wanted consumers to fundamentally change the way they thought about chocolate milk. All of the excellent taste, nostalgia, and functionality of protein and electrolytes, but none of the negative qualities that were popular in the media. When going through their competitive positioning, they kept finding ways to overcome/eliminate each of these negative qualities, so they were giving chocolate milk a "clean slate." They moved forward with Slate as it was not only a name that they could trademark, but it was short, simple, and easy to pronounce, which they thought represented the product well.

The messaging to support the brand name flowed naturally from the product design, following the three dimensions of competitive positioning explored above (see Figure 8.10). For functional positioning, messaging around taste and health was the first step. Manny and Josh found that consumers still primarily chose their beverages based on taste, so they led with a love for the delicious taste of chocolate milk. Then, the no lactose and much lower sugar content were clear, "hard" design drivers. Next, Manny and Josh wanted to rekindle the fun, youthful passion that they had as kids for chocolate milk (and continued into adulthood) in predisposed adult consumers. Finally, the societal positioning was equally compelling: the milk was sourced from family farms, where the farmers followed strict animal welfare guidelines, and were members of a dairy co-op seeking to support and sustain the tra ditional American farming lifestyle. The water stripped from the milk during ultra-filtration was also used back on the farms to pursue water neutrality. Plus, the founders chose aluminum cans, the preferred choice of environmentally focused drink producers, as an alternative to plastic bottles. Together, these three positioning dimensions combined to create a powerful *brand story*. With some thought and creativity, you can do this, too. In fact, as an entrepreneur, *you must*.

As noted earlier, by 2020, Slate offered three SKUs: classic chocolate, dark chocolate, and espresso (coffee) chocolate, and these flavors were also supported with functional positioning of Dutch chocolate and Colombian origin coffee.

Visuals are essential for any consumer product. For example, Slate chose its colors with variations of brown to connotate chocolate and coffee ingredients. Images of active use were also important, whether it was rich chocolate milk pouring into a glass, or Manny and Josh themselves going crazy over their own chocolate milk. This also shows that the founders believe and are passionate about their own products. Such imagery lends authenticity to a brand story.

These various elements of a brand strategy matter just as much for industrial products. We worked with a large tractor manufacturer connecting equipment with IoT. The visuals that the company chose were not of dry computer screens replete with boring data. Instead, the company chose active machines and people striving for greater worksite productivity. Or, we worked with a large defense contractor developing electronic warfare systems – rather than emphasizing the bits and bytes of EW (which is shorthand for electronic warfare), the company's brand message was "*We protect those who protect us*," showing a passion and com-

Target user: Adult chocolate passionates, Male and female adults	Brand name	• **Slate**
	Logo	slate.
	Message(s) following with the brand — Functional positioning — Emotional positioning — Social positioning	• Chocolate milk's clean slate (functional positioning) • Health and fitnessy stuff (more protein, less sugar, delicious) • We love chocolate milk (emotional positioning) • Milk sourced from family farms in the U.S. under the Animal Welfare Act regulations (societal positioning) • Sustainable cans (societal positioning)
	Product or service subbrand names (and ingredient/component names)	• Classic chocolate milk • Dark chocolate milk • Espresso chocolate milk
	Imagery, colors, other visual cues for website, packaging, displays	• Black and chocolate tone colors • Chocolate milk pouring into a glass • Founders drinking the product, showing their passion for it
	Community-building strategies, including web and events	• Ambassador program (for influencers) • Chocolate milk events (at bars and restaurants)

Figure 8.10   Slate's brand strategy

mitment to help the warfighter. This was emotional positioning even in the most high-tech of businesses. That message resonates with employees as well as their customers. It is both simple and powerful.

Another good industrial example is the leading environmental services firm in North America. The company is called *Clean Harbors*, with a heritage of cleaning oil spills near shore. Today, it has a wide range of services, including safely removing hazardous waste produced from factories and recycling common engine oil into "new" oil for cars and trucks. Yet, the Clean Harbors name sticks and fits across the broader range of services.

Together, as a team, sit down over coffee or beer and have a go at Figure 8.9. A powerful branding strategy will make *you feel good* about the innovation you have created. Be proud of your branding!

SLATE BECOMES AN OPERATIONAL, GROWING BUSINESS

Slate has posted a video on YouTube that reflects the company's startup experience. Look up https://www.youtube.com/watch?v=41tdO5B2Siw or any of Slate's videos.

An important part of Slate's startup was securing early-stage financing. They first received a $10,000 grant from Northeastern University's incubator and used it to help pay for the early formulation of their product. Manny and Josh launched the Kickstarter in February 2019, about a year after the formal startup. That year was filled with learning about the market, designing the product and the packaging, and to develop the supply chain described above. They made a short video, implemented the branding strategy on the website, created social media accounts, and produced sample products. At an official launch party at a venue in Boston (over 400 people showed up to this chocolate milk party), they hit their goal of $10,000 in the first 14 hours of the Kickstarter campaign. Within a few weeks, Manny and Josh had over $52,000 in customer orders! These first orders made the company real.

The next step was to raise more financing, set up their eCommerce website, and sell into stores for distribution. Josh was lucky enough to be randomly paired in a golf tournament with one of Chobani's first sales brokers and founding team member of the frozen Greek yogurt maker Yasso. This broker would eventually become Slate's lead angel investor. With his help, Slate received a commitment from a large retailer in the Southeast of the U.S., Harris Teeter. Josh and Manny also believed that a prime retail account for Slate was Whole Foods. They were able to find their way to a meeting with the head buyer for the New England region of Whole Foods and secured a commitment to launch in his stores as well. From this, Slate proceeded to sell into different regions across the United States in "specialty" channels, which includes retail chains that contain less than 25 locations, boutique grocers, and food retailers. The final step was to fully launch their website and get the products listed on Amazon. Once that was accomplished, the brand was officially made available online and in stores in November 2019.

Even with all this careful planning and execution in terms of financing and early distribution, Slate still had to perform well on the shelf. A great product needs to roll off the shelf in consumers' hands, or else the retailer will stop carrying the product.

Figure 8.11 shows photographs taken by one of the authors in a Whole Foods Market in Cambridge, MA in early 2020. Working with a company in a nearby Starbucks, he hopped over to the Whole Foods next door for a take-out lunch. Near the checkout counter, eye level, standing out on the shelf as good if not better than any other drink product, was Slate. Note the retail price of $2.99 in the figure. The first picture on the left was taken around noontime, and it was great to see such an active, full display in a premium shelf space. The author returned five hours later, curious to see the "spins" of Slate during the afternoon. The picture on the right tells the whole story. From a retailer's perspective, product performance means cans flying off the shelf to the checkout lane. Slate's cans were doing just that!

Figure 8.11   Slate on shelf: before lunch and at the end of the day

The next step for Slate was to achieve product placement in large mainstream national grocery chains (Publix, for example) or mass merchandisers or club stores (Costco and Walmart) – all the while, ramping up supply. These distribution successes are now a reality. Publix is the largest grocery chain in the United States.

Our hopes are high for these two determined, talented young men. By early 2021, they had raised $2.5 million from investors and had achieved shelf space in more than 3000 stores, with a plan to continue to rapidly improve store presence and distribution. Josh and Manny show the commitment and energy that an entrepreneur needs to see things through from initial idea, to functioning product or service, to launching a real company, and then growing sales. Towards that end, you must craft the market positioning, brand, and messaging for your innovation. These can be as powerful as the design of the innovation itself.

A FINAL THOUGHT: CRAFT A BRAND STORY

We believe that every great company has a strong brand, and behind these brands, an exciting story, particularly for startups. In this book, we have seen strong examples: Kevin's story of working his way into a leading university in Europe, then returning to his rural community to combine his skills in engineering with his passion for cleaning up his childhood environment, and then designing the recycled roof tile branded as EcoTiles. That is a powerful story. Or Kate and Jeff's experience as actual triathletes, as believers in nutrition and health, leading to an authentic story for Drink Simple. So is the brand story of Karthik's journey to apply vision AI to help the blind, branding it as Envision. And finally, Manny and Josh – creating a clean slate for the formulation and perception of chocolate milk as a healthy, tasty drink for themselves as well as for you.

In each of these cases, the entrepreneur's personal story lends authenticity to the product or service itself, the brand, and the positioning of the brand in what is typically a crowded marketplace. The story must be true, and as such, believable, engaging, and testifying to the founder's commitment to the enterprise, as well as to helping its users.

Reader exercises

The reader exercises are to apply the three steps in this chapter to your own idea. After completing these three steps, refine the Customer Value Proposition from Chapter 4.

STEP 1: PERFORM A COMPETITIVE ANALYSIS

Gather information regarding your close competitors, dimensionalize the performance of your products or services and theirs, and complete the template shown earlier in Figure 8.3. Again, be specific with the data.

STEP 2: DEVELOP A POSITIONING ALONG FUNCTIONAL, EMOTIONAL, AND SOCIAL DIMENSIONS

Refer back to the text in this chapter and complete the templates shown in Figures 8.6, 8.7, and 8.8 as appropriate for your innovation. Think about this carefully. Back up positioning in the functional domain with specific features and functions in your products – be they food, software, hardware, or some new type of material or chemistry. The same applies to the features and functions of a service. What can you do which is better than that already provided by direct competitors?

Then, see if there is some particular advantage that you might create in developing a disruptive innovation in terms of price–performance. An example might be a healthcare service that is efficient, community-based, and less expensive than sizeable hospital-based medicine due to new, Cloud-based technologies and telemedicine. The unique twist might be to break the tension between two traditionally conflicting design factors, just as Slate did by providing rich chocolate milk that was lactose-free. Doing something like this for your product or service might surprise and delight target users.

STEP 3: DEVELOP A BRANDING STRATEGY AND THE STORY BEHIND IT

Use the template shown in Figure 8.9 as your guide: brand name, logo and trademarks, primary messages along the three dimensions of functional, emotional, and societal positioning, subbrand names (we will look at filling out a product line more fully in the next chapter), and any colorization or imagery that you think helps express the brand. Also, think about the brand story behind the new product or service itself. This might be your own story of innovation and venture discovery.

STEP 4: REFINE THE CUSTOMER VALUE PROPOSITION

There is no better time to improve your Customer Value Proposition, having worked through competitive positioning and branding. Figure 8.12 shows, the Customer Value Proposition template (originally Figure 4.10). Now, please refine the row with "different than current (competitors/products)" based on the work done in this chapter. Also, think about the brand name and the benefits statement one more time. The clearer and sharper these statements, the better. Then, wordsmith the overall concept statement at the bottom. This is the ultimate 10-second elevator pitch that should get the listener to say, "Hmmm ... that's really interesting. Tell me more."

Refine the Customer Value Proposition

ABC *(give it a name)* is a family of (products/services/solutions)		Brand name
That *(solves what problem)*		
For *(which target customers)*		
For *(which target buyers)*		
The needs we expect to solve *(name primary needs)* and benefits we wish to provide *(name major benefits)*.		Sharpen this
And is different than current *(competitors/products)* because of *(why customers will buy it)*		And this ...
Now, put it all together:		*New draft*

Figure 8.12   Refine the Customer Value Proposition

9
Defining the prototype

THE PURPOSE OF THE CHAPTER[1]

Now that you have created a new product or service design with competitive positioning, let us create an even more detailed specification for that design and, hopefully, start some rapid prototyping. It is time to start bringing your idea to life. Then, following the lean design process, once you make your first one or two prototypes, to then reconnect with target users to show them your prototypes. As Eric Ries has said, this is the version of a new product that allows a team to collect the maximum amount of customer feedback and learning with the least amount of effort.[2]

Listen, observe, and ladder responses to learn what features, functions, and exterior styling might make your prototypes even better and more pleasurable for users. Think of this as creating a *minimal viable (and lovable) prototype* that you can use to learn more from users before a minimal viable product (MVP). It is your *alpha* on the way to a *beta*, and then onto your first MVP for the market.

LEARNING OBJECTIVES

After reading this chapter you should be able to:

1. Develop a specific design of your new product or service that identifies the different parts, pieces, or processes needed.
2. Develop a cost model for your design, which will be an essential input for understanding unit profitability later when you take a course on business modeling and comprehensive business planning. You also want to estimate how much it will cost to produce or provide in both small and then more significant volumes.

PROTOTYPING A NEW IDEA

A new product or service prototype is an initial hand-crafted example of what you wish to bring to market later on. The purpose of a prototype is to learn and mitigate risk before investing lots of money to build and sell fully complete products or services. When prototyping, you get direct experiential learning in design and construction. Then, as you show prototypes to target users, you get the opportunity to test both functionality and usability, as well as styling.

Prototypes can range from simple sketches all the way to fully functioning early examples of a new product, system, or service. The idea of a prototype is not to take too long to build it, using the resources at hand or that can be readily accessed. Do not let the perfect get in the way of the good. These are pre-production, pre-deployment examples.

From a previous chapter, you have an overall sketch and an underlying architecture. Now, let's get more detailed. Start drawing or computer drafting the significant parts or subsystems of your new product or service. For each significant part, think about how your drawing matches up against the needs of your target users, whether it is an easy-open lid for an older person or a tamper-proof lid for a child, or a light that is easily turned on or turns itself off automatically after a certain period of nonuse or movement. Or your design might emphasize eye appeal for your target user as opposed to function. For example, in the Honda Element SUV example from Chapter 7, the team deliberately chose large, oversized tires to connotate durability and an active sports character.

The authors once spent an afternoon learning how to design chocolates with "Mr. Chocolate" Jacques Torres, regarded as one of the best pastry chefs in America. For function, Jacques used a vacuum chamber to remove all the air from the chocolate paste, making it smoother in texture and eliminating air bubbles in the molding process. For form and styling, his trick was to create a specific "design language" for his chocolate shapes. "If you mold a rabbit's head, make the ears extra large; or for a molded fish, oversize the lips." In other words, Jacques would take one major part or feature and emphasize that part in size and shape. He knew that this would make what might otherwise be a standard commodity chocolate product a special, emotional experience for the user. Other designers, such as those at Apple or Tesla, seek minimalistic designs and work hard to remove the complexity of the operation of a machine. The internal cabin of Tesla is striking for its lack of switches and controls, and the driver can talk to his or her vehicle for many operations.

Think hard about the design of your prototype. What aspects provide function; what other aspects provide the form. As we learned before, you seek a synergy of form and function, and need both to succeed.

TWO SPECIFIC MVP DESIGN TEMPLATES

Look at Figures 9.1 and 9.2. Use Figure 9.1 to prioritize the functions or features that might be included in an MVP. We like to think of features in terms of "must-haves" and "nice-to-haves" from the user's perspective based on your customer discovery work. Note that at the top of the figure are two summary boxes – the first is a high-level description of the product, software, or service's purpose and functionality. The second box contains a sketch of the outward appearance or GUI of your innovation. You might want to have subsequent pages containing the drawings you create in this and previous chapters for the overall design and its significant parts or subsystems. Moreover, for a service, you need a separate page for your process flow diagram and another page to show the primary GUI for the software that typically goes hand-in-hand with a new service. This might be a wireframe of the GUI – a main user input screen or a dashboard showing analytic results. In summary, create sketches that best communicate your product, service, or software vision and design.

Product name: _____

Detailed Functional Description: What it does and how it works.	Insert Sketch or Drawing (use separate page if needed). For a service and a complementary app, show the process flow and the wireframe of the primary GUI)

Features/Functions

	Feature from the user's perspective	How that functionality is delivered/executed
Must have		
Must have		
Must have		
Nice to have		
Nice to have		
Nice to have		

Figure 9.1   The minimum viable prototype features and functions prioritization template

The concept of prioritizing the must-haves versus the nice-to-haves is very important for entrepreneurs. It is an essential first step before embarking on a more detailed design. Generally, you don't want to focus first on specific features that users do not prioritize. There are exceptions where the user might not fully appreciate the importance of a design or feature, such as a particular design that significantly decreases the cost of production or increases stability or shelf life for the consumer. Or a software programming library that makes it easier for other developers – as opposed to end-users – to build software on top of your own. But typically, the end-user is the driver. Delivering what they genuinely need and want should be your top priority.

In Slate chocolate milk, for example, lactose-free and good taste were must-haves. The aluminum packaging was a nice-to-have that Matt and Josh decided was important for a sustainability story. Karthik used the same reasoning. While he knew that someday he would want to embed the vision AI software into some type of wearable, but to get the software into the hands of users quickly, his first minimal viable prototype and then product was a mobile app running on the Android OS. It was an app for mobile phones to start with, not yet embedded in Google Glasses. Moreover, it focused on the shopping and commuting occasions instead of the myriad of other possible use cases uncovered. Later, Karthik hoped to secure venture finance and move onto the Google Glasses. This is precisely what occurred.

Working with limited resources, get your innovation into the hands of users with a base level of functionality that focuses on their most significant needs and concerns. Then, over time you can consider adding more features – those nice-to-haves specified in the template. Also, once you show an early working prototype to users, your understanding of the must-haves and nice-to-haves continues to improve. Nor does this stop once you release an actual commercial product to the market. Good companies are those where the innovators continue to learn from users to stay ahead of the competition. Importantly, for most new ventures, it is difficult to raise seed or early venture capital (VC) money without having the proof point of people using and testifying to the effectiveness of an MVP.

Once you have established design priorities in this manner, you can then specify specific parts, components, or processes that you think should be used. Figure 9.2 shows a method for this. The parts might be materials or electronics in a physical product, specific software tools, or libraries in a software product, or a combination of software, analytics, and detailed processes in a new service. The template in Figure 9.2 can be as simple or complex as you think appropriate – but as a general rule, try to keep it to a single page, with no more than ten significant components to start. Later on, you can get much more detailed. For each part, you then work across the template with an identifying description, the materials or components in that part, the source of the component (developed by you or purchased), any special processing or handling required, and any particular legal compliance needed for that component.

Figure 9.2 is a general template that can be used across a broad range of products and services. For example, the packaging for a given product might need to be made from particular materials to be recyclable. Or, as an example of chemicals in a therapy might need to be maintained at a specific temperature. Or, food ingredients might require FDA (U.S. Food and Drug Administration) approval as well as special labeling. Or software for healthcare applications might needs to be compliant with privacy standards and common database formats.

Part	Description	Materials, ingredients, or components used	Developed in-house (Y/N)	If supplied, source/supplier	Regulatory factors, if any	Cost per unit for the part, in low volumes (extra credit!)
1						
2						
3						
...						
N						
				Target cost of materials plus labor, per unit		

Figure 9.2   MVP specification

As a final step, the template can then be used to look at the cost of components or materials, or the cost license specific software development tools or gain access to streams of data needed for analysis. For a physical product, the bill of components and its cost comprises of the materials per unit for a new product. Then, you add estimated costs of labor or automated manufacturing to derive a total "cost of goods sold." Prototyping allows you to develop a target total cost estimate of what you think you should achieve based on competitive products or services in your category, as shown at the bottom of Figure 9.2.

The elements in the cost of goods for a food or drink product can be illustrated with Slate chocolate milk. The major ingredients used in the milk include the cost of purchasing and filtering the milk, the chocolate, other nutritional additives, and then importantly, the cost of packaging. There is the cost of these materials and then the cost of production or assembly of the materials into a finished product.

In software, the cost of goods sold is often minimal. There might be Amazon Web Services or some other hosting charges. There might also be the ongoing cost of licensing specific development libraries. Mobile app developers must license Android and iOS updates, and this can cost upwards of $10,000 per year, followed by the cost of licensing programming interfaces into the major social networks for about $5,000 a year. However, since software companies no longer provide printed user manuals and use the Cloud to distribute products, there isn't much else in the way of cost of goods. That is why the gross margin for most software products tends to be greater than 80% of sales.

The cost of materials provides insight into the commercial feasibility of a new idea. Let's say that you wanted to design the world's most robust umbrella that could withstand any wind or rainstorm. Your target consumer is an affluent professional. Your team decides to use a new, ultra-strong carbon fiber composite for the umbrella frame and ribs to achieve the strength requirement for a light umbrella. However, when you take the design to a composite molding supplier, or to a sophisticated 3D printing company that uses advanced carbon fiber materials, you soon find out that a carbon fiber umbrella is going to cost at least $700 to manufacture, which means that it would have to retail for over $1500. Not many customers for a $1500 umbrella, hey?

*** *** ***

Now, let's look at some specific examples. Find the one most relevant for your idea and use it as a model for your work in this chapter.

PROTOTYPE DESIGN SPECIFICATIONS FOR A PHYSICAL ASSEMBLED PRODUCT[3]

Specifying prototypes for physical, assembled products focuses on the functionality needed to deliver against the goals of the product for the user in the use case. If it is a new office chair, one specifies the different elements within the chair architecture against measures and goals for seating comfort, lumbar support, and styling. New exercise equipment must focus on the range of exercises to a body part(s) and ease of use and storage. Or, as another example, one of our former students is well on his way to making a small fortune designing and patenting new fishing lures that catch more fish, with components that include various materials, weighting, hooks, and motion-making attachments!

Let us use a simple example to illustrate this process, thanks to Steve Golden, our friend and valued colleague at Northeastern University. It is a handheld solar-powered flashlight designed for the active outdoorsman needing a waterproof backup lighting device, with multiple methods to build and maintain the charge. Based on conversations with target users –

active outdoor sportspeople – this design also includes a temperature sensor and an adjustable high-powered LED light. The flashlight is light and portable.

Figure 9.3 shows how features are prioritized according to the user's needs and the desire to create a flashlight for active sports users. Look at the must-haves (rugged and durable, a bright light, and solar-powered) and then the nice-to-haves (the temperature sensor, a light that can be dimmed or brightened, and a dynamo as a supplementary form to charge the battery). As the example shows, you don't have to make the prototype specification overly complex. Keep it simple, user-focused, and pragmatic in the sense that you are not trying to build something that will require unproven or undeveloped component technologies.

Next comes the specification of specific components, materials, suppliers, certifications, and in this case of the flashlight, a general total cost of goods target for the finished products (about 25% of what might be its retail price of $36). As you start building prototypes, the pricing and an availability for specific components becomes more detailed. This information is provided in Figure 9.4. Looking at the figure, you can see the prioritization of features before in Figure 9.3 translate into major components for the actual prototype. We could even group the specific parts into higher-level subsystems. For the flashlight, for example, there is a lighting subsystem that includes the bulb and the lens. There is also the power supply, which consists of the battery and the solar film to recharge a lithium-ion battery. Then there is the housing, which includes the plastic and the on-off switch. This design also features environmental sensors for temperature and motion, suiting the outdoor sports person. And we must not forget the retail packaging, which in this case, is a simple corrugated box, preferably made from recycled materials. With this specification in hand, you could then try to buy these components and wire together a functioning prototype – and even a 3D-printed housing for the entire assembly.

Most entrepreneurs build such prototypes themselves, gaining access to a machine shop or a 3D printer. This approach suffices for getting prototypes into the hands of target users for feedback and refinement. Even as early prototyping proceeds, the entrepreneur must begin to consider what it will take to produce the prototype in volume. Contract manufacturers – other companies that can assemble products for you – can reduce the need for significant upfront capital outlays that would be needed if you were to try to build an assembly operation yourself. If you select correctly, they will also have substantial prior experience making products such as yours with high quality and reliability. They can help you improve your designs.

PROTOTYPE DESIGN SPECIFICATIONS FOR A NEW FOOD OR DRINK PRODUCT[4]

Many students will develop innovative ideas for healthier, tastier foods and drinks. Note that health and taste must now go hand-in-hand, wherein prior decades, one was usually achieved at the sacrifice of the other (due to sugar and other artificial ingredients and preservatives). Drink Maple and Slate described in earlier chapters are examples of this dual demand.

Consumer products that are food and drinks are more complex than one might initially think. There are two major subsystems to consider, the food or drink itself and the packaging.

Project Name: Solar Flashlight

Detailed Functional Description

The Solar flashlight is designed for the active outdoor sportspeople needing a waterproof back-up lighting device that includes multiple methods of maintaining a charge and that acts as a utility device. This new design includes a temperature sensor module, a high powered laser lens that is adjustable and is light and portable.

Sketch or Drawing

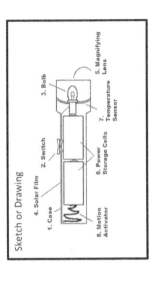

	Feature from the user's perspective	How that functionality is delivered/executed
Must have	Rugged	Worry-free casing/housing
Must have	Bright Light	Spotlight for bulb
Must have	Solar Power	Back-up solar cell, charging battery pack
Nice to have	Temp Sensor	Outside Temp Sensor
Nice to have	Adjustable Light	Flashing beacon switch
Nice to have	Motion Power	Kinetic dynamo—shake battery regenerator

Source: Used with permission of Steve Golden.

Figure 9.3   Features and functions prioritized for a solar-powered flashlight

Part	Description	Materials, ingredients, or components used	Developed in-house	If supplied, source/supplier	Legal compliance type (if any)	Cost per unit for the part, in low volumes. (extra credit!)
1	Case	High-grade PVC		Plastics supplier		
2	On-off switch	Copper		Cuverro	UL	
3	Bulb	Bulb (bright white)		Rexel	UPC	
4	Lens	Glass		Optiusa	CA AB341	
5	Solar	Solar film		Anderson	CASL	
6	Battery	Lithium-ion batteries		Targray	EEC	
7	Temperature	Temperature sensor		Texas Inst	TM	
8	Motion sensor	Motion sensor		Texas Inst	FCC	
9	Package	Corrugated box		Packaging supplier		
10	User manual	Electronic PDF	Yes			
				Target cost of materials with assembly		$12.00

Source: Used with permission of Steve Golden.

Figure 9.4   MVP specification for a solar-powered flashlight

The recipe for a food or drink typically has multiple ingredients and different functionality for those ingredients. The functionality to be defined includes:

- Nutrition: This often involves government or federal regulations and requirements. The specification needs to consider the health profile of the product (by type, such as the use of wholegrains, and by the sourcing and processing of the ingredients, such as organic). The formulation must also consider unhealthful ingredients (including sugars and other color additives or preservatives). Halo Top ice cream is an inspirational venture with a sugar substitute – erythritol – as its "hero" ingredient. As part of the nutrition profile, a food innovator must also be concerned with potential allergens affecting the general population – for example, nuts in energy bars.

- Taste and smell: This covers a broad spectrum, from sweet to savory, to spicy and less so, and for some products, flavors unique to different parts of the world. We often forget that despite the desire for increased health and wellness, consumers still seek good-tasting food. Innovation can occur in minimal processing or some more artful, flavor-enhancing process. Single-origin, organic coffee products can be one source of inspiration; baking products with tunable or adjustable frostings (more or less butter, for example), yet another.

- Texture: Some new foods have a truly crunchy texture, and other new foods, an extra-smooth, creamy texture. For drinks, Chong Cha tea with its tapioca bubbles illustrates differentiating a food/drink product with texture.

- Appearance: This is another sensory characteristic of a food or drink product, be it the toppings on a frozen pizza or the finishing touches of a cocktail. Increasingly, food innovators are making visible the ingredients in their foods to connote freshness – such as grains in bars, fruit in snacks, and inclusions in packaged sauces.

Designing new foods must take into account not only nutrition but the other human senses: you first see it, then you smell it, then you taste it, and perhaps there's an after-effect from the spice, the sour, or the fizz.

Moreover, unless the new food is "raw" and picked from the vine, nearly all food and drink products require some type of processing. That processing can diminish the healthfulness of the final result. Minimally processed is now part of the common lexicon, but there are interesting examples where certain types of processing can improve food-health outcomes. Slate is one such example, where ultra-filtration removes the natural sugars in milk, e.g. lactose. Mars, Inc. has developed a method for low-temperature processing in chocolate refining that produces clinically proven, heart-healthy results with certain types of cocoa. In contrast, even minimally processed foods such as fish can contain harmful levels of metals and other toxins discarded into the sea, such as the mercury found in tuna and swordfish.

Therefore, new food and drink design is complex. And it does not stop with the food or drink itself. Packaging is all-important. Here, too, some dimensions must be specified:

- Preservation period or shelf life.

- The labeling, such as a required nutrition label, and other claims.

- The branding, such as the brand name on the package and other artwork or imagery for emotional connection.

As noted in the prior chapters, many entrepreneurs do not concern themselves with the packaging for their prototypes until too far down the development process. You should start thinking about it relatively early. Packaging and ingredients have a symbiotic relationship. Try to find both food ingredient and packaging suppliers in your local area – these persons will have a wealth of information and expertise that can enable your concept development.

Let's look at an example of applying our two prototyping templates to a food product – a new artisanal chocolate chip cookie. Take a look at Figures 9.5 and 9.6, respectively. This example was contributed by friend and former colleague at Mars, Inc. for many years, Neil Willcocks.

You can see the description of our new chocolate chip cookie: a golden-baked exterior appearance, clearly visible chocolate chips, a moist and tasteful baked dough, and a minimalist ingredient deck that appeals to health-focused consumers who still want a tasty treat. We might even call it something like the Simply Good with a story around the origin of the cocoa used for the chip.

Figure 9.6 provides the recipe for the cookie and the materials for the packaging. We show this as a percentage of the total recipe. We would also want to do some additional digging to determine the cost of both the recipe ingredients in low-volume production and then higher-volume production. Fortunately, there are various baking cost calculators available for free on the web to get a per unit and 12-pack cost for a recipe. We would also want to speak with an experienced baker about the volume amounts of each ingredient per cookie. Given that gourmet chocolate chip cookies now sell for upwards of $3.00 per cookie, our goal might be to create a baked cookie, with all packaging, for 75 cents per cookie, so we can sell it to retailers for $1.50 per cookie, giving them the margin to price at a premium level. And of course, it needs to be a special-tasting cookie with quality ingredients, packaging, and messaging.

Project name: Chocolate chip cookie

Detailed Functional Description

The Cocoa Cookie provides a crunchy, tasty, buttery experience with large pieces of dark chocolate chips. Rugged in design for shipping. Sized to be part of a portioned controlled diet, yet indulgent in taste so as to be a real treat.

Sketch or Drawing

	Feature from the user's perspective	How that functionality is delivered/executed
Must have	Rich, buttery flavor with crunch.	Recipe contains butter. Baking process tuned to create the crunch effect.
Must have	Dark chocolate chips that are clearly visible.	Dark chocolate cocoa chips, more than 25% of recipe by weight.
Must have	A clean, undamaged appearance.	Packaging design for singles and multi-pack has robustness.
Nice to have	Healthy profile.	Minimal ingredients. Cocoa chip origin story.
Nice to have	Sustainable profile.	In baking and chip recipes, and packaging materials.
Nice to have	Less than 80g calories per cookie.	Cookie portion size.

Source: Cookie image sourced from https://www.deviantart.com/gnomesandcookies/art/Chocolate-chip-cookies-2-332701559.

Figure 9.5   Features and functions prioritized for a chocolate chip cookie

Part	Description	% Recipe	Ingredients Cost per Cookie
1	Flour	28	
2	Granulated sugar	14	
3	Brown sugar	8	
4	Dark chocolate chips	25	
5	Palm shortening oil	12.6	
6	Whole eggs	5	
7	Salt	.5	
8	Sodium biocarbonate	1	
9	Vanilla flavoring	.4	
10	Water	5.5	
	Target cost of ingredients	100%	.50
	Labor		.20

Part	Description	Packaging Cost per Cookie
1	PET formed tray for 12 cookies	.03
2	Heat sealed polypropylene wrap around the PET tray	.01
3	Cardboard carton for outer package, printed with Cocoa Cookie name and origin story	.01
		.05

Target cost target of materials and assembly	$.75

Source: Used with permission of Neil Willcocks.

Figure 9.6   MVP specification for a chocolate chip cookie

PROTOTYPE DESIGN SPECIFICATIONS FOR A SOFTWARE SYSTEM OR APP[5]

Software has the blessing of being much easier to prototype than physical products – and the curse of being more complex as it proceeds from prototype to commercial product. That complexity is driven by cascading features and functions as one digs deeper and deeper into a specific use case. Fortunately, software consumers expect frequent new versions. You don't have to get everything done upfront. If you try to do this, it will get in the way of rapid prototype development and delay getting feedback from users.

Software has externalities that the designer needs to consider but not necessarily try to build into the initial prototype. This complexity can be saved for the commercial release for the software later on. For example, your software might have to integrate with a half dozen other applications or databases to be truly functional. Or, if your target customer is a large company that has multi-tier security protocols, these must be included in your application for it to be useful. Or, your customers might be global, as in the Envision example, and you will need to support multiple languages. Fortunately, there are now easy-to-integrate language tools, just as there are libraries that provide enhanced security and database access to address all these external concerns. This makes conversion from prototype to actual first product less costly and quick than ever before.

For a software prototype, we think about three major components:

1. The underlying workflow or business process, and the primary outputs that the system must produce. This can be called the logical specification for a piece of software. Within this logical specification, you can identify the must-have features versus the nice-to-have features, either on a separate template sheet such as in Figure 9.2 or directly on the process workflow diagram itself.

2. The GUI, which is how the user interacts with the system – which is the look and feel, as well as the basic functionality behind each screen or menu action.

3. The underlying or external database to which the software must connect, including its data structures (its tables and the way the tables can be combined in database queries).

To summarize, to prototype software, we first create a logical specification of what the software does and what it produces (with some prioritization of critical functions and features), next its GUI, and then its database structures. Do not spend too much time trying to make any of these three sub-specifications "perfect" – all will rapidly improve once you bring the prototype to life. Software development, more than any other type of product development, is highly iterative. If you have done the user discovery work in earlier chapters, the prototype designs for the software should come relatively quickly.

To illustrate this process for software, we will consider a mobile app that allows the visitors to a museum to search for the art they wish to see, to get assistance locating that artwork once in the museum, and to submit their reviews and social experiences. This museum art finder app is one that many large museums have tried to develop and field – but it remains a clear opportunity for the aspiring art-loving student entrepreneur. While the app logic itself is relatively straightforward, gathering and indexing all the artwork either on display or in storage makes the actual fielding of such an app gnarly. The museum itself has to be digitally organized.

Let's take a look at four successive diagrams illustrating the software app prototyping process, contributed by another friend and cherished colleague at Northeastern University, Greg Collier. Figure 9.7 shows the logical workflow of the app, following the template in our design chapter for services innovation (Chapter 7). This is the desired, improved process enabled by the app. On the lower left side of Figure 9.7 are the must-haves and nice-to-haves for this application. You could do this on a separate page using Figure 9.1 as your guide – but you can also list these directly on the workflow figure. For complex applications, you can use colors or shading to differentiate between short-term versus longer-term development objectives.

With the logical workflow specified, we then turn to prototyping the GUI. Grab a free mobile app wireframing tool and begin building the top three or four screens. These tools do not require much expertise to create a basic prototype. If you are not a programmer and do not feel comfortable using a software tool, first hand-draw the GUI. Look at Figures 9.8 and 9.9. The first figure is the hand sketch; the second, the representative, not yet fully functioning GUI. This might include the user login or registration, the major search or query function, and the output or report desired from the app. Many applications – mobile or otherwise – now feature a summary type of dashboard for the user tuned specifically for the use case and the data processing done for it. If this applies to your idea, please sketch the primary dashboard

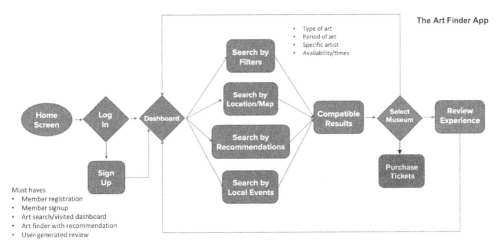

The Art Finder App

- Type of art
- Period of art
- Specific artist
- Availability/times

Must haves
- Member registration
- Member signup
- Art search/visited dashboard
- Art finder with recommendation
- User-generated review

Nice-to-haves
- eTicket purchase with member discounts
- Social network visit sharing

Source: Used with permission of Greg Collier.

Figure 9.7   A process flow chart for the museum navigation app with feature prioritization

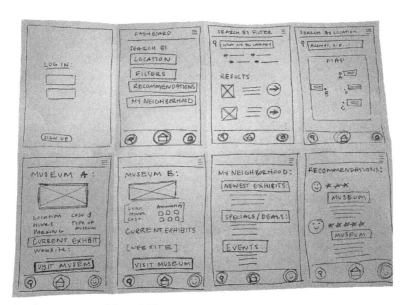

Source: Used with permission of Greg Collier.

Figure 9.8   A hand-sketched wifeframe

The Art Finder App

 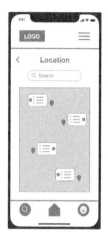  

Figure 9.9   A prototype wireframe developed with a free software tool

you would like your users to see. Then, with these hand-drawn references in hand, grab one of those free wireframing tools to bring the GUI to visible form. Don't try to make functionality behind the GUI just yet. For now, a "see how it looks and how it feels" is sufficient to show target users. We don't need "how it works" just yet.

You next need to define the underlying data required to drive the app. More specifically, you need to think about the specific data tables, the data structures or definitions for those tables, and that the APIs (application programming interfaces) to external databases often required to stream certain data elements into your app. For example, a consumer tech app will typically need to access an external financial database such as Equifax, Experian, or Plaid. Medical mobile apps will also often need to check specific external databases. Or, for the museum art finder application, the system needs to access navigation databases and ticket booking/credit card processing systems. In most cases, data must first be sent to external databases or services for correct information to be received. Moreover, these external data feeds often cost money at a price per click or a monthly or annual subscription. Many mobile apps now access major social networks, such as Facebook or Instagram, or LinkedIn through those companies' APIs.

These API's are often not free and comprise part of the "cost of goods" for a mobile app, just like the solar flashlight team must find the cost to purchase solar films and lithium ion batteries.

Figure 9.10 shows a data design for the museum app. On the left are the internal database – which can be stored in the Cloud and accessed by the app. On the right is a high-level specification of the external databases needed. If you are building an app, you will want to get quite detailed about the internal database structure as well as these external data feeds.

The Art Finder App

Visitor
Last name
First name
Member
Email
Etc.

Review
Review last name
Review first name
Review museum ID
Review date
Review rating
Review user comments
Review museum comments
Social pictures

Review
Museum ID
Museum name
Museum address
Museum URL
Museum hours
Museum reservation URL
Museum amenities
Museum special services
Museum facility photos URL

Art
Art artist
Art collection type
Art birthdate
Art status
Art location
Art owner
Provenance URL

APIs (Data feeds)

- For location-based services, Google Maps location, places, and other required
- Museum APIs for tickets purchasing
- Cost of any external data feeds, either per access or annual subscription

Figure 9.10   Data tables and data relationships, including APIs

DESIGN SPECIFICATION FOR A NEW SERVICE

Prototype design for a new service is the same as that for the mobile software app, with two additional items for the specification. For a new service prototype, like software, you must specify the logical workflow and prioritize those processes to be improved or delivered. And since most services are not self-managing, you need to specify the software-enabled process required to manage activity. That software-enabled process will require a GUI and underlying data structures, just as in the example above. In addition, there are two more elements needed for fully specifying a service prototype: metrics for process management and the actual types of people (if required) to provide the service.

Metrics: Services are processes where metrics are required to understand the operation in terms of quality, the cycle time for service delivery, and the cost of providing the service. *Quality, speed,* and *cost.* We also need to think about the source of the data or any outcome measures.

For example, a new type of educational service will want to understand how well students learn, how quickly they learn, and the teaching and technology costs incurred in training. A remote at-home car washing service will want to make sure its technicians do an excellent job on different parts of the vehicle, and do so in an optimized manner to generate an operating profit for each vehicle serviced. We have seen the same logic applied to new food services, environmental clean-up and remediation, and even life sciences services for drug testing and development. The trick is to define quality metrics in a way that genuinely measure the new

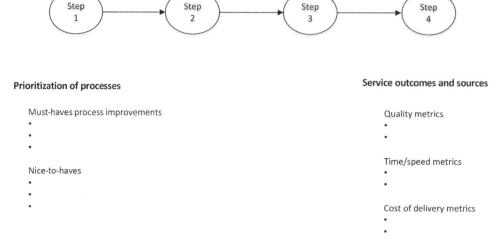

Figure 9.11   A generic process flow diagram with feature prioritization and outcome measures

service. Sometimes these are subjective, such as a user or customer rating – but far better are objective, empirical measures of quality, be they defects, returns, or the number and types of complaints. A hospital in the United States, for example, is now responsible for patients who have to return to the hospital for corrective surgery or infection remediation within thirty days. This measure is called "bounce backs" – and can be very costly for the hospital. Nearly all healthcare services now measure bounce backs from hospital surgeries.

Once you have considered your metrics, write them down on the right side of the process flow map as shown in Figure 9.11, using the simple categories of *quality*, *time*, and *cost*. Or, simply reuse the process flow diagram in Figure 9.7, adding the outcome measures on the right side of it.

People: In addition to workflow design and metrics, a service innovation must typically consider the people needed to deliver the service. Different kinds of people might be required for different parts of the service. As a simple example, the same car mechanic can diagnose and repair a car for different mechanical and electrical problems when equipped with computerized diagnostic tools and sensors. However, the typical solar panel installation service needs different types of staff: first, the salesperson, who also designs the specific installation; next, the roofer, because it is not uncommon that older roofs need first to be replaced to handle a solar panel installation; and then third, the solar panel installation and test technician. These are three different kinds of people, and not always from the same company.

Developing a service is one matter; scaling it another. At the prototyping stage, we are most concerned with a "unit of one" service. This is the who and what needs to be done to please a single customer. However, the reality of scaling a service in volume typically means specialization of people and equipping them with good physical and computer-related tools to make their work efficient and effective. That is why in the template in Figure 9.12 we show

Role	Primary responsibilities	Qualifications	Cost per person, per year	Supporting hardware & software tools

Figure 9.12 The people and supporting tools needed for service delivery

not just the people roles required for the service, but the tools and information services they need for service delivery. Imagine how that simple template might apply to the excellent car mechanic and then to the solar installation service described above. If your innovation concept has a service element to it, this is an important template to apply.

DEFINING THE LEVEL OF THE PROTOTYPE YOU SHOULD BUILD FOR THIS CLASS

Prototyping new products and services is often seen as a matter of degree. A fancier term for this is the "fidelity" of the prototype, much like the word fidelity refers to the clarity and quality of the sound from a speaker system.

Designers often think of the degree of fidelity of a prototype as progressing from (a) "looks like," to (b) "looks like and feels like," to (c) "looks like, feels like, and works like." These terms were developed for physical products such as the flashlight or cookie examples in this chapter, but you can easily stretch them to apply to software products and services.

At one end of the fidelity spectrum – "looks like" – are the sketches you did for your idea in Chapter 7: Product and Service Design. These sketches fleshed out your ideas – to help shape and crystalize the ideas for further refinement through user and competitive research. We can consider these low fidelity designs – aspirational as opposed to highly detailed prototypes. None of the specifics are yet worked out.

At the other end of the spectrum is a highly refined prototype that is good enough for a pilot test with actual prospective customers. Such products are well designed and substantially engineered across many dimensions: the major functions and features, as well as the styling or form. These are functional, working prototypes, whether for the electro-mechanical flashlight, that cookie, or the software app. The difference between the high-fidelity prototype and the actual MVP is the final work needed to solidify the manufacturing cost, long-term quality, serviceability, repair, and support of the product or service. Still, a "looks like, feels like, and works like" prototype is a high-fidelity execution of your new product or service idea. *It has real functionality.*

Your prototyping for this course falls somewhere in the middle of this spectrum – a medium-fidelity prototype. It is a "looks like, feels like" prototype. You already have your sketches and drawings. Now, you need to bring it to concrete shape or form. It might have a bit of functionality as well.

For a physically assembled product, you should have the exterior styling, a mockup of the packaging, and even brand names and messaging. You should also gather and assemble by hand representative components for the major parts. In the flashlight case, this might be rechargeable batteries, the switch mechanism, and the lens. 3D printers can be used to make housings. Be creative. You can scrounge around for parts from other products readily available in stores. In some cases, separate prototypes are created for specific subsystems.

For food and drink, you can design that drink bottle for food products and even try some flavoring of the liquid to meet the desired palette. It would be best if you had the recipe and made a range of different samples. The packaging should contain the ingredients as if they were being sold on the shelf. Later, the more complete functional prototype includes final dialing in on the ingredients and packaging for taste, food safety, and shelf life. This last step is a lot of work and may require help from a local food incubator. You can rent time in such facilities for not much money to gain access to the nutrition and food safety personnel, as well as packaging experts. Plus, you can learn how to better source and prepare ingredients within a recipe. Again, you don't need great this high-fidelity prototype for this class – it comes afterwards should you decide to start a real venture with this class project. We hope you do!

For software, the "looks like and feels like" prototype is a set of wireframes with some limited functionality of what might happen when certain menu choices are selected. You should have your back-end databases and processing logic relatively well-defined but not operationally implemented. The "works like" prototype is also later, including a functioning GUI, databases, logic, and basic user security running up the Cloud.

For a service innovation, the medium-fidelity prototype might also have a bit of functionality. The "looks-like" is simply a detailed process flow diagram; the "feels like" a walkthrough of the user experience in the service, showing the transformation that occurs during the service process. Having an initial set of metrics for time, cost, and quality in delivering the service should also be defined. Plus, a medium-fidelity prototype of the user software needed in the service. Your team can take the extra step to test the service with another ten target users to get the feedback needed to fine-tune and improve it. To create a high-fidelity prototype of a service, the user and process management software will have to be more fully developed.

Of course, your ability to produce a medium-fidelity prototype might be limited by the prototyping facilities and resources at your disposal. Here's the challenge: what can you do quickly in two weeks, and then, within two weeks later? Stage things out in a manner that fits within the time remaining in this course. Then, later, you can make your innovation the basis of an actual company. Think in terms of short development sprints.

The type of product, systems, or service impacts the fidelity that can be achieved in these short development sprints. For assembled products such as the flashlight, your university should have CAD (computer-aided design) software and 3D printers for use. If not, there are relatively inexpensive 3D printing service bureaus that can produce models within a day or two. For food, for modest money, you can buy most raw ingredients, take them to your kitchen, and be a prototyping chef. However, take extra precautions to avoid any process that might lead to food safety issues. This would include hot-filling packages with liquids or crushed fruits with bacteria contamination risk. Do not leave samples on the kitchen table overnight before bringing them into class to show and taste with other students. Put samples in the refrigerator! Cleary, one way to not get an A is to get everyone sick!

Keep things simple – aim for the shape, or taste, or texture that you wish to achieve. Develop the packaging with a hand-drawn or printed brand name, messaging, electronics, or ingredient information. Those of you working on software and services have the fewest barriers. There are many excellent wireframing, database, and reporting tools available either for free or at marginal cost.

Well … perhaps it is time to stop reading and just get to work! Good luck, and most of all, have fun with your teammates.

Reader exercises

STEP 1: DEVELOP THE MUST-HAVES AND NICE-TO-HAVES LIST FOR YOUR IDEA

Use Figure 9.1 for a physical product, Figure 9.7 for software, and Figure 9.11 for a service. Develop a list of must-haves and nice-to-haves. Remember, the nice-to-haves can become part of a future roadmap for product or service development. There is no need to try to do everything all at once in a prototype for the first commercial release of a product or service. However, it is important to try to address at least one clear latent need or frustration and solve that need cleverly and well. This will set your design apart from others already in the market.

STEP 2: DEVELOP THE MINIMAL VIABLE PROTOTYPE SPECIFICATION

For a physical product, proceed to Figure 9.2. For software, use Figures 9.8, 9.9, and 9.10 as templates. For services, use get even more specific about the process steps in Figure 9.11 and specify the people and metrics with Figure 9.12. If the service also employs software, you must specify it, too.

STEP 3: CREATE HAND SKETCHES OR SOFTWARE-BASED MODELS, AND THEN BRING THE PROTOTYPES TO LIFE

Bring your ideas to life either first as a sketch or computer model and then as an actual prototype with limited "looks like, feels like" functionality. In some cases, computer models can rather quickly be converted into 3D printed parts for a physically assembled product or a wireframe for an app.

If you are working on a new food product, it's a trip to the grocery or specialty grain and spice supply stores and then back to your kitchen for experimentation. If you do this, PLEASE be careful with liquors or any material that is in the slightest way flammable. And watch your fingers! Perhaps most important, make small samples of your desired product to dial in on the taste and texture. And if you intend to share these samples in class or with consumers to gain further insight, once again, MAKE SURE to store things safely in the refrigerator overnight. Making anyone ill during the sampling process will land you and perhaps your teacher in hot water. Beyond taste, texture, and appearance, food safety and shelf life are the most significant challenges in food or drink innovation – and to get these correct, you need access to an experienced chef or food biologist on campus or a local food incubator. Before widespread sampling, you need a professional to review your recipe and formulation process. This is not a step to skip. Chefs at your University will probably be delighted to help during their break time after lunch.

For both assembled product and food teams, hand sketch or computer draw the packaging you think might suit your product. Not all products need packaging – for example, a new type of bicycle or scooter – but if a product is going to sit on a shelf in a retail store or be shown on the web, it will need it. That packaging is an integral part of brand communication.

How do you prototype a new service? Most teams simply try to perform the service themselves for a limited number of trial users. For example, for student-focused services, such as apartment or roommate finding or furniture storage – we have seen teams try to provide this service to other students in a manual way to learn what matters or not. Other teams have developed new learning methodologies in areas such as art and music, and have found new students to test teach with their innovative methods. To innovate a new service, you must try to provide the new service in a series of test runs. Given the time constraints of this course, a preliminary first pass or two should suffice. And you do not have to do a test run of the entire service. For example, if the service idea is a new type of highly automated self-service restaurant, you can design the points of automation with our various templates, but for an actual prototype, perhaps test the types of meals to be prepared with the robots but prototype them first by hand. A semester is not sufficient to prototype an entirely automated food assembly line!

STEP 4: DEVELOP A SIMPLE COST MODEL FOR YOUR PROTOTYPES

This step is to develop a ballpark estimate for the cost of materials for your prototype design *in a unit of one* – for example, a single flashlight, or snack food, or a single delivery and use of a mobile app, or the cost of materials and labor for delivering a single unit or execution of a new service. We call this a "unit of one" cost model for your new product or service idea. Use Figure 9.2 as your guide for products; Figures 9.7 and 9.10 for software that needs to access/subscribe external programming libraries and external data feeds; and Figure 9.12 for services requiring using labor other than yourself to fulfill. Your teacher may consider such a cost model an optional extra credit assignment. However, if you have any plans to make your innovation the basis of a real venture, it is best to gather data from suppliers and create an initial estimate, or at least set overall cost objectives based on anticipated retail or other form of customer price.

STEP 5: DEVELOP PROTOTYPES, SHOW THEM TO USERS, AND LISTEN

This step should make the entire journey worth the ride. You've created a new product or service grounded in your personal passions, with a multi-talented team of classmates, gone deep with users to learn their greatest needs and fears – and now, based on your ingenuity and hard work, you have the opportunity to see users' reactions and, hopefully, that smile on their face as your innovation solves their specific problems. Push yourself here. Aim for another ten target users for the show and tell, but be satisfied with at least six.

If you get an adverse reaction at first – well, join the club and go back into the studio and make the prototype better, more functional, and more appealing.

At some point, target users will say "YES!" – and when that happens, you should feel a warm, glowing shine not just in your head but in your heart. All of your teachers, your authors included, wish this moment of deep satisfaction for each of you. When based on customer discovery and clever design, a solid prototype that pleases users is an accomplishment that you will remember for many years to come.

NOTES

1. This chapter has examples contributed by our colleagues, Steve Golden, Neil Willcocks, and Greg Collier. Thank you, gentlemen! And thanks in particular to Steve, whose articulation of the fidelity of a prototype is imbued throughout this chapter.

2. Ries, E. (2011). The lean startup. *New York: Crown Business,* 27, 2016–2020.

3. Steve Golden provided this flashlight example.

4. Neil Willcocks provided this cookie example.

5. Greg Collier provided this mobile app example.

10

Understand the broader market opportunity and industry ecosystem

THE PURPOSE OF THE CHAPTER

You have achieved much up to this point. You have developed a new product or service idea based on profound user insight – as well as your passion for a particular field of work or societal concern. You have also started digging into the design for a prototype of that idea. You are hopefully working on bringing it to life to show target users. This prototyping will take some time, particularly since you should iterate with target users to improve your prototypes. As this prototyping work proceeds, we now want you to work in parallel to understand the larger market opportunity and the industrial ecosystem surrounding your innovation idea.

Understanding the market opportunity for an innovation is crucial if you decide to create a new venture. Most entrepreneurs think of this market opportunity as the "total addressable market", or TAM. This is the amount of actual money spent each year by all the consumers or buyers in your target market in your product or service category. With some searches on the web and carefully considered assumptions, you will be able to create a TAM for your project. However, as we will see, you need to focus the TAM at a level more detailed than the broader market. This is called the "serviceable addressable market" (SAM). And then, one step further, called the "serviceable obtainable market" (SOM), which is the portion of a specific market segment that you intend to reach in your customer focus in the first five to seven years of your business.

In addition to market sizing, you must also gain insight into the other major players in your target market. This is the "industrial ecosystem," which includes the major suppliers, resellers, investors, as well complementary innovators in your product or service category. Having developed specifications for a prototype in the previous chapter, you should already know a few major suppliers of components, raw materials, or the software tools you need. In this chapter, we learn about a few other major actors in your ecosystem and then put everything together into a single, powerful template.

TAM, SAM, SOM: SIZING YOUR MARKET NICHE

Look at Figure 10.1, which provides the basic terms for market sizing.

- TAM: the total addressable market. This is the annual spending of all the customers for a broad category of products or services. It refers to the entire market, today and in the five to seven years ahead. TAM is the *entire global market* for a product or service. TAM is the customer (buyer) spending in the entire market. For example, if we were innovators in the plant-based food business, TAM would be the total global market for plant-based foods. It is already large and growing rapidly!

- SAM: the serviceable addressable market. This is the annual spending of those customers for your specific category of products or services. To continue the plant-based foods example, our SAM might be the Italian-style frozen poultry-look-alike part of the larger plant-based foods market. SAM is the target *market segment*.

- SOM: the serviceable obtainable market. This is the annual spending of those customers who fall directly within your target use cases, distribution channels, and geographical reach by the end of that same five- to seven-year time window. Since most ventures start as specific *niche* players, the SOM represents your target market niche. The SOM for the frozen Italian-seasoned chicken plant-based substitute market might the U.S. Again, the customer spending estimation goes beyond startup – five to seven years out in that selected market niche.

To illustrate the use of these terms for sizing a market opportunity for an innovation, let's use a fun example of two pet food innovators, Rob and Deb. They started Polkadog Bakery in the South End in Boston about twenty years ago. Rob and Deb are shown in Figure 10.2. At that time, rent was inexpensive, and the South End was seen as an "adventurous" place to live. Today, the South End has become perhaps the most expensive real estate in Boston.

They started baking treats for their dog, Pearl, who they found as a stray animal while vacationing in San Juan, Puerto Rico. They took Pearl back home to Boston. Pearl had just one eye and had the habit of appearing to polka dance from side to side because of her single eye when saying hello to new people or pets. When Rob and Deb decided to start a pet food business, Polkadog Bakery's name was personally meaningful.

Template: TAM, SAM, SOM

Step 1	Current annual spend in the entire market	TAM
Step 2	Expected growth rate in that spend	TAM
Step 3	The segment of the market for your category of products or services.	SAM
Step 4	The niche within that market segment represented by your target users and use cases	SOM
Step 5	Geographical constraints in your business strategy.	SOM

TAM: annual spending of all customers in the entire market, considered your "industry," today and what is expected in 5–7 years. *The total market.*

SAM: annual spending for your category or products or services in your industry, today and expected within 5–7 years. *The target market segment.*

SOM: annual spending of those customers representing your specific set of use cases, geographical distribution focus, once again today and expected in 5-7 years. *Your target market niche.*

Figure 10.1   TAM, SAM, and SOM

While carrying premium main meals and treats from other suppliers, Rob and Linda also began designing their own unique dog snacks, baked fresh right behind the counter. Their snacks often looked like people's snacks, such as cookies or mini-cakes, but made with healthy ingredients for dogs. The retail store itself was a destination point for dog owners, with every sized animal bone that one could imagine. It was and remains a fun place to shop.

Young professionals began flooding into the South End, some with kids and many with dogs and cats. Rob and Deb expanded their baking operation to produce all-natural chicken and beef chips and strips, shipping them through wholesalers to small specialty pet stores and Whole Foods Markets across the U.S.

Source: Rob Van Sickle. Reproduced with permission.

Figure 10.2   Rob and Deb, founders and owners of Polkadog Bakery

They also expanded their retail footprint, to six stores in and around Boston. Their signature snacks also achieved international distribution, such as in South Korea.

Several years ago, Rob and Deb developed a new snack based on extensive pet owner interviewing in their stores, plus their intuitive insight into the pet snack category. It is a fascinating food innovation, integrating a New England natural by-product from the sea – the skin of the codfish removed as the filet is prepared for the market – with a sustainable fishery supply

Source: Rob Van Sickle. Reproduced with permission.

Figure 10.3 Cod Skins from Polkadog Bakery

chain. The new product was called Cod Skins, made from otherwise discarded fish skins from fish production operations. Figure 10.3 shows the snack itself as it comes out of the oven and its two forms of packaging – in a tube and in a bag. The Customer Value Proposition for Cod Skins is a fine example of building a total experience as well as a product:

> Cod Skins are a fish jerky for your dogs and cats. Healthy and nutritious, Cod Skins are made from wild-caught cod in season by fishermen on small boats in Alaska. We hand-roll and slowly dehydrate each skin in our Boston kitchen to create these crunchy, savory, healthy cod skin treats. *Pets love them. And they are made for people who love their pets!*

Let's say we are hired as consultants to help Rob and Deb expand their pet snack business, focusing on the market opportunity surrounding Cod Skins. The market opportunity emerges quickly with some web searches. Let's build the story of that market opportunity together.

First, the current total size of the pet food and snacks market is over $100 billion, growing at about 4% a year. This is the TAM for pet food and snacks. We find with further web research that in 2020, over 71 million households in the U.S. owned a pet, comprising more than half of all households. A rather remarkable number. It comes from publicly available studies, which we find in about 2 seconds on our first web search.[1]

Next, of this total market, according to further readily available market studies, more than 20% is spent on pet snacks, or $21.5 billion in 2020. For Rob and Deb, this is the SAM, that is, the specific market segment for pet snacks versus all pet food. Even though it is only 20% of the total spending, studies show it is growing at approximately 19% a year, nearly five times the growth rate of the pet food market as a whole. No wonder Rob and Deb are focused on snacks as opposed to main meals! By 2030, some industry experts expect the size of the global pet snack market to grow to over $70 billion, and in the U.S. alone, to over $50 billion.[2]

Third, and to get to the SOM, we focus on that portion of the snack segment attributable to healthy, natural snacks such as the Cod Skins. Pet snacks have historically been unhealthy, in the form of heavily processed and preserved animal skins or parts – such as "rawhide" leathers that dogs never actually digest and that pass through the stool. Consumers are now demanding something different for their cherished pets. Another recent study showed that nearly 49% of pet owners in the U.S. are highly concerned about the ingredients used in their pet foods, including snacks. "Limited ingredients," sustainable sources, and humane treatment of animals raised for pet food are all vital consumer concerns. Retailers are responding in kind. They want an all-natural, planet-sustainable story for new products. Cod Skins fit right into this trend.[3]

Another indicative measure might be the percentage of all pet food sales going through premium or specialty channels in which a product such as Cod Skins will sell. It is unlikely to be sold in a general grocery store or mass merchandizer because of its price and the type of consumer it wishes to attract. Once again, we go to the web and find that in 2020, premium channels (such as PetCo, PetSmart, and smaller independent stores) comprised 43% of all sales and were growing faster than other pet retail channels.

We now have two highly relevant data points: consumer interest in healthier, sustainable products and a channel-focused selling of such products, both standing at above 40% of all pet food sales. While we can continue to labor away to find other market studies, our time is valuable, and these are legitimate data points. Therefore, we make a reasonable estimate and move forward with an estimate that 40% of the pet snack SAM wants this type of premium, healthy product. For Rob and Deb, 40% of the $21.5 billion pet snack segment comes to $8.6 billion as the SOM for the global market.

This SOM can then become a key assumption in the revenue projections for a company that achieves scale. No single pet snack or product line has ever gained more than 10% of the SOM – it is a fragmented industry. However, significant players in the pet snack category comprise more than 50% of the SOM globally, including Purina, Nestlé, and Mars. But with a fully developed line of snacks like Cod Skins, broadly distributed, Polkadog might seek to capture even just 1-2% of the niche. That product line might be envisioned as a dozen different SKUs of premium pet snacks for dogs and cats using clean ingredients from our natural environment.

We might then further refine SOM by a venture's geographical focus. Rob and Deb were already distributing across the country as well as internationally. Still, the U.S. accounts for about half of pet snack sales globally. Even just 1% of the niche is about $40 million in the U.S. and $80 million globally. This revenue projection would interest a knowledgeable food investor. Of course, Cod Skins would need some darn good follow-on products for this to be possible – but this becomes part of the venture's business plan and the basis for execution as well as investment. As a current benchmark, the top pet snack product line is Greenies, a small company in St. Louis acquired by Mars (of M&Ms fame) in 2006 and that is now producing hundreds of millions of dollars in sales each year by dominating the same premium channels that are growing so rapidly.[4]

As you can see, market sizing is an imperfect science. The entrepreneur must search the web for market studies from respected sources – be it an industry trade association or professional market research firm – and use these data to tell the story of the larger market opportunity surrounding her or his new products or services.[5]

A B2B EXAMPLE

Let's take a B2B example, perhaps for the engineers taking this course!

Suppose we are designing energy management and monitoring systems for commercial buildings, mostly software and some best-in-class sensors scattered throughout the building and external to it. As stated before in this book, IoT is a very hot area for innovation and there is no more active venue for it than in making buildings "smart" in terms of energy in the form of HVAC and lighting. With a quick Google search, we learn that our TAM for money spent on energy management systems for commercial buildings globally is a large number: about $7 billion worldwide in 2020 and expected to grow to about $11 billion by 2027.[6] We learn further that it is dominated by ABB, Honeywell, Johnson Controls, Signify, Schneider Electric, and Siemens. To provide building owners with the best analytics from using our software, we will have to integrate with at least some of the systems of these multi-billion-dollar equipment and systems manufacturers.

Next, we learn that related data services are about 50% of customer spending for energy management systems, with energy systems' design and maintenance services being the other 50%. Software is our market segment. As a result, the $11 billion is halved to $5.5 billion for the SAM. That's still a very large, attractive number for customer spending each year.

Finally, let's further posit that software will focus specifically on LED lighting applications, as opposed to managing the HVAC (heating, ventilation, and air conditioning), the elevators, the data center, or other general electricity syncs. This focus is realistic for a startup and still not unattractive. Lighting comprises about 20% of the energy costs for building owners. All this lighting has shifted to LED-based luminaires and lighting control software. Moreover, as a startup, we will try to conquer the U.S. and Canada in the first five years, a geography that is about 20% of the world's building energy consumption.

This gets us to the SOM – our market niche. We multiply $5.5 billion times 20% (lighting costs) times 20% (North America – Canada, which business people refer to as NACD) to get an approximate $220 million – the annual customer spending in our target market niche. For those that are entrepreneurially inclined, that number is sufficiently large to be attractive to "angel investors," but perhaps too small for larger venture capital (VC) firms that prefer to see a billion-dollar-plus SOM.

If our company can capture 10% of that SOM, then revenue would approach $22 million – sufficient enough for a software company to perhaps attract the interest of one of the large equipment manufacturers listed above for acquisition. The manufacturer, with its global market reach, might have the expectation of growing that revenue to $100 million in revenue per year. As this example shows, market sizing has investment implications.

BUILDING THE STORY FOR TAM, SAM, AND SOM

Each team will have to do its data search for market sizing, preferably using the web to find free sources of data. Look for government and industry reports or data sets. Trade associations for a category of products or services often have great data. Once you scope the pieces of data needed, your search becomes more focused and efficient. The reference librarian at your university might also have access to specialized industry data sources, such as Statistica. It never hurts to ask.

Build a story with the numbers. In fact, outlining that story ahead of time will focus and refine your search. Textualize how you think about the total market (TAM), the market segment (SAM) for your products or services, and then your target market niche (SOM) in terms of users, use cases, and geographic focus. An approach to storyboarding the market sizes is on the right side of Figure 10.1. While we provide five steps, in practice, you can make the steps fewer or greater. Any less than three steps will not convey serious thinking, and more than six steps may prove challenging for others to follow your reasoning.

As the examples above show, you might want to work geographical targets into the story. Geographical considerations can be fascinating.

For example, we have a team of engineering graduate students designing an electric scooter and in-store charging systems for corner grocery stores in India. They have won business plan competition grants in the United States and have angel investors in India. These electric motorcycles are seen as more eco-friendly and cost-effective for the millions of small corner grocery stores in India. The team's TAM is worldwide sales of electric motorcycles; its SAM, the sales of such motorcycles in India; and its SOM, EV motorcycle purchases by businesses in India versus consumer purchases.

There are close to 13 million grocery stores in India, the vast majority of them small and nearly all of them owning a small motorcycle of some sort. These grocery store owners are the venture's SOM – their initial market niche, with the average price of a scooter about $1000. In fact, over 70% of all the vehicles registered in India are two-wheelers of some sort. This is a very different world than the U.S. or Europe.

To get to SOM, the team's geographical target in the first five years are the adjacent states of Tamil Nadu and Andhra Pradesh, whose combined population that is about 10% of the entire country. Using this, we estimate the SOM as 13 million scooters in all India, times the 10% population share of the two target states, times $1000 per vehicle. This comes to $1.3 billion. This does not include repair services.

Then, to get to a revenue estimate, the team believes that only 5% of grocery store owners in their target market will purchase an EV scooter over the next 5 years. And the team has achieved a $750 price point with its design, which would be highly attractive to store owners as well as less expensive to operate. They will also offer grocery carrying accessories and make a small fee on battery recharging through their special charging stations, also sold to the grocery store owners. Running the numbers, they estimated that they could have a $50 million dollar a year company with a 5% adoption rate, or a $100 million with 10% adoption.

This case is a great example that if the territory or region has its own special dynamics, bring these into your story and make them work to your advantage.

Experienced listeners will want to have a conversation with you about your reasoning. They will want to understand your assumptions and provide their insights. There is a delicate balance between being too "wild-eyed" with rosy projections on the one hand, and short-selling the promise of your venture on the other. Your teacher and mentors can help you walk this fine line.

INDUSTRY ECOSYSTEM MAPPING

It is also essential to know all the industry's key players that serve as the larger context around your new product or service. This method is called *mapping the ecosystem*. The "industry" is used broadly to refer to any cohesive group of product or service providers. An educational service for early learners has its "industry" ecosystem, comprising schools, teachers, government bodies that provide funding, and the parents and children who are the buyers and consumers of such services. The world "industry" is simply a construct – every innovation exists within an industry of suppliers, innovators, investors/funders, and users/buyers. Understanding these key players is as important as sizing TAM, SAM, and SOM.

Industry ecosystems are living, breathing meta-entities – an aggregate of players that influence, work, or compete with one another, just like plants, insects, and animals on an island in the South Pacific. The players can be individuals, companies, corporations, government organizations, and investors. And as a product is produced and placed into the hands of users, there are specific steps in converting a set of raw materials into a finished, polished product for the market. The same is valid for services where data are refined, just like oil, into finished information and decision-making services.

There is a tried-and-true structure for examining an industry ecosystem called *value chain mapping*. One of its earliest uses was to understand the dramatic changes made by Henry Ford with the Model T in the early 1900s. He "vertically integrated" and automated the production of a passenger car to reduce costs and make the final product more affordable to the average person – including his factory workers. The classic flow of a value chain proceeds from gathering raw materials (iron ore), to finishing raw materials into functional components (such as steel), to assembling these components into a product design (the frame and chassis of the car), to adding additional parts and accessories from other suppliers, to selling these products to customers. Then there is the "aftermarket" where the customer adds additional complementary products or services. For example, Harley-Davidson bikers purchase upwards of 20% of the cost of their motorcycles in various accessories and motorbike customizations.

Value chain mapping works just as well for services. Newspapers or websites take raw news feeds from organizations like the Associated Press, add their reporting, and then produce "stories" that are packaged into print or web content. Specialty eCommerce sites gather and refine content from product suppliers to create their web catalogs for consumers. Credit bureaus reach out to many financial data sources such as credit card companies and banks for loan information. Fans of hit music groups, such as the South Korean group BTS, rush online after performances for value-added merchandise. The "BTS Meal" led to such a rush on McDonald's restaurants in Indonesia during 2020 that branches had to close because there were no more burgers left!

Value chain mapping is, therefore, the process of identifying and understanding the sequence of how value gets added to a raw material – be it a food ingredient, music, software, or chemistry – on its way to becoming a finished product or service in the hands of the user. This can be done by looking at the various prominent suppliers and distributors involved in your category of products or services. Industry ecosystem mapping builds on value chain mapping by going beyond just manufacturing and distribution. For example, it adds investors and government regulators, as well as aftermarket complementary innovators.

Figure 10.4 shows a simple framework for industry ecosystem mapping. The work here is to fill in the framework from the perspective of your idea/venture, putting your team in the center of the ecosystem map. There is no need to list your direct competitors on this chart.

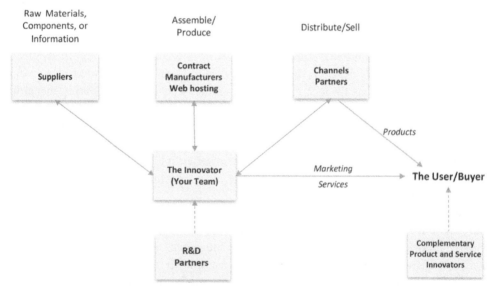

Figure 10.4   Value chain ecosystem mapping

Then, consider the suppliers or the raw ingredients or electronics you might require for your innovation. Or, for a software company, the tools you might wish to use, or as an information service, the data feeds you need.

Next, you might want to have a contract manufacturer produce your products. Or, if you are developing a web-enabled app or data service, a Cloud hosting service provider such as Amazon or Microsoft. Or, you might want to use eCommerce service providers such as Shopify or Squarespace if your innovation is a specialized online store.

Next comes the major distribution partners for your type of innovation. Once again, it could be an eCommerce provider, such as Amazon, or a retailer, such as Staples, Target, or Whole Foods Market.

If you are an analytics/database type of venture, you might want to become part of a large company's partner program to gain access to their customers. Oracle, SAP, and most other large software companies have invested heavily in such partner programs to crowdsource innovation around their "platforms."

Industry ecosystem mapping puts these potential partners on the map – raw materials or information partners, co-manufacturers or production partners, and distribution partners.

A web search for publications or industry reports on your product or service category will quickly reveal the significant players. Often, you can get a ranking of which corporations have the largest market share in your TAM, SAM, or SOM. These might be your partners in some aspect of your business.

Also, keep in mind that other companies often develop and sell additional products or services that work on existing products, systems, or services innovation. Sometimes these companies are referred to as "complementary innovators." If you think this might occur for your innovation, make a note of it on the ecosystem map. The same holds for potential R&D partners that you might need for certain technologies within your new product or service.

This framework provides a simple, powerful method for getting smart, quickly, about the partners needed to succeed in a particular market. It provides context that any good investor will want to know.

Reader exercises

The reader exercises follow the flow of this chapter. First, do the market opportunity sizing and next, the industry ecosystem mapping. The method works just as well for nonprofit sectors such as education or public health. Every product or service has a value chain with suppliers, innovators, some form of investment, and distributors or implementers with actual users.

STEP 1: DEVELOP THE STORY BEHIND YOUR MARKET SIZING

Use Figure 10.1 first to develop your story for your market size and potential. Write down a single brief sentence for each step. Keep the number of steps between three and six, with an ideal number being four or five. Read through your steps two or three times to see what you might have left out to further focus and refine the numbers. This might be your specific use cases, a geographical region, or an underlying technology platform that you will target for the initial growth of your business.

STEP 2: GET THE DATA

Now, as efficiently and inexpensively as you can, go to the web and do a series of searches for each one of your steps. Don't forget to look at the free information from the website of industry trade associations, government agencies or research bureaus, and other public bodies. Also, most universities have a "research librarian" who helps students find data that include industry and market studies. Go say hello to that person, be extra friendly, and ask for help. Typically, these research librarians are very skilled and genuinely enjoy helping students.

STEP 3: CALCULATE ESTIMATES FOR TAM, SAM, AND SOM

Run the math on your data to arrive at TAM, SAM, and your SOM. In the event that you eventually seek outside investment, your TAM will probably have to exceed $1 billion given current investment norms. Your SAM or market segment for your category of products or services should see its way to $500 million or more, and your SOM or target market niche should hit $250 million or more, of which you can then argue that you plan to achieve 10% or more over five years to build a healthy business. And this is for the smaller early stage venture capitalists (VCs) and angel investors. For the larger VCs, double or triple the numbers!

For small lifestyle types of low-tech and largely services-based businesses, such large numbers are not necessary. Please, however, try to make sure that your SOM ends up above the $50 million so that you can have the assurance that if you design outstanding products or services and execute them well in the market, you can generate enough revenue as a small business. To get to $50 million SOM, you will probably need to define your business as national in reach, and not just in your local city or region.

STEP 4: DEVELOP YOUR ECOSYSTEM MAP

Ecosystem mapping should be an exciting journey into learning about an industry. Develop a version of Figure 10.4 that reflects the dynamics of your market space. Keep an eye out for new, interesting entrants to your industry. Look at their innovations and business models.

For potential entrepreneurs, knowing the key players in an industry ecosystem is essential for success. Nearly every startup needs to bring in some type of materials or supplies for its business – as you perhaps realized in defining the MVP in a prior chapter. The prototype might contain proteins or starches, or some form of packaging; electronics or finished materials for systems and structures; or data or specific software tools for apps or enterprise software; or certain chemistries or sensors for life science or environmental innovations. We have students who partner with other companies for basic R&D or software development. That partnership often takes the form of licensing completed technology or paying another company cash for R&D services to take advantage of their own engineers or scientists.

In the same vein, most new companies use other companies for final assembly or web application hosting. And there are always different options for distribution partners, be they various retailers, distributors, eCommerce giants, or large systems manufacturers who might include your specific technology into their systems. It's the same thing with investors, who tend to be highly specialized in the types of technologies and ventures in which they invest.

The bottom line is that not having a mapping of the key players in your field of endeavor is working half-blind. So, please make an effort now to become more expert in your industry, as savvy about potential partners as you have become about users, buyers, and direct competitors.

The web helps here. But so does identifying a few seasoned mentors that have worked in your industry. If your university has a mentor network, and you are serious about starting a venture based on the innovation in this course, now would be a good time to find the person running it and ask to be connected to an industry mentor.

   In addition, if you are developing a consumer product such as a food, electronic game, or device, spending some time in a retail store with an experienced salesperson is worth its weight in gold. Tell them you are working on a new venture and would like to learn from them if they have the time – just 15 minutes. That will probably turn into 30 minutes or more if you engage the person and listen well. Perhaps even buy an inexpensive item as a way to say thank you to your new friend.

NOTES

1. Go to www.mordorintelligence.com and look up the industry report for the global pet food industry. Read the free data summary.
2. www.petfoodindustry.com
3. www.petfoodindustry.com
4. www.petfoodprocessing.net
5. A fun side note to this story is that lightly grilled cod skins have been a long-standing traditional snack food amongst certain Asian cultures, such as in South Korea, where people have snack on dried, grilled pollack skins as a lighter, tastier alternative to potato skins. One of your authors was promoting the Cod Skins as a new food innovation example for "pets" to a group of Korean businesspeople. He was duly corrected . He also had to literally eat his words in considerable volume that evening at a bar. Fortunately, there was enough beer to help wash down the mistake.
6. Do a Google search yourself on Building Energy Management Systems for the latest data.

11
Creating a product line and platform strategy

THE PURPOSE OF THE CHAPTER

Very few entrepreneurs can make and sell just a single "killer" product to achieve success in their chosen market. Instead, it takes a product line – a series of closely related products and services. That product line has a standard, shared internal architecture and common subsystems within that architecture. Final products or services result from relatively minor changes made to or on top of the common core, creating different or customized products or services. Offering choice and a variety of products or services to the customer – while at the same time basing them on common cores – is a hallmark of hyper-growth businesses. Experienced investors look for it, too. In this chapter, we learn the basic concepts for developing and communicating a more complete product line or service strategy.

LEARNING OBJECTIVES

After reading this chapter, you should be able to:

1. Understand the importance of creating product lines or a suite of services.
2. Understand the meaning of "platforming" for a product or service.
3. Define "good, better, best" within a product line.
4. Tackle new users and use cases with common product platforms.

GIVING CUSTOMERS CHOICE WITH A PRODUCT LINE, NOT A SINGLE PRODUCT

Rarely does a single new product or service appeal to everyone in a target market segment within any reasonably sized industry. It is far better to have multiple offerings tuned to different price–performance preferences within your target market, especially for users and buyers who believe they have specific needs and uses beyond the standard, entry-level product or service. The old Henry Ford adage regarding the Model T – "you can have it in any color as long as it is black" – doesn't apply any more. Choice and variety are essential for just about any set of users, and it is up to you as the innovator to define the nature and extent of that variety.

Perhaps Google is the leading example of a "one-trick pony" – a single blockbuster product or service that, year after year, produces enormous amounts of revenue. For Google, this is Google Ads. Google also tries to leverage databases and "eyeballs" into a more extensive range of information services, and that new revenue now accounts for tens of billions of dollars each year. However, Google still derives more than 80% of its revenue from advertising fees on Google search, where customers buy sponsored advertisements keyed to certain types of searches.

Your authors once had as a classmate at MIT the founder of one of the greatest "one-trick ponies" in computing history: Lotus 1-2-3. Its founder, Mitch Kapor, left MIT in 1983 to make a back-end graphics plotting package for the leading spreadsheet software, Visicalc. He then integrated a competitive spreadsheet with the graphics plotting software, which became Lotus 1-2-3. It became the most popular software sold on the IBM PC and other MS-DOS compatible PCs – a "killer" software product. Mitch sold his company in 1995 for over $2 billion to IBM. The reality, however, is that even though Lotus 1-2-3 was a single product, it was perhaps the most flexible multi-user software ever created. One can do just about anything in a spreadsheet!

Examples like Google search and Lotus 1-2-3 are so rare that it is far better to think of creating a product line or a suite of services to scale a company. This broader range of products and services can still use a common technology foundation. Specific common subsystems can be standardized and leveraged across all products. We call this *platforming*.

Remember from our earlier examples that those common subsystems might be ingredients and packaging for food products, programming modules or databases for software applications, or specific workflows and tracking software across different services. An example might be the chocolate for a line of indulgent cookies with different flavors, a database management system within a family of accounting software for different types of small businesses, or a risk assessment expert system for different but related lines of insurance, such as individual and group life, or individual health and group health. For example, having diabetes, or working as a fireman, or jumping out of airplanes for fun adds risk (and higher premiums) to both life and health insurance underwriting.

Figure 11.1 presents a framework to capture this platforming idea. It shows the architecture framework from our design chapter (Chapter 7, Figure 7.7 for physical products) with a set of different products emerging on top of the architecture (and its major subsystems).

Already in this book, you have seen example after example of entrepreneurs who have embraced a platform approach in their businesses.

- For Kevin in Eco Blocks & Tiles, his major subsystems are glass, plastic, and sand that are crushed, melted, and combined in a proprietary process that produces roof tiles of different shapes and colors (based on the color of the sand), and "pavers" as walking steps on the ground. These two product lines serve the same user but for different use cases (roofing versus walkways). These two product lines share the same basic architecture and subsystems but have a different format (roof tiles versus pavers) and a standard process for crushing, melting, and forming both types of end product. That shared process is also a fundamental "process platform," while the glass and plastic are Kevin's "product platforms."

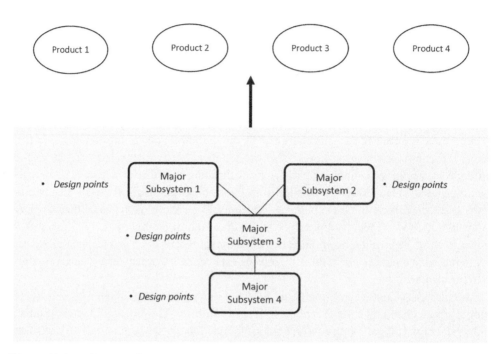

Figure 11.1   Product line architecture as the foundation for product lines and services

- The same reasoning can be found for Kate in Drink Simple. She has a product line featuring noncarbonated and carbonated beverages, which in addition to the fizz, further vary by flavoring and serving size. The common product subsystem or platform is tree water! Serving all products is also an underlying common supply chain and production process for filtering and stabilizing the tree water. Accordingly, while the tree water is the product platform, the proprietary production process is the common process platform for all her products.

- For Neil and his My M&M's team, the M&M's candy is the platformed subsystem upon which food ink is printed to create customized text and photo images. This process produces an infinite variety of end products for consumers.

- Karthik in Envision has a different yet analogous approach for the software for the visually impaired. He has two product lines: the mobile app and the same software embedded in the relatively expensive Google Glasses. Supporting both products is a common software architecture featuring object databases, image analysis routines with ML (machine learning) capabilities, speech/language input and output in multiple languages, and a Cloud infrastructure with user security mechanisms. Product line expansion comes in the form of adding new use cases for activities of daily living, such as going shopping for clothes as opposed to groceries.

- With Slate, Josh and Manny are very similar to Kate from a product strategy point of view. Slate has just one product line with three different flavors based on two underlying shared subsystems or platforms: the lactose-free milk and the aluminum cans. Supporting the milk is a unique supply chain that becomes a barrier to entry for others who wish to copy Slate. While the milk and the cans might be called "product platforms," the supply chain processes can be considered "process platforms."

And Rob and Deb are the same, but their platform is cod skins, dried, and then packaged into different formats. These examples are a similar approach: platforming, leveraging standard products and or process subsystems across a range of products or services. Now you know platforming!

As a consumer, you see this approach in successful products. For example, a popular cereal such as Cheerios has many different varieties based on the standard format. These varieties range from plain, to honey-nut (our favorite), to apple cinnamon, to frosted, chocolate covered, and then the multigrain "healthier" one (although this healthier version has six times the sugar per serving as the original Cheerios). Again, these varieties have the same signature donut shape and, for most, a shared ingredient deck for the core recipe. And yes, the cereal box and moisture shielding lining comprise another shared platform.

Most consumers of a new product or service want to have some choice in their final purchase, to find the version that meets their needs. Or, in other cases, consumers want to buy accessories or software plug-ins to tailor a product or service to their tastes and preferences. The critical idea is how to achieve this variety and choice for users and buyers with *relatively simple means*. That means designing and using those common, shared platforms across multiple products or services.

Even though you are innovating your first product or service, we want you to think forward to multiple products – two or three years out – as hard as that might seem at this very moment. But imagine with us for a bit. You will be graduating from school, your minimal viable prototype (MVP) from this course not just in-hand but well-developed, and you might even have done a small production run and conducted a limited market test. You have in front of you an angel investor who wants to provide upwards of $1 million for your company. Part of your pitch to this investor will have to be the complete product line or suite of services that can grow the company into a $10–20 million-plus business over just five years. To create multiple products, you want to do it cleverly and cost-effectively. That means designing a product line based on a solid product line or services architecture, with shared subsystems within, and that drive variety for your customers.

PLATFORMING: MORE DEFINITIONS

Let's use Figure 11.1 to define the words platforms and platforming. The common architecture and its subsystems are shown in the bottom half of Figure 11.1.[1] The specific products at the top part of the figure are typically gathered and organized as particular *product lines*. The combination of product lines, their particular product or service elements, and the underlying platforms in the design and production of these products is collectively referred to as a *product strategy*. You might prefer to call this your *new product strategy*.

Today, some pundits write about industry platforms (which are business models, like Uber, and not technologies), brand platforms (like M&M's or Nike, as brands that support multiple subbrands), and technology platforms (such as mRNA, or messenger RNA, in various new vaccines, which teach our cells how to make proteins that trigger an immune response to specific diseases).

Here, we are focused on product and process platforms as part of a new product strategy. You should consider both, carefully. A product platform is a single major subsystem shared across multiple products. An example would be Kevin's crushed glass and plastic, or Kate's tree water, or Josh's cow milk. Also, all three examples have a unique manufacturing process, which is a *process* platform as opposed to a *product* platform. Karthik has product platforms, too: his image processing and machine learning code, developed as programming libraries, are a powerful product platform applied to many different use cases and leveraged across the mobile app and the Google Glasses. His process platform – well, it is made by someone else, e.g. Google Cloud.

Therefore, think of a shared subsystem – the product platform – as a building block, just like a small plastic shape in Lego. You assemble the pieces with a standardized interface between the components, and voila, you can make just about any final form (or product) you want. The process platform can be thought of as common methods for either producing the Lego blocks or assembling them together if that was ever done through automation.

Note further that a product platform does not have to use just a company's own technology. In fact, in most cases, a team will work with external suppliers for some of its essential shared subsystems. Mars, for example, has external suppliers for its printheads and edible inks. Karthik, uses Google as a Cloud provider and for the Glasses. Kate and Josh both use external flavor houses to tune their drinks and other suppliers for the flavor ingredients on an ongoing basis. The idea is to build best-in-class technologies or components into the major subsystems that you will use in all products. In other words, it is composite design used for any subsystem, including a platformed subsystem.

Platforming is, therefore, the process for defining (a) the common product line architecture, (b) the shared product and process building blocks that can be used within the architecture, and (c) developing the product strategy that takes advantage of (a) and (b).

A FOOD EXAMPLE

Enough definitions. Let's look at another simple, tasty example! We want to share this story to inspire you to think out of the box, even in traditional product categories.

Consider Figure 11.2. The product on the left has been around for decades. It is a Vlasic pickle. Company lore has it that the stork on the front of the label grew from the myth that women like to eat pickles when pregnant. Yes, we find this lore both offensive and dated, too. We also think it ill-advised as a branding image when the single, highest value consumer for most consumer product companies (CPCs) is the Millennial female shopper who might already have young children or perhaps wants to do so in the future. There are also many good things about this legacy product. The pickle is "crunchy" to the bite, primarily because the company has direct supplier relationships with farmers in different parts of the country. Fresh-picked and into the jar with the brine, sliced or whole – that is the recipe for success. Also, the legacy product remains a pretty good deal for the money and is the pickle category leader in the U.S.

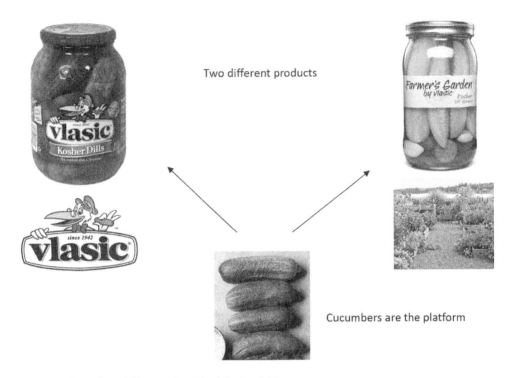

Two different products

Cucumbers are the platform

Figure 11.2   Good. Better. Best for Vlasic pickles

A few years ago, the CEO of this company asked your authors to work with an internal, entrepreneurial innovation team to create a product precisely for that Millennial/Gen Y female consumer. The CEO formed a team of a half dozen individuals from different functions and sent them up to Boston for an innovation boot camp. We gathered a dozen female consumers in the target consumer segment. There were three small consumer panels: the first was single women shopping primarily for themselves; the second, women shopping for themselves and their significant others; and the third, women shopping for their families with young children. The team did full-cycle ethnographies, going on shopping journeys and tasting all sorts of high-priced, mid-priced, low-priced, and spiced pickles, all the while having conversations about choice, competitive options, price preferences, and different occasions of use for pickles.

It also had access to all tiers of food retailers, from Dollar Value stores to Walmart, Target, Trader Joe's, mainstream grocers, and Whole Foods Markets. The team purchased what seemed like every pickle product and package in existence and brought these into a design studio. We worked in an open lab at a university – mixing and matching cucumbers with different brines and hand-drawing new labels. Fortunately, several team members were chefs, and one of your authors also cooked his way through college. We knew enough not to hurt anyone with our brines!

Imagine a team of diverse, food-passionate individuals trying to brainstorm their way to innovating a legacy pickle product. The immersions with consumers truly helped: all three subgroups desired a healthier lifestyle, less processed pickle preparation, a simpler ingredient deck, and a desire for farm-to-table offerings. The product line architecture was also obvious: the pickle, the brine, the jar, and the label. Some of the pickle products lacked the crunchiness of the Vlasic. Some consumers complained about the brine and the label on the legacy product. "The brine is yellowish – it looks like pee!" "The jar has garish colors." "What's all that stuff on the ingredient list on the back?" And for Vlasic, "What is the stork doing there? It is not suggesting what I think it is, is it?"

The moment of insight came on the second day of debriefing on these ethnographies. We were taking a break and having a cookout in a backyard up in Boston. Right in front of our eyes was a hobbyist-type vegetable garden with lots of variety. After some beers, the team took a fresh run at the innovation challenge. Someone said something simple yet brilliant: "We are all just looking at the cucumber – the pickle. We are tunnel-visioned! Why don't we put everything into the jar from the garden right in front of us? Make the product itself be the experience of the entire garden? Let's bring the garden to the consumer in a fresh, shelf-stable, enjoyable format!" Well, that was it. We were all intrigued, and sold.

The team ran back to the kitchen studio that same evening. A run to the vegetable store delivered a range of fresh vegetables of different colors. Different brine mixtures were made, including some without the color dyes. The team sketched labels with various names. One of these was "Farmer's Garden." That name combined the heritage concept of working with farmers and putting the entire garden, not just the cucumbers, into the jar. We all loved it. Later, this brand name proved strong in broader concept testing.

The product was launched fairly soon thereafter. The retailers liked the concept and slotted premium shelf space for it (eye level). Target consumers, the young professional female, responded favorably. Farmer's Garden soon won several food innovation awards and generated the $100 million-plus type of new revenue that CEOs crave for internal, company-generated growth.[2]

That is the Farmer's Garden story. The cucumber is the "hero" ingredient with other vegetable inclusions, a new brine, a new jar, a new label, and a new brand name. But it also used the common product platform – the pickle – and the common canning/sterilization process, e.g. the process platform of the legacy Vlasic product.

Can you foresee leveraging your core technologies and subsystems into different products or market applications? What is your "cucumber," and how can it be used to create your "Farmer's Garden" analogy?

SOFTWARE APPLICATIONS

There are many fine examples of a robust product strategy in software products, or software products sold as service. Microsoft has its office productivity suite: Word, Excel, PowerPoint, Access (for the database), OneNote (note-taking), Publisher (for graphic artist-quality publications), and Outlook. Each has a different use case or purpose. But underneath each application are shared software and services for security, database, and Cloud access. Another favorite example is Intuit, which for decades has stood independently from the giants in the software industry to become the industry leader in accounting for small businesses. Its core product is QuickBooks. The company has variety and choice in its product line in terms of features and functions, which also translate into price. It also has a specialized version of QuickBooks for nonprofit organizations, which have their own set of accounting rules and procedures, and for small retailers, as well as a beefed-up "enterprise" version for medium-sized businesses.

To achieve efficiency in development and make life easier for end-users, successful software companies build underlying subsystem platforms and add additional code to these subsystems to create final products. A robust internal database is every bit as consequential for a product line of software products as the cucumber is for a product line of pickles. The same applies to other critical subsystems – the user interface libraries, the logic processing engine, and the security layers that all good software products now need to offer.

Figure 11.3 shows our earlier framework for software architecture as containing these platform elements at the bottom of the figure. Then, the different market applications (shown as just two generic ones) are at the top part of the figure.

For Microsoft, the bottom part of the figure contains its shared libraries for critical functions, and the Microsoft Office Suite, the top layer. The same applies to Intuit: core functions on the bottom and the different versions on the top.

Sometimes there are general-purpose applications for software and then special-purpose applications. For those of you who are engineering students, you might have already used or will use a software product called Matlab, and its sister product called Simulink. Matlab and Simulink provide a sophisticated scripting language for creating and simulating complex equations using math and data for an incredibly broad range of applications. These are general-purpose software tools for engineers. Then, MathWorks provides a range of plug-in modules for specific applications to save the engineer time and money. These plug-ins are use-case specific: designing controls for things such as anti-lock brake systems, test and measurement systems design, and even a 5G electronics-communications design and test toolbox. MathWorks' product strategy is quite remarkable as an example of product variety and diversity in software.[3]

If you think about it, often the end-user rarely sees any form of the code platformed at the bottom of Figure 11.3. However, users benefit significantly from its functionality. In this way, software platforms are analogous to the engine underneath the hood of a car. We rarely ever see it, but we enjoy its performance every moment behind the wheel of a car with a good engine.

These shared, platformed subsystems allow a small company, such as Envision, to add new use cases to its product portfolio quickly. For example, it started with shopping for food in

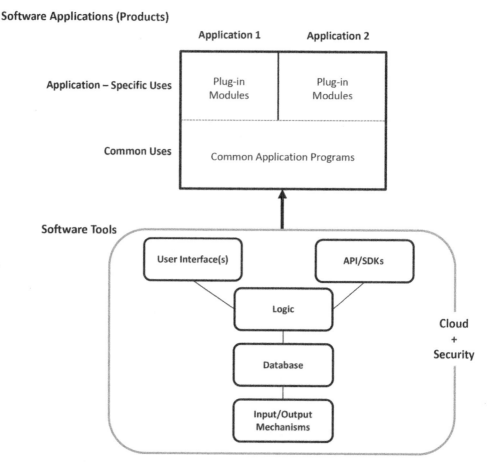

Software Applications (Products)

Figure 11.3   Software platforms (tools/building blocks) enable different software applications

a grocery store and promptly advanced to reading a menu to order food in a restaurant without writing all the code from scratch.

Software also provides the rather special opportunity to enable other software developers to build their applications using your tools, packaged up as an API (application programming interface) or software development kit (SDK). APIs and SDKs are different terms for the same thing – a developer's library. The purpose of this is to get other companies or independent programmers to build their applications and make them available to customers as part of a larger meta product portfolio. This strategy allows the software company to look and act much bigger than its actual size.

Figure 11.4 shows a framework to express this strategy. On the right side of the figure are arrows emerging from the API/SDK box to entities, generally called "third parties," who then create and sell their products directly or through the API-owner's "Partners Program." Typically, the lead software company has already developed its own set of core applications.

The third-party developers tend to create niche applications that surround or complement those core applications. Then there is typically a business arrangement that provides a percentage of the sale or subscription fee to the platform-owning software company for selling these third-party applications through its channels. This business model can be powerful in terms of growing market presence. Every major software company has an API or SDK externalized for use by others. Salesforce, SAP, Oracle, Apple, Microsoft, and yes, The MathWorks, are but a few examples. It is a form of a crowdsourced new product strategy.

Many software entrepreneurs work the other side of this equation, as the third-party innovators that integrate a larger company's API/SDK into their own code. For example, students building mobile apps include Google Duo's API for two-factor authentication for user login. Others incorporate the Slack API to allow their software to be accessible by Slack users and teams. In fintech, some of our students have integrated the Plaid API to access financial account information in banks and other institutions. In software, there is an API for just about everything and every purpose. This API approach is shown as "Toolkits from other companies" on the right side of Figure 11.4.

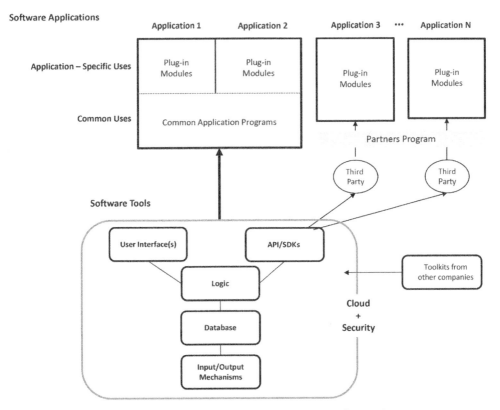

Figure 11.4 Software APIs/SDKs become potent elements of a product strategy

If you are developing software, think through the API/SDK options that make the most sense as part of your product strategy. Is there a toolkit that you will wish to provide to others that helps customers integrate and customize your software or data from it? Or for other software companies to build plug-ins for your software? Are there other external toolkits that would help your software? They might even be free, open-source software for programming and data access. Or, an innovator might have to license and pay for an industry-leading toolkits. Or a combination of both. For example, many game and metaverse application developers start with the free version of a development toolkit called Unity and then migrate over to an $1800 per year subscription for the professional version.[4]

For example, another software venture – LinkSquares – focuses on improving the mundane area of contract creation and revision in corporations with a Cloud-based document change control system with activity analytics. The company experienced difficulty gaining traction in the market until it integrated with Salesforce. The Salesforce plug-in gave the venture a foothold across the corporate community because Salesforce is essentially *everywhere* for specialized workflow management. Integrations with DocuSign, AdobeSign, and HelloSign came next. With this plug-in strategy, LinkSquares' offering was much more complete. Sales accelerated.[5]

The irony is that we try to design software with the robustness of a physical product – with clear structure within a layered architecture and plug-in modules as end-user applications, and yet, we then often sell the product *in the form of a service*, with a monthly or annual subscription.

Suppose, for example, that you are a city manager and purchase 10,000 LED lampposts for your municipality. You buy the lamppost hardware and a monthly or annual subscription to gain access to the data gathered by sensors embedded in those lamp- posts. Those streaming data services quickly become essential for managing the 10,000 lights, but because extra sensors that can be purchases to fit into the lamppost, you can can also monitor traffic, air pollution, crime, and offer 5G services through the city. These are all data services. These days, customers most users think software should be cheap, if not free, but they do not believe the same about data. Just the opposite, in fact; data are increasingly powerful and valuable. Therefore, rather than license a software product to run on servers, entrepreneurs instead make the same software available as a subscription service over the Cloud, as an SaaS (software as a service), where the emphasis is on the workflow enabled and the data generated by it.

A SERVICES EXAMPLE

If data services are one form of service, how can we generalize to more traditional types of services? What do product lines and platforming shared subsystems mean for services?

We mentioned a student venture discussed in Chapter 7, Pure Solutions that provides "premium" pest control services for both residential and commercial applications. Its core mission is to use eco-friendly and pet-safe remedies to control mosquitoes, ticks (and the diseases they carry), indoor pests (rodents, ants, cockroaches, spiders, etc.), and deer them-selves, which can ruin a flower or vegetable garden. Its products feature plant extracts and natural oils. As we learned before, these alternative treatments have proven so effective that the company is now producing them as a standalone product offering called PROGAEA™. This chemical alternative is a product platform shared across its various services. The method for engaging clients is also standardized and carefully measured in terms of services and lawn treatments. This has allowed Pure Solutions to scale its business without sacrificing quality in service delivery. These processes are its service platforms.

Take a look at Figure 11.5. It shows Brian and Trevor, the co-founders, and their services strategy. On the left side of the figure are major customer/market segments: residential, commercial, and franchisees (Brian and Trevor are now franchising their business in different geographical areas). There are different services packages for homeowners versus commercial building owners. There are also different pesticide treatments for different types of pests. Each of these services leverages specific "product platforms" in the form of the natural pesticides and inhibitors. And then, there are common process platforms for onboarding new customers and treating their properties, tailored for commercial versus residential customers. In other words, product platforms are the foundation for a range of specific services.

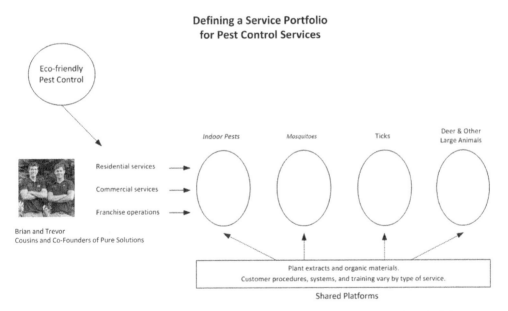

Figure 11.5 Service variety based on common processes, systems, and materials

PROVIDING VARIETY AND CHOICE WITHIN A PRODUCT LINE OR SERVICES

The next step is to work on the top part of the basic framework shown in various formats in Figures 11.1, 11.3, and 11.5. Just like car companies have different packages to upgrade a base-level vehicle, or Uber offers a suite of ride-sharing services at various price points, you can plan this for your innovation. This step defines the variation expected in a future product line of suite of services.

The basic approach to provide variety in a product line or service suite is to launch your product to market not as a single monolithic product but as a product line with tiers of functionality and price, even if one of these is freemium in the case of a mobile app to induce trial. We think of it as providing options for "good, better, best."

A more extreme approach is to leverage your underlying technology, materials, or ingredients to entirely different users or use cases. This second approach involves greater complexity and tends to be part of the next phase of growth for a new company. It might not occur until after the first product line or service has gained traction. Rather than build a new product line or service from scratch, you leverage product and process platforms into the new products or services. This approach makes its development much faster and the results more reliable because it uses proven elements from your first product line. We think of these new users and new use cases as *new market applications* for a company's technologies, products, and services.

Let's look at a few simple, powerful examples of each approach.

Good, better, best

Figure 11.6 shows the classic example of Stanley Black and Decker Power Tools, where a single electric motor design has been the internal product platform for a wide range of different power tools. In the figure, you can see three different drills: the basic level of Black and Decker, the somewhat more expensive Firestorm, with more power and durability, and the much more costly DeWalt (for tradespeople who use power tools all day long). The different levels of power come from a standardized motor that delivers added power by increasing the stack length of the copper wire in the coil within the electric motor. This extra stack length generates greater torque. Notice the stack length in the bottom right picture of the motor subassembly.[6] The longer the stack length, the greater the torque produced. Three different price points, three different levels of power, three different colors – all based on a common, scalable subsystem – the motor. The motor itself comprises 25–30% of the total cost of goods in a power tool and the common motor design creates a significant point of leverage. Using the same motor subsystem across the millions of power tools produced each year substantially lowers the cost of goods sold, based on more significant volume procurements of materials and running manufacturing machines at higher volumes. The company extended the common motor to circular saws, jigsaws, sanders, and other power tools, generating even greater savings. These lower costs were used to dramatically lower prices on the shelf, through which Black and Decker grabbed leading market share.

How does this example apply to your innovation? How can you create good, better, best with simple means based on a single, scalable underlying architecture? What are those common subsystems that can be scaled, just like the motor in the drills? Figure 11.7 presents a template to help you organize your thinking here.

Branding *good, better, best* is both fun and important to consider. Some companies use special acronyms to connote basic versus premium, such as "value" or "basic" on one end of the spectrum, and "premium" or "platinum" on the other. One of our students is the brand

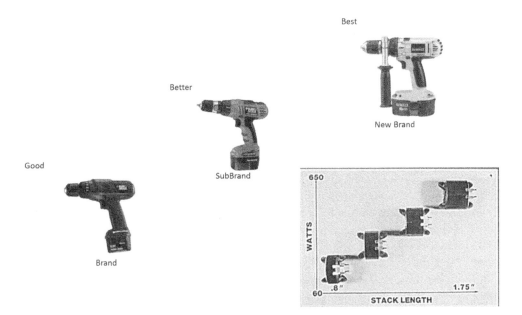

Figure 11.6   Good, better, best at Stanley Black and Decker

For product variations within a single target user/use case

	Name/Brand	Features / Functions	How the variation is accomplished Visible and not visible to the user	Pricing Implications
Best				
Better				
Good				

Figure 11.7   Define good, better, best for your product or service

manager for one of the largest cannabis companies in California and works on its premium product line, Monogram. The company secured the rapper Jay-Z as the brand personality and offers better, best, and out-of-this-world varieties, using THC (tetrahydrocannabinol – the psychoactive substance in cannabis) and specifically its concentration to connote strength (No. 1 or No. 96, for example). Or, "bronze, silver, gold" are common expressions for levels of service in services businesses. Uber has Pool, X, Comfort, Green, and Black, all representing different price and ride experience levels. Make sure that your good, better, best branding is easily understood and comfortable for the target user. Look for analogies in your industry. Leading companies do this well.

New market applications – creating new product lines

New market applications involve targeting new use cases either for the same set of users or new types of users.

In Stanley Black and Decker, the power tools product line includes drills, sanders, circular saws, straight blade saws, routers, and so forth, comprising a single product line addressing different use cases.

However, companies also often create new product lines for new market applications. In a car company, passenger cars, SUVs, and crossovers are all considered separate product lines, even though critical subsystems are shared: the power train, the driver controls or driverless control systems, the seating, and the entertainment and navigation systems. Many companies even share the underlying frames, suspension systems, and tires between passenger cars, SUVs, and crossovers. Each product line is tuned for a different use case, even for a distinct type of persona: e.g., a branded type of SUV that is luxury-focused versus another that is value-focused, such as the Acura MDX versus the Honda Pilot, both made by the same company and that share substantial chassis and other technology.

For software, new market applications – new use cases and often different users – are often easier to accomplish due to the modularity and flexibility of software relative to hardware products. This is achieved by leveraging most of the underlying software subsystems – the databases, the GUI, the Cloud, and security – and adding to these new application-specific programmed logic, knowledge bases, or data sets.

Figure 11.8 shows an example of a Korean venture, Crescom, which has launched a series of highly sophisticated software applications that apply AI/ML techniques based on deep learning algorithms to provide automated diagnosis of bone diseases. Working with physicians, the founder, Jae Joon Lee, first developed a product for detecting slow or fast bone growth disease in young children. Many hospitals now use his software (as a service, to send images and received diagnoses through the Cloud.). Crescom also leveraging its platform to other bone diseases. These include micro-fracture detection in an emergency room, shown on the right side of Figure 11.8. Jae-Joon Lee can also detect the progression of osteoarthritis in the elderly through the decay of cartilage between bones. Osteoarthritis is an enormous market segment for diagnostic tools and treatments. All three of these bone disease applications leverage the same underlying software, with specific "plug-ins" for each particular disease.

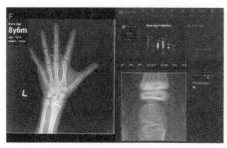

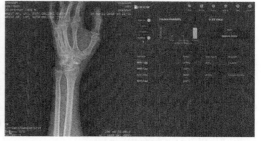

| Medical imaging: bone growth in children | Small fracture detection |

Source: Images provided by Jae Joon Lee, CEO Crescom. Reproduced with permission.

Figure 11.8   Different market applications for a medical image AI software product

New market applications in terms of new users and use cases applies equally well to services. In South Korea once again, Kakao Talk is a wildly successful application for messaging, text, Wi-Fi calls, and video. The chat emojis and other animations are fun. On top of this basic service, Kakao has developed a wide range of new mobile services. These include Kakao Taxi, Kakao Bike, Kakao Driver (the country has stringent drink driving laws, so this app brings a driver to the restaurant to drive the person home in their own car), Kakao Parking, Kakao Bus, Kakao Train, and even Kakao Carpool. All serve different use cases, but leverage common user registration, GUI, messaging, and database software.

For product variations across multiple target users/use cases

	Target User	What is different about the use case?	Timing implications The amount of work to get there
User/Use Case 3			
User/Use Case 2			
User/Use Case 1			

- Not much work
- Moderate work
- A lot of work

Figure 11.9   Define different market applications for your innovation

Now, let's generalize the new market applications concept and apply it to your innovation. Take a look at Figure 11.9, a simple template to think about future market applications. The two most important considerations are the technical feasibility and financial attractiveness of an adjacent market. How much work do you think it would take to develop the new solution, given that you can leverage much of what you have already created for your first product or service? You can use the words "not much work," "moderate work," or "a lot of work" to provide a gut estimate on the effort needed to address the new opportunity.

Developing new market applications based on common core technology and processes goes to the heart of strong technology platform-based companies.

*** *** ***

A final thought on product lines: provide choice but do not go overboard. Consider just two or three different levels of functionality and price within their product or service portfolios. Those two or three levels of choice for customers are your "good, better, best." This way, if a customer thinks a particular offering is too expensive, you might not have to lose that customer by providing an option that is less costly with a bit less functionality. On the other hand, if the customer needs more functionality or style, you can provide it but the buyer must pay more for the value delivered. That might be your "best" version. The idea here is to maximize your sales by having different offerings that appeal to different types of buyers with your target market, yet have these offerings share a lot "underneath the hood."

Reader exercises

We have presented several simple templates in this chapter. Now it is time to use them to build your product or services strategy.

STEP 1: PRODUCT LINE STRATEGY

Define the higher-level product strategy for your innovation over the next three to five years. This is the product line(s) you think you might create, based on a standard product line or service architecture and common, shared subsystems or processes within that architecture. Use simple descriptors for the types of products or services developed with those shared subsystems. Remember, a subsystem can be a component, an ingredient, an electronic subassembly, a software module or tool, or an essential process within a service.

Refer to Figure 11.1. If your innovation is primarily software, use Figure 11.3, and if you are brave and ambitious, use Figure 11.4.

STEP 2: DEFINE "GOOD, BETTER, BEST"

Apply Figure 11.7 to your innovation concept, be it a product line, a suite of services, or a pure software product or mobile app. What is the reasoning behind the tiers of price performance? More specifically:

- What features distinguish better-featured products from those with fewer features if you are making a product line of foods, mechanical, or electronics solutions?
- For software or apps, is a tier free to induce trial? What additional features warrant charging users later?
- If you providing data services similar to the LED lighting example, could these data services be segmented into types of services, where some are more valuable than others?
- Last, if your innovation is primarily a service, are the services individualized or bundled as a suite of all-inclusive services?

Think freely and broadly about these questions. Use the Black and Decker example to guide your thinking regarding a product, the MathWorks for software, or Uber for a service. Try to derive a strategy that flows naturally and that you can explain easily to others. You might also want to tweak the very first row of your Customer Value Proposition (Figure 4.10) to capture the idea of a family or product or services, as opposed to a single offering.

NOTES

1. Meyer, M.H., and Lehnerd, A.P. (1997). *The Power of Product Platforms*. New York: The Free Press.
2. https://www.businesswire.com/news/home/20130208005758/en/Consumers-Vote-Farmer's-GardenTM-by-Vlasic®-2013-Product-of-the-Year. Published February 8, 2013.
3. https://www.mathworks.com/products.html.

4. Unity Technologies IPO'd in 2020 and will surpass $1 billion in revenue in 2021! Based in San Francisco, it was actually founded in Denmark in 2004 as Over the Edge Entertainment and changed its name in 2007. An IPO is an initial public offering of a company's equity.

5. LinkSquares, based in Boston, raised over $40 million in venture capital during 2017–21.

6. Meyer, M.H., and Lehnerd, A. (1997). *The Power of Product Platforms*. New York: The Free Press.

12
Conducting a Reality Check

THE PURPOSE OF THE CHAPTER

Each year, a multitude of innovators come up with ideas that they believe could be the beginning of a great startup or the foundation of a new business unit within their current company, like My M&M's. While a new idea may seem outstanding from a 50,000-foot level, the innovator must test, refine, and improve the innovation concept with target users and buyers to make sure the effort is worth everyone's time.

One way to do this testing is to develop and show prototypes to people. Hopefully, you are well on your way in that activity based on our earlier chapter. Another method is to do a more extensive survey based on the refined Customer Value Proposition developed and refined throughout this book. We call this a "Reality Check." Marketing professionals who work in companies also refer to it as a "Concept Test." We want you to do both: develop a looks like, feels like and works somewhat like prototype based on ethnography and direct user interaction, and also conduct a broader, survey-based Reality Check. Each provides important insights.

In this chapter, we will learn how to design and conduct a Reality Check and present the results. It is a structured survey with some specific analyses. Reality Checks should be fast and effective. Unlike our ethnography and user walkthroughs with the prototypes, a Reality Check requires a larger number of respondents. In this course, we ask you to aim for at least 30 respondents, and if you wish to impress, more.

LEARNING OBJECTIVES

After reading this chapter, you should be able to:

1. Plan a "Reality Check."
2. Define specific questions to test your Customer Value Proposition, as well questions to test your product or service solutions, the revenue dimensions of your business model, and your go-to-market strategy.
3. Organize customer panels – the interviewees.
4. Conduct the field research itself – using methods that can help build the required sample quickly.
5. Analyze and present the results of the field research.

THE FIRST STEP: TUNING THE CUSTOMER VALUE PROPOSITION

We have been working with the Customer Value Proposition (CVP) since the fourth chapter of this book. You then refined it with a crisper definition of users and buyers, a more precise statement of needs and benefits, and a clear product or service design. We also improved the competitive positioning statement. The CVP, along with a prototype and the "serviceable obtainable" market, goes a long way towards defining the new venture. Now, the icing on the cake is a more empirical validation of the innovation idea – and that is this Reality Check.[1]

As we have learned, the Customer Value Proposition has a specific structure with the following components:

- The brand name (of the group of products/services).

- The specific problem solved.

- The particular target user and specific use case.

- The specific target buyers (this can be optional in the survey if the user is the buyer).

- Specific benefits for users (in terms of features, performance, quality, or price/revenue model.

- Competitive differentiation from current products/services and what is the basis for customer preference when buying.

The final integrated statement at the bottom of the CVP is what can be used here. It belongs at the beginning of the survey is in the last row of the Customer Value Proposition template. It integrates all of the rows of the CVP int a concise two or three sentence statement. The generic form is:

> ABC is a new family of products (or services) that [*solves what problem*] for [*which target customers*] in [*which specific use cases*]. The benefits that we expect to provide include [*name the* significant, specific *benefits*]. ABC will stand out from competitors because of its [*positioning on functional, emotional, and social dimensions*].

You can look at some of the other CVPs in previous chapters, such as those for Kate and Jeff, or Rob and Deb.

Accompanying the concept statement at the beginning of the survey should be a sketch of the new product or service idea. For an assembled product, such as the flashlight, an image of the product itself suffices.

For a food or drink, the packaging design is as important as the product itself, even if it only shows a desired bottle design and label. For software, this sketch might be the wireframe or GUI. For a pure service, perhaps it is a single illustration representing the primary use case for the service. Some teams find it better to have a separate page for such illustrations, at the very front of the survey, and then follow that page with the specific questions.

These images help respondents understand the concept statement. They should read the concept statement and look at the picture, and say, "Oh, I get it!" This is not as simple as it sounds. We suggest you practice testing the surveys on people other than yourself, whether they be roommates or classmates on other teams in this course. No one gets it right the first time. It is not easy to convey to first-time readers the design and benefits of an innovation idea, particularly when you may not be speaking to them face to face. They will have to read the concept statement, look at the visual illustration, and then quickly understand the basic focus and purpose of your design. This is actually an excellent first pass at marketing communications for a new company, where a picture can be as powerful as a thousand words.

THE QUESTIONS NEEDED FOR THE REALITY CHECK

The next step is to develop specific questions that test different aspects of a Customer Value Proposition.

Look at Figure 12.1. This figure contains questions to ask customers. You should start by asking the respondents who they are regarding demographics or job titles that might be important for sharpening your customer focus, B2C or B2B. This can be an open-ended response line or conversation that you can code later, or you can use decennial age selections or a range of job relevant job titles. You can view these as screener questions that place respondents into an appropriate user/buyer group or filter a potential respondent out from the survey. These screener questions can cover areas such gender and marital status for consumer products. A behavioral question may also be a screener. For example, do you exercise five days a week? Do you meditate occasionally or regularly? Are you a regular user of public transportation? Such questions can quickly help segment respondents. A good on-line questionnaire development tool will have a branching mechanism where if the respondent does meet a certain criteria programmed into the survey, the session is terminated. Or, even better, different demographic or B2B buckets can be used to sort data in subsequent analyses, perhaps showing how one group of users/buyers responds more favorably to your idea than others.

Then come the questions in Figure 12.1. These are a similar to the ethnography questions but tuned to get more empirical results. We show nine in all. If you want to add an additional question, do it. However, any more than ten questions tend to yield incomplete surveys. You should report data only from completed ones. All the questions are important. However, if three questions were more important than others, it would be the level of dissatisfaction with current products or services, perceived distinctiveness of your innovation, and purchase intent (Questions 1, 2, and 8).

It is naïve to think that people simply will switch to a new product or service just because it is new. Your innovation needs to be a lot better, perhaps twice as good, to get most users to try something different. Perceived distinctiveness relative to current products and services and purchase intent typically must score above 50% "top-two box" to successfully break into a market. (Top-two box simply means either the fourth and fifth choices in a five-choice scale, such as "Likely to Buy" + "Definitely will Buy.") Having said this, some innovation ideas are simply so wild and different that the typical respondent might not know how to evaluate them.

First, can you tell us a little bit about yourself or your company? (Open-ended, but look for key demographic descriptors to align with your market segmentation and user/buyer groups. This can also be supplemented or replaced with one or two screener questions for consumer demographic or job type/level information. A behavioral question might also be a screener.)

This is what our product or service generally does. (Provide a quick description or a picture/sketch on a separate page.) Do you view yourself as a potential customer of this offering? (If yes, continue.) What would be the different ways that you would want to use the product or service?

1. How satisfied are you with the current products/services you use now?

    Very dissatisfied   Dissatisfied   Neither Dis/Sat.   Satisfied   Very Satisfied

2. Do you see the proposed offering as distinctive from the competitors?

    Not different   Marginally different   Somewhat different   Very different   Strongly different

3. How much would you be willing to pay for this offering compared to the current products/services you use now?

    A lot less   Somewhat less   About the same   A little more   Considerably more

4. How often do you buy similar products or services? (Open-ended.)

5. How much do you spend each time you make a purchase? (Open-ended, but looking for a dollar amount.) Do you prefer to buy, rent, subscribe, etc.? (Try to validate the structure of revenue.)

6. Where is the best place to buy products/services such as this? (Open-ended, but look for a specific preferred channel and ways in which they test or try products/services.)

7. Where do you get your information about products/services such as this? (Open-ended. Look for preferred information sources.)

8. How likely is it that you would be willing to buy this offering?

    Very unlikely   Unlikely   Neither   Likely   Definitely

9. What additional features do you think are important in a product or service such as this?
    What other products or services would you like to see sold with this (product or service)? Open-ended.)

Figure 12.1   The field research instrument for the Reality Check

Discerning investors might want to see a top-two box score that is even higher, in the range of 70%.

The other questions are also powerful. These questions test for pricing and competitive positioning, preferred points of purchase, and channels for promotion and information. Think of these as go-to-market questions. The survey also asks for frequency of purchase and amount of spend per purchase for this type of product or service. Consider these revenue estimators for annual and even lifetime revenue estimations later on in business planning. Then, by multiplying these annual spending numbers by the number of potential buyers in a target market, you can get a granular, "bottoms up" estimate of revenue, as we considered in market sizing in Chapter 10.

Last, the survey asks respondents to consider what additional features or services they would like to see in your innovation. Or the responders might have ideas about other products or services they would like to see sold with your product or service. This can give you new ideas for your final product or service design.

All of this input is important – and that is why we call it a *Reality Check*.

Now, take a few minutes to work down the questions in Figure 12.1 with a pencil in hand. Jot down some notes on how you might modify these questions. What might be your screener questions to quickly get you the types of respondents needed for helpful input? You can also add one or two additional questions – but be forewarned. As noted, questions are about the limit for respondents. They will want to complete a survey of this type in 10-15 minutes, maximum. Partially completed surveys will not do you much good.

ORGANIZING THE PANELS OF RESPONDENTS

Throughout this book, we have been careful to use the words users and buyers instead of customers. The reason for this is that for a pet food innovator, for example, the customer might be the pet retail chain, and the man or woman the buyer, and the actual pet, the user. While an innovator who becomes an entrepreneur needs to know the retailer's needs, the most crucial dimension at this point are the needs and wants of the target users and buyers, and in this case, the pet owners.

If your user can read and respond, that is the individual upon whom to focus for this Reality Check. There are rare cases in which this is not possible. For example, if your innovation is to help people with dementia, you must try to find those responsible for his or her care, typically a spouse or children. Or, if you have developed an innovation for a machine or system of some type, such as an AI-based diagnostic tool or software agent, you must find those responsible for that device or system. These persons might be plant engineers or IT professionals. These are people in the user organizations involved in the use case and responsible for purchase decisions and implementation.

Fortunately, you have already spoken to a number of these individuals for your field research. Now, you just need to reach more. You have several options for doing this. You can collect the data by:

- Personal interviews (face to face) following a structured discussion guide.

- Telephone interviews also following a structured discussion guide.

- Emailed surveys that respondents complete and send back to you.

- Online form surveys, using one of the popular survey tools offered on the web.

Personal interviews (face to face) have the significant advantage of enabling you to ask probing questions or see the respondents' reactions. Any face-to-face time with a target customer is an opportunity to learn more and the unexpected. You simply cannot get enough of it – and this is our preferred method for testing Customer Value Propositions, product strategies, revenue models, and go-to-market approaches. As we also learned, try to do this research in situ – in the the user's or buyer's actual environment.

As for the other methods – speaking on the telephone, emailing surveys, or sending respondents to an online form – do the best you can with the time you have remaining in the course. Use the technique that makes the most sense. Most schools have a license to SurveyMonkey or a similar form package available at no cost to students. Google Forms is another option. You can send the survey results to Google Sheets for a simple statistical compilation.

Whatever the method, the goal for the Reality Check/Concept Test for the number of persons in the survey panel is 30 individuals, at least. This is the minimum number generally considered necessary to achieve statistical validity – and you will be compiling some statistics from the survey. We also have students who have used Facebook and other social network groups to quickly get to 100 or more respondents. One hundred respondents will undoubtedly impress most teachers. Note that some instructors feel that statistical significance comes only with 100-plus respondents. Professional market research for new consumer products aims for 200 completed responses. However, this course is not *that*.

Another way to think about setting a goal for the number of respondents is to get 30 qualified respondents to complete the survey within each specific user group. For example, suppose we were designing a consumer product for households. In that case, we might wish to get 30 responses from women (who do most of the shopping) with children, couples without children, and then single nonmarried individuals, males and females being distinct groups. Or if our innovation focuses on college students, 30 females and 30 males. Then, we can contrast the differences in purchase intent and perceived distinctiveness between the two potential target groups. This understanding of the difference between a primary target user group and adjacent ones not only validates your idea but shows where you might logically expand later. You can therefore structure potential users into a few distinct groups and target 30 responses for each group. We will show an example of this from an actual Reality Check in the pages to follow.

Getting to 30 respondents for B2B innovations can be difficult. Work with your teachers on an adequate sample size. For example, reaching a dozen physicians for a medical innovation is a good accomplishment in a semester, or a dozen city officials for a public-sector innovation. If, on the other hand, your innovation focuses on small businesses, there is no reason why you can't reach 30 completed responses with dedicated effort. Each team should set a goal with the course instructor that is appropriate for its innovation project.

LET'S EXPLORE THE SURVEY METHODS WITH AN EXAMPLE

We can share an example to show how survey design, administration, and simple statistical analysis works. Since your authors love their pets and know many pet innovators such as Rob and Deb, let's continue this theme forward. We also assume many readers grew up in households with a dog or cat and have empathy for the category.

We call this example HealthyWags. *It is not Polkadog Bakery*. It was a project pursued by another student team with a similar premium healthy positioning, but instead of fish skins, offered a wholegrain-based dog cookie with tasty, genuine meat inclusions and minimal processing. It played into a clear market trend for wholegrains, and a limited ingredient deck.

The team felt the need to test its dog cookie concept against three potential, adjacent user groups: a Millennial female without children (married, or not, and the inspirational user for the design phase of the project); a female with young children; and an older male above 50 years old (married or single). The team's ethnography had shown these three groups as the most significant potential consumer types for premium snacks. The survey was administered face to face in local dog parks in Boston.[2] This translated into three groups of respondents with a target of 30 completed responses for each group, or a total of 90 completed questionnaires. Note that the team did not see young Millennial males as likely targets for this premium treat and, therefore, skipped them as a subgroup for the study.

Place yourself into the context of the team's three personas.

- The first group, mothers with children, is a strong potential buyer for a healthy dog treat. So let's be that Mom for a minute. We have two kids and buy pet food and snacks while shopping at the local grocery store for the rest of the family. We seek a combination of good quality and reasonable price, and for this, prefer well-established pet food brands such as Purina, Pedigree, or Iams. For us, the pet is another family member. When it comes to food, we treat the pet at a level below that of the children – but the pet still matters a lot. For the fun of it, let's give this persona a name: *Mother Goose.*

- Next, imagine that you are a young professional woman, single or married, who doesn't have children yet, and have a dog with whom you have a special, almost mother–childlike relationship. You tend to shop at Whole Foods Market or Trader Joe's for food, buy all-natural pet food brands, and spend whatever time it takes at your veterinarian to keep your pet healthy. You are skeptical of mass-manufactured, non-local products made with mysterious ingredients. When it comes to snacks for yourself and your dog, you explicitly read labels and look for natural, healthy ingredients. You want something for your dog that feels like the types of snacks you purchase for yourself. For some of you, these might be vegetable-only proteins instead of meat. And over the past several years, you have been shopping at a pet specialty store such as PetSmart or PetCo and have seen a much wider variety of premium pet foods and snacks made by smaller, independent manufacturers, some of them local to your region. For the fun of it, let's give this persona a name: *Dog Mommy.*

- Last, let's pretend to be a 60ish-year-old male. You view your dog as a companion, a "buddy" of sorts. You shop anywhere convenient and even buy snacks and treats for your own consumption at places like Walmart or Target. Moreover, you never really bought into the health food craze for yourself, let alone your pet, despite constant and sometimes annoying encouragement from your Millennial children. You know that you are not going to live forever, and neither is your dog. And you know that certain vitamins are recommended for longevity and to help stop certain aches and pains. However, with retirement approaching, you will not spend $20 on a bag of dog cookies! Yes, the dog is special but more like a buddy than a real family member. The persona name for this older male? Of course, *Pet Buddy.*

Millennial males are a very different persona. If you have ever been to a pet store selling ice cream designed for dogs at the front register, it may well be these younger Pet Buddy dudes who are doing the buying. Ice cream is an indulgent snack. Most young Millennial males think they will live forever, rarely ever see a doctor, and think that ice cream or beer is just fine for their dogs! We over-state in jest here, but there is more than a small bit of truth to this stereo-type. The young males are not a primary target for our new healthy dog snack.

Now, let's see how the three target personas that are our focus emerge in their responses to the survey.

ANALYZING YOUR DATA AND INTERPRETING THE RESULTS

Assume that you were able to get 30 completed responses for each of the target consumer groups. You must first consolidate all the data from the survey into a simple, single spreadsheet or database to run some basic statistics. Also, you need to carefully read the answers to the open-ended questions.

Figure 12.2 shows the first outcome: a detailed restatement and refinement of the persona or personas used for the Reality Check. You need to do the same for your project. Also, state the N of the sample size for each group, whether it is a user or a buyer, or both.

Opening General Question. Can you tell us a little bit about yourself or your company? (Open-ended, but look for key demographic descriptors to align with your market segmentation and customer groups.)

Results: (Combination of earlier ethnography and the Reality Check field research.)

Mother Goose (Attitude: Dog as family member, but still a pet.) Customers are health conscious when purchasing at the grocery store, and many are going to Whole Foods. They expect quality ingredients, but they are not label readers. They are explicitly focused on taste but value is also important because dog snacks are part of the overall household food budget. They will accept fortification of ingredients, as opposed to all-natural recipes. Tend to trust large brand name manufacturers. Shop in grocery stores or Target. Key motivation for feeding snacks: "I feed my dogs just for love." Key target customer. **Estimated 50% of market based on industry reports. N=30.**

Dog Mommy (Attitude: Dog as family member, dog as child – and may be a surrogate child for some.) Customers are very health conscious. These customers want quality ingredients and not at lot of fat and calories. All-natural is another key driver. Distrust large manufacturers. Want locally sourced food. They want all-natural ingredients, good taste, and minimally processed products. They are deliberate shoppers that read the ingredients list. Shop in Wholefoods, Trader Joe's and for pets, PetSmart, Petco, or independent pet retailers. Key motivation for feeding snacks: "I want my dog to be as healthy as I am." Key target customer. **Estimated 30% of market based on industry reports. N=30.**

Pet Buddy (Attitude: Dog as pet friend.) Predominantly male. They are focused on ingredients on a more scientific basis. All-natural is less of a concern. He does not mind using a dog snack as an indulgence. Milk Bones will do for this customer. Key motivation for feeding snacks: "If he is happy, I am happy." Looks at dog as exercise buddy. **Estimated 20% of market based on industry reports. N=30.**

Figure 12.2 Pet snack consolidated field research data: personas refined

VALIDATING YOUR PRODUCT OR SERVICE DESIGN

The next step is to show the results for "the big three" Concept Test measures: (a) the extent to which the customers are dissatisfied with their current solutions, (b) the extent to which they find your solution distinctive (memorable and meaningful for their use case), and (c) their purchase intent.

The stars align for an innovation if target customers are highly dissatisfied with current solutions, the proposed product or service is perceived as highly distinctive, and target users/ buyers show high purchase intent.

If people are already pleased with their current product or service, it will be hard to get a high percentage to switch. Or, they might be dissatisfied with existing solutions but perceive your innovation as not all that different. And this is why we must ask all three questions and why you should report them together.

Turning to Figure 12.3, in this case, it is clear that certain target customers appreciate the premium, all-natural, healthy positioning more than others. Looking at Question 1, the Dog

Question 1: How satisfied are you with the current products/services you use now?

Very dissatisfied   *Dissatisfied*   *Neither Dis/Sat.*   *Satisfied*   *Very Satisfied*

Mother Goose: 30% Dissatisfied or Very dissatisfied
Dog Mommy: 50% Dissatisfied or Very dissatisfied
Pet Buddy: 10% Dissatisfied or Very dissatisfied

Question 2: Do you see the proposed offering as distinctive from the competitors?

Not different   *Marginally different*   *Somewhat different*   *Very different*   *Strongly different*

Mother Goose: 50% Very different or Strongly different
Dog Mommy: 80% Very different or Strongly different
Pet Buddy: 30% Very different or Strongly different

Question 8: How likely is it that you would be willing to buy this offering?

Very unlikely   *Unlikely*   *Neither*   *Likely*   *Very Likely*

Mother Goose: 40% Likely or Definitely
Dog Mommy: 70% Likely or Definitely
Pet Buddy: 20% Likely or Definitely

Figure 12.3   Pet snack consolidated research data: results for the big three questions

Dog Mommies were the most displeased with current snacks, and the Mother Gooses next. The Pet Buddies didn't seem to care!

Next, looking at Question 2, having read and looked at the concept image, the respondents responded to this question on concept distinctiveness. Once again, the Dog Mommy target is strongly validated. Mother Goose – not bad. And Pet Buddy – did not think the proposed concept was all that different than current products.Next comes purchase intent, in Question 8. These data affirm Dog Mommy's strong interest. Combined with the previous two questions, the team had validated its focus. The Mother Goose saw the snack as special, but not as a regular treat, probably due to the perceived cost and the need to feed the rest of the family first. Pet Buddy stayed true to form. Often in innovation, it is just as important to know who doesn't like your idea as much as who loves it. The Reality Check across different adjacent user/buyer groups provides this insight. This helps with both the design and the branding for a new product or service.

VALIDATING THE GO-TO-MARKET STRATEGY

Testing the commercialization approach for positioning, pricing, and channel is important. Innovators often focus so hard on their products or services that they short change the go-to-market aspects of the business. Go-to-market is the hidden genie. An incapable salesperson or low-quality retailer can make the best products appear inferior. Strong go-to-market, on the other hand, can be a huge differentiator. Today, developing a community around a new product or service can create the buzz needed to generate critical momentum in a marketplace.

The Reality Check for the go-to-market strategy includes getting customer feedback on five elements:

- Price level relative to current in-market products/services.

- Frequency of purchase.

- Amount typically "spent" for each purchase.

- Preferred place of purchase.

- Preferred information channel for product or service information.

Price level (Question 3) validates the competitive positioning. Frequency of purchase (Question 4) and amount typically spent (Question 5) provides an estimate of the "annual value of a customer" – in this case, how much money is likely to be paid for these new pet snacks. Learning whether target users/buyers agree with your channel strategy is also very important (Question 6). For example, do customers want to buy directly from you? Or would they prefer to purchase from an already established channel, such as a retailer?

The last question is the media channel(s) by which target users prefer to learn about new products or services such as yours (Question 7). How does social media play versus traditional advertising? The majority of ventures launched today, whether B2C or B2B, have some form of influencer strategy designed to get the word out on the web from persons other than the venture itself.

Now, take a look at Figure 12.4, which shows the go-to-market question results. The Dog Mommies fit an ideal pattern for the HealthyWags concept: willing to spend considerably more money than already spent for current products; shopping primarily at pet specialty stores which tend to carry premium products; and trust influencers on the web more than traditional mass advertising from the major brands. It all fits.

The Mother Goose consumers were a mixed story: less willing to pay more. They expected to find snacks in a grocery store along with their other food items, and were interested in more traditional media channels to learn about new products. Given the "slotting fees" required to get shelf space in grocery store chains and the cost of advertising in traditional media channels – this was not good news for the HealthyWags team. Finally, the responses from the Pet Buddies did little to make this type of user more attractive as a target for a healthy, premium pet snack.

PRODUCT LINE OF SERVICE EXTENSIONS

Question 9 provides another chance for users to give you additional product ideas.

What additional features would make you more likely to buy this (product or service)? What other products or services would you like to see sold with this (product or service)? (Open-ended.)

Figure 12.5 shows the results for the pet snack example. The target user – Dog Mommy, was, not surprisingly, highly focused on authenticity of ingredients and sustainability in packaging. Also, locally made was seen as another important feature in the overall story. The Mother Goose wanted the ability to lower costs through bulk purchases. She also wanted smaller portion sizes as training aids for new pets – the practical side of matters. Not much useful came from the men; make it less crumbly and throwable, and remove the smell (even though dogs have amongst the best noses in the world!).

Question 3: How much would you be willing to pay for this offering compared to the current products/services you use now?

Mother Goose:	30% A little more or a lot more
Dog Mommy:	50% A little more or a lot more
Pet Buddy:	10% A little more or a lot more

Question 4: How often do you buy similar products or services? (Choice or open-ended.)

Mother Goose:	Generally, once a month
Dog Mommy:	Generally, once a month
Pet Buddy:	Once every two to three months

Question 5: How much do you spend each time you make a purchase? (Open-ended, but looking for a dollar amount.) Do you prefer to buy, rent, subscribe, etc? (Determine method of payment.)

Mother Goose:	$20
Dog Mommy:	$30
Pet Buddy:	$10

Question 6: Where is the best place to buy products/services such as this? (Open-ended, but look for a specific preferred channel and ways in which they test or try products/services.)

Mother Goose:	Supermarket, Pet Specialty Store
Dog Mommy:	Pet Specialty Store
Pet Buddy:	Supermarket

Question 7: Where do you get your information about products/services such as this? (Open-ended. Look for preferred information sources.)

Mother Goose:	Print, television, friends
Dog Mommy:	Internet, friends
Pet Buddy:	In-store

Figure 12.4   HealthyWags consolidates field research data: go-to-market questions

Question 9: What additional features would make you more likely to buy this (product or service)? What other products or services would you like to see sold with this (product or service)? (Open-ended.)

Pet Buddy :	Make it tougher and heavier so I can throw it or play with it with my dog. I don't like the smell of fish. Can you eliminate the smell?
Dog Mommy:	More information about the source of grains and meats. Provide a clear statement about sustainability. Back it up. Prefer a local sourcing story. How does the package perform in terms of recycling?
Mother Goose:	Bulk packaging to buy it for less money per lb. Want smaller portion treats for training purposes.

Figure 12.5   Pet snack consolidated field research data: other features, products or services

TESTING A BRAND NAME

A good innovation deserves a brand name and tagline that amplifies the purpose and benefits of the product or service itself.

We recommend that you do this *after* you ask all the questions to respondents for the Reality Check. If they seem willing, tell them you would like to test a few brand names to get their opinion. It is also a fun way to end the interview process! Heck, they might even give you a better name or tagline message.

To do this, you need to first come up with two or three possible brand names for your products or service and then the short, powerful message following the name. For example, the MX-5 Miata is a convertible roadster "engineered for the heart". That simple message tells the purpose and emotional benefits from what would otherwise be a small, low-priced passenger car. Tesla's motto is "to accelerate the advent of sustainable transport" through electric vehicles and the name itself is derived from Tesla, a unit of measurement for magnetic fields, itself named after Nikola Tesla, a brilliant electrical engineer who helped invent the alternating current (AC) power supply system in the second half of the 19th century. Or, Nike makes sneakers and other athletic wear to "bring inspiration and innovation to every athlete in the world."

To prepare for this:

- Go on to the web to find brand names for leading, competitive products or services. You might also want to browse the startups in your industry niche and see what they are calling their new products and services. Look for the most impactful, standout brand names in your category. Also, look for messaging.

- Brand name testing can be done whether interviewing is synchronous or asynchronous. If it is live in some form – face to face, Zoom, or a telephone call – have the interviewees first look at what you think are the best competitor brand names. Then have them look at yours. Setting this up as a simple table might be the best approach: the various competitors' names and messaging in the first column, your possible brand names and messaging in the second column, and the third column open for notes. If the process is asynchronous, e.g. a web survey, you can list three potential brand names and ask respondents their favorite, plus any other suggestions they think might be better for the concept.

The type of responses you are looking for are:

1. Of all the names and messages in the table, which are the clearest and most powerful?
2. If your brand names and messages "pop," what are the reasons? What do respondents like about your branding?
3. If your brand names and messages seem a little off, what don't respondents like, and what might they recommend?

Continue to note the type of user/persona that the respondent represents. Different types of customers often react to the same branding in very different ways. Your goal is to develop and validate a brand name and messaging that truly resonates with *your* target user/buyer.

SUMMARIZING EVERYTHING INTO SEVERAL IMPORTANT TEMPLATES

Figure 12.6 summarizes the information gathered from the Reality Check and other templates in earlier chapters. We think of it as an Innovation Dashboard. It is the target user persona slide from a prior chapter amped up with additional, important information. The only new element compared to prior chapters is called a preliminary business model on the right side. This includes a few bullet points for product variety, price level, and channels to market. All the rest of the sections in the Dashboard build on what you have already learned. For example, the Industry section comes from the market sizing chapter. The other sections build on our customer discovery and design chapters, but now validated with real data from the Reality Check.

The power of summarizing your insights and information on a single page cannot be under-estimated. You can quickly show a friend, mentor, or colleague the innovation idea – tested

The Innovation Dashboard

Industry Information

- $20B in US; $8B health-focused
- Big three mass manufacturers: Nestlé Purina, Mars
- Lots of snack innovation
- Low volume, very high margin with premium products priced at $15+ per pound on the shelf

The User/Buyer Insight

- Seeking ways to show care/love for pet
- Health through nutrition; taste, too
- Snacks should be as healthy as main meal
- Sustainable source for animals and grains used in snacks
- Local production of food is important, distrusts mass manufacturers

Target Users and Use Cases

- Young females without children are primary target, estimated 30% of consuming market in the U.S.
- Shopping for snacks once a month at PetSmart, Petco, or independent. Also some Whole Foods
- Snacks for dogs and cats, as treats and for training

Preliminary Business Model

- Small packs and large packs
- Premium-priced
- Specialty stores and eCommerce

Product Design

- Naturally sourced
- Minimally processed
- Locally processed and not by a large manufacturer
- No nasty animal byproducts
- Artisanal packaging
- Engaging website – story behind products

Figure 12.6   The innovation dashboard for HealthyWags

with target users and buyers, against their perceptions of competitors – and talk about how the different pieces of the Dashboard reinforce one another.

The picture of the ideal target user makes an important contribution to quick, effective concept comprehension by the viewer. Find or create a good one for your project. Wherever possible, include other images of target users and use cases in presentations. If the buyer is different than the target user, create a separate personal slide for that buyer. In short, use this slide to bring your audience into the world of your users and buyers.

Reader exercises

Now to the reader exercises for the Reality Check. These exercises are important because they result in field-based validation of everything you have done so far. You will assess the quality of your choices for target users and buyers and use cases, their purchase intent and distinctiveness scores for your product and service designs, and their levels of dissatisfaction with current offerings. Plus, the Reality Check covers positioning and branding strategy, provides insights into channel design and promotional mechanisms, and gives guidance on annual revenue likely per user/buyer. If done well, a Reality Check is a wonderful capstone to this course. That, and your prototypes, of course!

STEP 1: EDIT THE CUSTOMER VALUE PROPOSITION FOR THE REALITY CHECK

Finalize the Customer Value Proposition and specifically the bottom row that is the summary. It should be two or three sentences. You should be able to communicate the essence of your innovation to potential customers in about 30 seconds. Polish that single drawing or photograph of your product or service concept. Include it underneath the concept statement on a separate page/screen before getting to the survey questions. Practice on yourselves first and then on friends outside of your team. Did those friends understand the concept in 30 seconds? If not, keep reworking the text statement and picture until your friends can clearly understand it.

STEP 2: CREATE THE DISCUSSION GUIDE/SURVEY

Using Figure 12.1 as a reference, prepare your survey instrument. You should cover all the various elements shown in that figure. Once again, practice with teammates and friends outside your team.

Above all, try to keep your survey short and focused. Most customers won't give you much more than 10–15 minutes to complete the survey. But of course, if it is a synchronous survey on Zoom or in person and the user wants to talk more, set the survey aside for a while, listen hard, take notes, and then come back to the survey to wrap things up with a big thank you.

Always show your appreciation to each and every respondent, whether it is verbally or with a warm statement at the end of an online survey. If they want to stay involved with your project, take their contact information and be sure to follow up, or if it is an online survey, give them an email where they might contact you to share more ideas. These individuals will help you test your new products or services when your prototypes become true MVPs.

STEP 3: CONDUCT THE FIELD RESEARCH

Talk with at least 30 potential customers for each user group. Why that number? If you have distinctive user groups, try to talk to people in each group (e.g. three customer groups, 30 each = 90). If you still have unanswered hypotheses or unclear results, find more prospective users to complete the survey. Here, the more, the better. Those teams that talk to more than 50 and even a 100 or more prospective users tend to have the most robust results. Don't be afraid to use Zoom!

A few additional comments: if your users are different than your buyers, make these two distinct survey groups and compare results for each group. Buyer insights are as crucial as user insights.

If you are working in a B2B market space, you must try to talk to a sufficient number of users and buyers in target corporate customers. Our rule of thumb is to also aim for 30 respondents, but to achieve this number by getting multiple respondents in a single company or organization, for example, six clinicians in five hospitals (for a healthcare innovation) or five IT professionals in six companies (for a new software security related product.) Try your best and keep you teacher informed. And at the end of the day, you have your earlier ethnographies to complement these empirical results. Those buyer personas are important.

Remember, check in with your teacher so that everyone is clear on a reasonable survey sample for your particular project and how that might have to be adjusted once you get into this part of the field research.

STEP 4: ANALYZE AND SET UP THE SPECIFIC REPORT STRUCTURE FOR THE RESULTS

Now begin to analyze what you have discovered. Use Figure 12.7 (below) to organize the data and present the results as part of an interim or final project presentation. What do the data tell you? For example, are users interested in the concept? Are they likely to buy? How much are they likely to spend on each purchase? Through which channel do they prefer to make purchases? How do they hear about and learn about new products or services in this category? Imagine, with a proper Reality Check, you can march through all the major questions one by one. This will impress.

Start with the purpose and design of your survey, including the sample size and group-ings. Show the concept statement that results from it and an image(s) from your prototype design. Then group the statistical or opened-ended responses into the three blocks used in this chapter: the "big three," the go-to-market questions, and the other features/other products or services. You can use a page for each one – the survey and sample design, the concept statement and image, the groups of statistical results, and a final slide with a half dozen bullets showing the major take-aways – *good or bad* – from the Reality Check.

Don't forget to use the language of "top-two box" for the five-point scaled questions. It will make you look like a pro. Perhaps explain what it means first, just in case one of your listeners does not know the term. In a larger group, the chances are that there will be engineering types who have never seen the term.

STEP 5: CREATE THE INNOVATION DASHBOARD AND DO A FINAL TWEAK ON THE CUSTOMER VALUE PROPOSITION

Create your Innovation Dashboard (Figure 12.6). Then, do a final tweak on the Customer Value Proposition based on what you learned from the Reality Check. Figure 12.8 is your guide. It is a repeat of Figure 4.10 with some arrows indicating specific improvement points for the Reality Check. Create a sharper definition of the Problem Space, the target user, buyer, and use case, or to convey a crisper benefits and positioning. The CVP and Innovation Dashboard reveal focus and clarity of your idea, improved through the work done in this course. This work, if done in earnest, can serve as the foundation for an exciting venture.

*** *** ***

The Reality Check should be a focused sprint. It's the end of the semester, your last bit of heavy lifting for this course. The final and last chapter provides a set of final presentation guidelines.

Reporting the Results of the Reality Check

Intro: Describe yourself or your company. Do you view yourself as a potential user of this product? Or add one or two screener questions to group or filter out respondents.	Validate primary and secondary customer groups.	
How satisfied are you with the current products/services you use now? Very dissatisfied Dissatisfied Neither Dis/Sat. Satisfied Very Satisfied	Report percentages. Look for top-two box scores: Very Dissatisfied, Dissatisfied.	Top-two box
Do you see the proposed offering as distinctive from the competitors? Not different Somewhat different Highly distinctive	Report percentages. Look for top box scores: Highly Distinctive.	Top-two box
How much would you be willing to pay for this offering compared to current products/services you use now? A lot Less Less Same More A lot more	Report percentages. Look for top-two box scores: More, A lot more.	Top-two box
How often do you buy similar products or services? (Open-ended.)	Report time frequency of purchase.	
How much do you spend each time you make a purchase? (Open-ended, but looking for a dollar amount. Try to validate the structure of revenue – e.g. does the customer want to purchase, license, subscribe, try before buy, etc.)	Report money spent range, with average. Report preferred revenue type.	
Where is the best place to buy products/services such as this? (Open-ended, but look for a specific preferred channel and ways in which they test or try products/services).	List channels with percentages. Validates go-to-market model.	
Where do you get your information about products/services such as this? (Open-ended. Look for preferred information sources.)	List sources with percentages. Validates build awareness model.	
How likely is it that you would be willing to buy this offering? Very unlikely Unlikely Neither Likely Very Likely	Report purchase intent. Look for top-two box scores: Likely and Very Likely.	Top-two box
What additional features do you think are important in a (product or service) such as this? (Open-ended.)	List the desired features, with most popular and percentages first	
Extra: Provide an estimate of revenues for a scaled up business (after five to seven years). (Target persona as a percentage of market, shopping frequency and desired price).	This should show your assumptions.	
Final checklist on key aspects of your venture strategy and business model.	Check them off! Final slide.	

Figure 12.7   Reporting the results of the Reality Check

Refine the Customer Value Proposition

ABC *(give it a name)* is a family of (products/services /solutions)		Brand name ←
That *(solves what problem)*		
For *(which target customers)*		
For *(which target buyers)*		
The benefits we expect to provide *(name the major benefits)* will make ABC stand out from similar products and/or services.		Sharpen this ←
And is different than current *(competitors/products)* because of *(why customers will buy it)*		And this ... ←
Now, put it all together:		New draft ←

Figure 12.8   A final edit of the CVP based on the Reality Check

NOTES

1. There is more required to launch a business, of course: the business model, financial projections, supply chain and distribution channel strategies, and perhaps most important, the team needed to implement all these things. We hope there are additional courses at your school that address these matters. If a class is not readily available, your authors have written other books that present straightforward methods for developing these other elements in a business plan.

2. To help the team, we brought our own pet, Amber, to the park to break the ice with respondents. *Amber, we miss you and often still think of you.*

13
The final presentation: guidelines and next steps

INTRODUCTION

Your teacher will want you to make a final presentation. This presentation integrates all that you have done, and all that you have learned. It is best done as a story of innovation rather than a dry, formal readout. You now have your story about the target users/buyers and their needs, a story about your specific innovations, a story about market potential, a story about yourselves as a team, and perhaps even some early prototypes to show. Weave these stories together into an attractive, compelling presentation. People tend not to remember PowerPoint decks; they do remember stories and well-designed prototypes. Stories and images stick in the mind. This is not to say that the final PowerPoint style and layout is not important. The chances are that a significant portion of your final grade is based on that final PowerPoint. Design it well.

The rest of this chapter is a style guide for the PowerPoint and the presentation itself.

A STRUCTURE FOR THE PRESENTATION: A STORY WHEEL

Figure 13.1 shows a story wheel for the final presentation. We like to think of it as a wheel where the innovative product or service is the hub, with various dimensions for it as the spokes. At any time, you can jump to a different spoke if the listener is so interested, rather than march down a straight order. Suppose you want to start with your team, that is OK. Or, if you want to end the presentation with your current team and who else you need to add to it, that's fine, too. Follow the flow that makes the most sense to your team.

You have already done a lot of work researching and completing various templates for this course. The templates are no more or less frameworks for considering different aspects of innovation: the user and buyer, the innovation design, defining the prototype, sizing the opportunity, and the goals and shared passion of a team, the innovation team. The first draft of the final presentation should be easy to create – it is the assembly of templates you have already created for your project, continuously improved with the feedback you have received from your teachers and classmates.

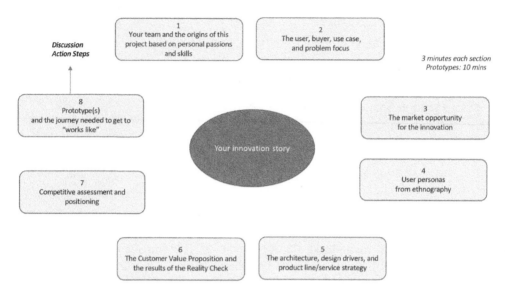

Figure 13.1   The story wheel

Open up a new PowerPoint or similar tool. Create a title slide with the name of innovation, a short one- or two-line description of its focus, and then your team members with contact emails for your teacher on it. And a date as well. Then, let's do the first draft.

Gather your work for the course and find existing slides for:

● Your team backgrounds, skills, and career and societal motivations. This comes from your work in Chapters 2 and 3.

● A picture of the target user and buyer and a clear statement of the specific problem to be solved within your larger Problem Space.

● The TAM, SAM, and SOM template (Figure 10.1). Note that even though this topic was covered in one of our later chapters, it makes sense to move it up here. Having stated the Problem Space, listeners will then want to under the market opportunity that solving the problem represents.

● The persona(s) for your target users and buyers, highlighting what you learned from the ethnography in terms of not just their obvious needs but their deep frustrations and latent needs across the full case. (Figures 6.4 and 6.6.)

● The CVP (Figure 4.10, and improved in Figure 12.8), and then, the specific new product, system, or service design, which is the architecture template with its design drivers (Figure 7.7 or 7.9), improved with the application of composite design (Figure 7.14) and packaging, where appropriate (Figure 7.16), or the process redesign and services innovation templates (Figures 7.10 and 7.11), followed by the product line or services strategy diagram (Figure 11.1 or its equivalents for software.).

- The Reality Check results from the previous chapter, starting with your Customer Value Proposition statement and an illustration or photo of the product or service concept. State what validations or surprises emerged from the Reality Check, good and bad, and how they affect your CVP and the product or service design. (Figure 12.7.)

- The competitive assessment matrix and the positioning map. (Figures 8.3 and 8.6.)

- Last, your prototype design (referring to the must-have, nice-to-have template, Figures 9.1, 9.2 and their equivalents for software, or Figure 9.11 and 9.12 for services). Include photos or illustrations of your various prototypes. While you might include these as PowerPoint slides at the very end, you might turn off the computer after the must-have, nice-to-have slide and show your prototypes by hand. These might be cardboard or 3D printed prototypes, food or drink to taste (careful, you won't get an A if someone gets sick!), or a wireframe on a computer or mobile phone. If you are doing a pure services innovation, you might show the before–after use case in the form of a small skit. Live demonstrations leave lasting memories.

Taken altogether, assemble no more than fifteen or so slides, with four to five pages reserved for the Reality Check section.

If you have additional slides you wish to include, put them into an Appendix. Too many slides in the main presentation often defocus the listener. In other words, it is best to have a fifteen-slide main presentation, followed by a twenty-slide Appendix, rather than a 35-page slide deck. You want a clean, straightforward, easy-to-digest story.

Appendix materials might be more additional information on competitors, more detailed designed sketches, more prototype examples, and specific bills of materials and cost estimations. Depending on your teacher's background, s/he may wish to have more detailed information on subsystem designs and materials. This is supporting information for the next level of detail questions that might arise during a presentation.

Once you have assembled the various templates applied to your project, take the first pass for content and completeness. Fill in missing gaps. Build your Appendix, too. Then, edit all pages for style. Hopefully, you have a team member who has a good eye for such matters. We prefer the clean, Apple-like appearance: not too much text on any given slide, please!

Important: don't just have the templates for your final presentation. Use the templates as a first pass, but then edit and simplify them. Think about a listener who is not part of the class, such as an investor some day in the future. Make an easy-to-understand presentation for them that is grounded in the deep work and thinking that you have done with the help of the templates. As part of this, create a design theme as a header or background for all the slides, with a logo or color tones tastefully placed in background. Make the presentation have visual appeal, clean and simple. In the main presentation, the font size should not be less than 20 pt. In the more detailed Appendix slides, smaller fonts will be okay, but certainly not font size 10. Your teacher will have to read at least ten of these PowerPoints – make it easy on them!

Whatever you do, do not make your PowerPoints painful to read or understand. Slides should be professional, clear, and engaging. If you have actual pictures or videos of the use case, by all means include these in the earlier part of your presentation because they will make the ethnography authentic. Moreover, a good prototype will make the presentation shine. Later, should you have investors as the audience, prototypes will be as important as the PowerPoints.

As important to any listener is you and your team. Personal passion for a Problem Space and your solution for it are essential, as is a balance of skills on the team. These are concepts from our earliest chapters that impress the listener as much as anything else. Think of yourselves not just as students in a course but as the founders and leaders of dynamic new ventures. Take pride in this and make sure your slides reflect a sense of genuine purpose.

THE VERBAL PRESENTATION

Standard rules of thumb apply here. Talk to your audience, not to your slides. This means look at your audience and make eye contact. Do not read your slides. Instead, provide additional context and stories around images and bullet points. In other words, loosen up a bit. Engage both yourself and your listeners in the story that you are telling. Practice the slides more than once, more than twice – about four or five times.

Ask your teacher for guidelines regarding time allowance. The final presentations for this kind of course tend to be 30 minutes each, with 20 minutes to present the slides and 10 minutes to show prototypes and answer questions. This time goes quickly, so please, be prepared to the point of scheduling the 20 minutes slide by slide.

Given the number of teams in a course and the number of class meetings reserved for readouts, your teacher may give you more or less time. They are the boss!

Your authors prefer to hear from every team member for these final readouts. Your teacher may have a different preference.

*** *** ***

Well, dear readers, we have come to the final pages of this book. *Thank you for participating in this journey of innovation and for allowing us to be your guides.*

Hopefully, you have learned something about yourself along the way. We think about this as a few crucial questions that you might wish to ask yourself in a moment of quiet reflection:

- *Do you like to innovate?* Does innovating make you smile? There are many jobs in industry and government where you do not have to innovate and can still do very well. However, if you have enjoyed this experience, perhaps you should set your sights on an innovative job in innovating industries. If you are not starting your own company right away, work for a company known to be innovative and that seems to share your own core values. If you get stuck in a job where the company that does not support creative thinking, neither you nor your employer will be pleased.

- *What aspect of the innovation process do you like the most?* The methods in this book represent different types of jobs in companies. Interfacing with users to gather insights is typically a product management or designer's job. Building architecture and specifications usually lead to a hardware, software, or materials engineering career path. Doing broader scale user studies lands someone in market research groups, or well-known business consultancies or market research firms. If you relished your project's branding and communications aspects, brand management and marketing jobs are the places to explore. Or, if you had the most fun organizing the entire team – well, that tends to be a program or project management function in a company. It is also an essential skill for an entrepreneur.

It's OK to enjoy all of these activities. However, is there an activity you enjoyed the most, and what does this mean for your career path? What internships can you get while still in school to validate a potential career path, both in terms of industry focus and the type of job you might like to have in that industry?

- *What type of innovation do you like to do?* Your team worked on a specific project representing either a product, software-based, or pure services type of innovation in a particular industry to address certain problems. You dug deeply into the Problem Space. However, you also heard from other teams throughout the entire semester. Is there another project that caught your fancy? Where you might have said, "I wish I were working on that project because the application area is so compelling and interesting to me." Now that the semester is coming to its conclusion, there is nothing preventing you from exploring other pathways for innovation. You now know the innovation methods and have practiced and applied them repeatedly. These methods are your personal play-book for innovating systematically. Is there another team that you can join which plans to continue its project? Or, is there an internship or job in a company working in that area of keen interest? Who can you speak with about the innovation area that has piqued your interest? This is called *networking*. Start now!

- *What do you need to learn next?* This last question is about learning new skills. As you worked on the project for this course, was there a particular design skill you wish you knew better? This might be a technical skill in programming, digital IoT, nutrition, or life sciences. Or, doing consumer research and branding. Remember how Kevin went to get a Master's degree in design engineering? Or Kate a degree in nutrition science even though she was a salesperson selling software? You don't have to wait until after college to do this either. Take control over your own education. Use electives or even add or change majors to pursue a new-found interest. If you are an engineering student, you might want to learn something about business finance or marketing. Or, if you are a business student, consider an elective in data science or web services design. There are both complete courses or short-form professional study courses where you can pick up these skills. The next two or three years are the time to engage in the learning you need to be a more effective innovator.

Perhaps the biggest life–work question that you might consider is *do you want to become an entrepreneur?* This might mean creating a new venture based on the project for this course. You might have even found one or two teammates who wish to do the same. To support this dream, many schools have a venture incubation program on campus. After the semester winds down, speak to people there to find out how the incubator works and the resources it offers, financial and otherwise. Having learned innovation deeply in this course, you now need to add skills in business model design, creating financial projections, and strategies for venture finance. There should be a course at your school or online focused on these topics. Beyond courses, try to get direct coaching from experienced mentors working in the incubator at your school or nearby in your community. Proceed with a certain confidence that if your project did well in this course, there is a reasonable chance that it can serve as the foundation for a new venture.

If you are serious about starting a company, continue to work on the prototype. This means going from the current looks-like, feels-like, works-a-bit-like prototypes – those minimum viable and *lovable* prototypes – to well-functioning works-a-lot-like prototypes and even better, a true minimum viable product or service nearly suited for commercial release. That functioning MVP should then be test marketed, be it on the web, in a store, or sold directly to businesses or consumers. If some money is needed to create that MVP, look for resources in your school's Entrepreneurship Center or incubator. Or, like most entrepreneurs, ask friends and family for help. *Do not stop working on your prototypes!*

You can start building your venture now, test and improve it while still a student, and then launch it upon graduation. There is no need to drop out of school to start a company. Use this time as your test and learning period. Get work internships to advance your learning in certain skill areas as well to gain industry experience and ecosystem understanding. Then, if by the time you graduate, you have a good business plan and a great prototype, you can commit to the venture to make it a reality. Otherwise, you should find an innovation-focused job in a good company working in the Problem Space that you have come to cherish.

*** *** ***

In closing, it is our deepest and most sincere hope that the lessons learned in this book will have a lasting impact on your thinking, and from this, help shape your careers. Think beyond just personal benefit and instead towards work that achieves broader societal impact and that improves the human condition in some clear way.

Seek a productive, happy life. Innovation should challenge the mind, take advantage of a person's natural skills, and help discover purpose in life. With that discovery comes deeper meaning and satisfaction.

Reflect on this course, and the experiences you have had prior to college and those that you will over the next few years as the part of your personal discovery. Find the type of work that feels deeply good, does good, and in which you can be highly and naturally productive. Then perhaps, work won't feel so much *like work*, but rather, a fulfillment of your purpose in life and at many moments, a joy regardless of the hours and sheer effort you put into the endeavor.

We hope you have been inspired by the stories of our former students, now, entrepreneurs. Perhaps someday, your own venture will be one of these stories! Please, *let us know*.

We wish you the best of luck on your life's journey.
Thank you for allowing us to be part of it.

INDEX